OKINAWA: THE LAST NAVAL BATTLE OF WW2

OKINAWA: THE LAST NAVAL BATTLE OF WW2

THE OFFICIAL ADMIRALTY ACCOUNT OF OPERATION ICEBERG

John Grehan

FRONTLINE
BOOKS

First published in Great Britain in 2022 by
FRONTLINE BOOKS
an imprint of Pen & Sword Books Ltd,
47 Church Street, Barnsley, S. Yorkshire, S70 2AS

ISBN: 978-1-39909-193-0

CIP data records for this title are available from the British Library

For more information on our books, please visit
www.frontline-books.com, email info@frontline-books.com
or write to us at the above address.

Printed and bound by CPI Group (UK) Ltd, Croydon, CR0 4YY
Typeset by Concept, Huddersfield, West Yorkshire
Pen & Sword Books Ltd incorporates the imprints of Pen & Sword
Archaeology, Atlas, Aviation, Battleground, Discovery,
Family History, History, Maritime, Military, Naval, Politics,
Social History, Transport, True Crime, Claymore Press,
Frontline Books, Praetorian Press,
Seaforth Publishing and White Owl

For a complete list of Pen and Sword titles please contact
PEN & SWORD LTD
47 Church Street, Barnsley, South Yorkshire, S70 2AS, England
E-mail: enquiries@pen-and-sword.co.uk

Or

PEN AND SWORD BOOKS
1950 Lawrence Rd, Havertown, PA 19083, USA
E-mail: Uspen-and-sword@casematepublishers.com

Contents

PUBLISHER'S NOTE

The text that follows has been extracted from Battle Summary No.47, 'Naval Operations in Assault and Capture of Okinawa (Operation ICEBERG) March to June 1945', which is held at The National Archives, Kew, under reference ADM 234/368. It is reproduced under the Open Government Licence Version 3.0.

As far as possible, the extract has been faithfully reproduced in the format it was originally produced. As a result, some of the phraseology may seem dated and the use of some third-person pronouns will be seen to be incorrect. These have been retained to maintain the authenticity of the reports.

A small number of appendices have been excluded and a new index has been added plus a photograph section which was not in the original document.

Chapter I

THE PACIFIC THEATRE IN APRIL 1945

1. Situation in the Pacific, April 1945

In April 1945, the chain of advance bases flung by the Americans westward across the Pacific from Hawaii, and by the Americans and Australians northward from Australia, needed but the addition of a last link before the final assault upon the Japanese homeland could be undertaken.

Operations in the Pacific during the previous year had been directed towards the establishment of air and supply bases for this final assault. From Hawaii a chain now extended through the Marshalls and West Carolines; from Australia another ran through the Solomon Islands and Manus in the Admiralties; both converged at Leyte and Mindoro in the Philippine Islands, a geographical focus of lines of communication not only from the U.S.A. and Panama in the East, Australia and New Zealand in the South, but also from the United Kingdom and India via the Moluccas in the West.

The capture of the Marianas in the previous summer and the establishment during the winter of firm bases in the Philippines, had placed the Allies on a strategic line some 1,300 miles from Japan, across her direct routes of communication to the south where lay her oil supplies, vital to the prosecution of the war. The occupation of Iwo Jima where organized enemy resistance ceased on 16th March 1945, provided an air base at the eastern end of the line within 640 miles of Tokyo. The line was now to be advanced, at the western end, to Okinawa, in the Nansei Shoto, an island possessing potential airfields from which almost any type of aircraft could reach industrial Kyushu, 850 miles distant; and where space, both land and harbor, were adequate for the mounting of the final assault upon Japan.

To this advance the enemy could now offer no effective naval opposition. The overwhelming defeat of the Japanese Fleet at the Battle for Leyte Gulf in October 1944 marked the beginning of a decline in the importance of their Navy, so that six months later it possessed little more than nuisance value. In the Pacific, Japanese submarines had never held the governing position assumed by these craft in other theatres. Consequently, Japanese opposition was limited to aerial and static defence.

2. The Allied Plan

The directive by the Joint Chiefs of Staff to Fleet Admiral C.W. Nimitz, Commander-in-Chief U.S. Pacific Fleet and Pacific Ocean Areas, is stated in the following extracts:

(a) I. DIRECTIVE

The Joint Chiefs of Staff have directed the Commander-in-Chief, Pacific Ocean Areas, to occupy one or more positions in the Nansei Shoto, target date 1st March 1945.

(b) II. PURPOSES

To establish bases from which to: (i) attack the main islands of Japan and their sea approaches with naval and air forces; (ii) support further operations in the regions bordering on the East China Sea; (iii) sever Japanese sea and air communications between the Empire and the mainland of Asia, Formosa, Malaya, and the Netherlands East Indies. To establish secure sea and air communications through the East China Sea to the coast of China and the Yangtze Valley. To maintain unremitting military pressure against Japan.

(c) III. TASKS

Immediate: Capture, occupy, defend and develop Okinawa Island and establish control of the sea and air in the Nansei Shoto area. Eventual: Extend control of the Nansei Shoto by capturing, occupying, defending and developing additional positions.

d) IV. CONCEPT OF OPERATIONS

The following is the general sequence of operations in the Nansei Shoto:

Phase I: Capture the southern portion of Okinawa including small adjacent islands and develop base facilities.

Phase II: Seize the remainder of Okinawa and Ie Shima and develop additional necessary base facilities in favoured localities.

Phase III: Exploit the position in the Nansei Shoto by seizing and developing additional positions with forces locally available.

The operation was known as "Iceberg". This consisted of all those combined operations which had as their object the capture of Okinawa Gunto. Throughout their operations in the Pacific the Americans had acted on the principle of allowing the enemy no respite between blows. On 14th March 1945, the flag was raised officially on Iwo Jima, in the Nanpo Shoto, after 24 days of fierce fighting.

On the same day the American fast carrier task force, which had been supporting the operation, sailed from Ulithi, after 10 days spent in regrouping and replenishment, for operations preparatory to the attack on Okinawa. Mine sweeping of the island waters under the guns of the battleships of the fast carrier force, which comprised a completely balanced fleet, commenced ten days later. L-Day, the date for the assault, was set for the 1st April; difficulties in maintaining shipping schedules, and the possibilities of unfavourable weather in the target area were the influencing factors which prevented the adoption of an earlier date.

3. The Nansei Shoto

The Nansei Shoto, or South-Western Islands, which Admiral Nimitz was directed to occupy, lies on the arc of a circle 790 miles long across the approaches to the East China Sea, extending from Formosa, which at that date was in Japanese hands, to the southern extremity of Kyushu. It comprises eight large islands, about 20 smaller ones, and numerous islets, exposed reefs, and rocks.

The chain of islands is divided into five groups, named from south to north, Sakishima Gunto, Okinawa Gunto, Amami Gunto, Tokara Gunto, and Osumi Gunto; the first two groups are known collectively as the Ryuku, and the last three as the Satsunan Islands.

Owing to its geographical position, the chain provides a barrier against the invasion of Japan from the south. As long as it remained in Japanese hands, it was a threat to future Allied operations against Formosa, the China coast, and Japan itself. With positions in the Nansei Shoto, the Allies would be able to control the East China Sea. Moreover, an operation against this objective was expected to divert enemy pressure from the Philippines, where operations were still continuing, and from Iwo Jima, where mopping up was in progress.

All of the islands are within 750 nautical miles of the southern edge of the Japanese industrial zone; and all of the Satsunans, including

Amami, the southernmost large island, are within a similar distance of Tokyo. The northern islands of the chain are closer to the enemy's central industrial zone than any other overseas area except Korea, Vladivostok, the southern tip of Hokkaido, and the northern part of the Nanpo Shoto, in which Iwo Jima lies.

Okinawa, the largest and most populous island in the Nansei Shoto, afforded numerous sites for airfields from which Formosa, the great Central China ports, and the southern part of Japan would be within range of fighter-escorted medium and heavy bombers as well as B.29s. The islands also provided ample sites for naval bases and anchorages, including a major fleet anchorage, and sufficient land area for mounting Operation "Olympic", the proposed final assault on Japan.

During the five or six months from October to February/March the Nansei Shoto is under the influence of the winter monsoon which is from between north and north-east. Over the open sea its strength when at its height averages force 4 or 5, but it often freshens to force 7 and at times reaches gale force, causing rough seas in exposed places such as Nansei Shoto. From June to the end of August the summer monsoon prevails, with mainly light or moderate winds from directions between south-east and south-west. The intervening months are periods of transition. During the winter monsoon average to undesirable flying weather rules throughout the chain. April to the end of September good average flying conditions prevail, except when typhoons or local storms occur.

At this time of year, seas and swells are low to calm. The varying topography of the islands results in a marked difference in weather at individual points in the Nansei Shoto chain. All through the year the Nansei Shoto lies in the danger area of typhoons, twelve of which pass somewhere near Japan in an average year. Half of them occur during the three months August to October. They are infrequent near Nansei Shoto between November and May.

4. The Enemy Forces

(A) NAVAL

Japanese naval strength on L-Day was thought to consist of the following combatant ships: 4 battleships, 2 converted battleship-carriers, 1 light carrier, 4 heavy cruisers, 4 light cruisers, 30 destroyers, 25-30 submarines.[1]

---

1 *Cinpac Report April* 1945, p.22.

Actually, only three Japanese battleships were still afloat,[2] namely the *Yamato, Nagato,* and *Haruna.* Of these, the former alone could be considered comparable to the 10 great modern American battleships of the *Iowa, South Dakota,* and *North Carolina* classes, and to the *King George V* and *Howe* of the British Pacific Fleet which was to take part in the operation.

The three Japanese battleships, two battleship carriers, *Ise* and *Hyuga,* each of which still mounted 8 x14 in, guns after the removal of their after turrets for the fitting of flight decks, with two heavy and two light cruisers and 25 destroyers comprised the 2nd Fleet or First Diversion Attack Force, under Vice-Admiral Ito. The Japanese 3rd Fleet (Vice-Admiral Jisaburo Ozawa) had 4 carriers and one escort carrier; and there were still afloat the *Hayataka* (*Junyo*) which had been heavily damaged on 9th December 1944 off Nagasaki and was still out of action, and the *Ryuho* which suffered heavy damage on 19th March 1945, at Kure, during the preliminary operations by U.S. fast carrier aircraft in connection with the assault on Okinawa. But the Japanese carriers were inoperative through lack of air groups; in fact, the entire Combined Fleet was practically immobilized through lack of oil.

The 6th Fleet (Vice-Admiral Shigeyoshi Miwa) disposed of some 15 operational submarines. The enemy had made little offensive use of this weapon during the war. In the present operation it was assumed that enemy submarines would be active along the Allied supply routes, and such Allied escort vessels as were available were used up to the maximum in the waters nearest to the Japanese submarine bases and operating areas, but no movement was ever cancelled for lack of escorts. When these were not available some risk was accepted.

It was expected, however, that midget submarines and suicide craft would be encountered in the objective area; and indeed, suicide boats were encountered in large numbers in the course of the operation, though the measures taken against them nullified their effect. Seven Allied ships were damaged and one sunk by suicide boats out of totals of 371 and 36 respectively by all means. It was believed that the greater part of the enemy's naval strength would be based in Japan at the commencement of the operation, and that whilst he would not commit his major surface units, hit and run raids on the amphibious forces were a distinct possibility.

2 U.S. Intelligence probably included in their calculations the *Mutsu*, which, perhaps unknown to them, had been sunk on 8th June 1943, in Hiroshima Bay by accidental explosion.

(B) AIR

The most serious threat to the Allies lay in the very factor for which the operation was undertaken, namely the closeness of Okinawa to the Empire where lay the main Japanese reserves. This threat was never completely mastered, though heavy losses were caused to the Japanese air forces. The fact that the Allies would be able to strike Japan to better effect after securing Okinawa, also operated conversely and implied that the Japanese could strike the Allies during the amphibious operation.

The particular menace was suicide air attack, to the combating of which the Americans had given much thought since it made its first appearance, in concerted form, during the assault on the Philippines in October 1944. It was to cause fantastic damage during the present operation resulting in the sinking of 27 and damaging of another 164 Allied ships, for the Japanese airfields within easy reach of Okinawa were too numerous to permit more than their partial and temporary interdiction by Allied air strikes, ceaseless though these were.

The U.S. estimate of the Japanese combat air strength, including combat types in operational training, in the Empire, Nansei Shoto, Formosa, and China on 1st March 1945, was as follows:

	Fighters	Bombers	Light Bombers	Medium Bombers	Patrol	Sea planes
Japan	1200	300	30	450	50	250
Nansei Shoto	24	12	-	12	-	30
Formosa	110	36	10	60	10	90
China	200	30	50	24	6	150
	1534	378	90	546	66	520

This gave a total of 3,134, a figure which was evidently much too low.[3]

The effectiveness of the suicide ("Kamikaze") type of attack, revealed during the Philippines and Iwo Jima campaigns, decided the Japanese to set up a definite organization for the employment of suicide tactics in the defence of the Nansei Shoto, and certain air forces, both Army and Navy, were combined in a single tactical command under the

[3] The chart of Production, Wastage and Strength of the Japanese Naval Air Force *only*, which accompanies Interrogation Nav. No. 86, U.S.S.B.S. Well. 414, gives figures for 1st April 1945, as follows: Fighters – 2,778; Ship board attack and bomber – 904; Land attack and bomber – 516; R/C and patrol – 177; Special attack (Baka aircraft) – 750; Transport – 100; Float reconnaissance – 830; Flying boats – 84; Trainer – 4,290; Total: 10,429. Of these numbers, about 20% were in "Kokusho" (storage). Of these, some 65-75% were under repair, 10-15% were unassigned or awaiting delivery to commands, and the remainder were obsolete aircraft.

Commander-in-Chief, Combined Fleet, Admiral Toyoda. These two air forces, the 6th Air Army and the 5th Air Fleet, operated from bases in Kyushu. The 5th Air Fleet (Vice-Admiral Ugaki) had approximately 250 aircraft. It was kept up to establishment as required, by the transfer of pilots and aircraft from the 3rd Air Fleet (Vice-Admiral Teroka) (which disposed of some 300 aircraft) and the 10th Air Fleet (Vice-Admiral Maeda) (The Training Command, about 900 aircraft).

Aircraft from the American fast carriers had raided Tokyo in connection with the assault on Iwo Jima on 16th and 17th February 1945, and again on 25th. Lack of enemy opposition to these strikes, together with other information, indicated that most of the Japanese offensive air strength was based in the Kyushu area. Approximately 700 aircraft, including 250 fighters, 150 single-engine bombers, and 300 medium bombers, were believed to be based in southern Kyushu: the fighters at Kagoshima, Kanoya East, and Miyazaki: the single-engine bombers at Miyazaki and Kagoshima: and the medium bombers at Kenoya, Miyazaki, Nittagahara, and Miyakonojo.

It was thought that the American landings in the Nansei Shoto would hinder but not stop the enemy's air ferry route from Kyushu to Formosa via the Nansei Shoto, for there was a possible alternative route to Formosa via Shanghai. The Americans expected to knock out quickly the small enemy air force in the Nansei Shoto, which thereafter would probably not be re-stocked. But the airfields of Formosa, Kyushu and the Shanghai area were within practicable operating range of Okinawa for all types of Japanese combat aircraft except short-range fighters, and the Expeditionary Force expected to be attacked accordingly. It was thought that continued strikes on the enemy's factories and air facilities might compel him to commit most of his air forces against the attempt to land on Okinawa, in order to inflict the maximum amount of damage before his air force deteriorated under the Allied air strikes.

(C) GARRISON FORCES IN THE NANSEI SHOTO

Second only to the air in importance was the opposition to the assault expected from the enemy garrison in the Nansei Shoto. Before the commencement of the operation, it was estimated that the Japanese had approximately 55,000 troops disposed on Okinawa. It was estimated that the enemy force consisted of at least one Division and a reinforced brigade together with necessary service troops and artillery and tanks.[4] This estimate proved too low and had to be revised after the landing on Okinawa.

---

4 Admiral King, *Final Report*, p.8, says it was estimated the Japanese would have 80,000 troops on Okinawa by L-Day.

The large native population of the island was assumed to provide an unlimited labour supply, but an estimated 10,000 to 20,000 conscripted Okinawans were not taken into consideration owing to uncertainty. Including these conscripts, and Construction and Line of Communication troops employed as infantry, Okinawa was defended by 120,000 men, the principal units being the 62nd Division, the 24th Division, and the 44th Independent Mixed Brigade, under the command of Lieut.-General Mitsuru Ushigima, Commanding 32nd Army.

The enemy was reported to have, in addition, 57,000-62,000 troops in other positions in the Nansei Shoto, the largest concentrations being at Amami and Miyako, where it was estimated there were approximately 10,000 and 16,000 troops respectively. Further possible sources of reinforcement were 75,000 troops in the Shanghai area, 84,000 in Formosa, and 110,000 in Kyushu.

Okinawa could be reinforced from within the Nansei Shoto by troops transported in barges or small vessels. It was believed, however, that the most likely attempt at reinforcement would be by flying troops in from the Shanghai area, Formosa, or Kyushu, all of which were within two hours' flying time of the objective; but this expectation did not materialise.

5. Special Features of the Operation

The Ryukus operation was the largest of its kind as yet undertaken in the Pacific and the greatest long-range combined operation[5] in history, necessitating mounting and assembly being carried out at a number of widely separated advance bases. The operation differed from those carried out by the Americans in the past in the Pacific Ocean Areas mainly in its greater scale; whilst the objective was so close to the enemy's principal bases that combat conditions were expected to continue for an extended period.

An entirely novel feature was the establishment, in the space of no more than three days, of a repair and supply base in the islands of the Keramo Retto, off the S.W. extreme of Okinawa Shima.

The American fleet in the Pacific had for some time been operating far in advance of its forward anchorages and bases. The nearest Allied

5 The Americans use the term 'Amphibious Operation' to describe any operation involving landing on hostile shores: *Combined Operation* to describe an operation in which U.S. forces are operating with Allied forces of other nations: and *Joint Operation* to describe one which involves the different services, Army and Navy. Thus the U.S. Amphibious Operation is, broadly speaking, equivalent to the British Combined Operation.

permanent bases to Japan were Pearl Harbor, distant 3,700 miles, and Sydney, distant 4,800 miles. The fleet used the advance base at Ulithi, in the west Carolines, during the operations against Leyte and Iwo Jima, distant 840 and 900 miles respectively. Between Ulithi and Okinawa there extended no less than 1,200 miles of open water.

The British Pacific Fleet, in its first operation, "Iceberg", used an advanced anchorage at Leyte, distant 780 miles from its target. Its nearest shore base in Australia was 3,500 miles away. Later, it was to operate off the coast of Japan between Hokkaido and Kyushu, with advanced anchorages at Manus and Eniwetok (Marshall Islands). "The distances involved," wrote the Commander-in-Chief, Admiral Sir Bruce Fraser, "are similar to those of a fleet based in Alexandria, and with advanced anchorages at Gibraltar and the Azores, attacking the North American coast between Labrador and Nova Scotia."

Despite these distances, the United States Fleet had evolved a method of operating its task forces more or less continuously off the enemy coasts. A great logistic organization ensured supplies for the operating fleets, and a system of replenishing at sea ensured for their ships the ability to keep the sea for periods which extended up to two months. The intense rate of striking which was thus rendered possible, together with the extremely crowded accommodation of the American ships, and the scant facilities for leave and recreation that could be made available at any of the advance bases, imposed a very heavy strain on the officers and men, the psychological effect of which the U.S. authorities studied with their usual thoroughness. They found their remedy in "bread and circuses" – in the modern American counterpart ice-creams, cinemas, and mails. It would be vain to ridicule these amenities, for on them the Pacific war was fought, and successfully fought. The Americans "have concentrated on three things", wrote Admiral Fraser:

(a) Good food, which includes, for the Americans, ice-creams.
(b) Good entertainment, which primarily consists of universal cinemas, with a constantly changing programme.
(c) Rapid and reliable mail service.

In the British Pacific Fleet, the regular delivery of mail at sea went far to maintain the general morale.

It was on the air crews of the fast carriers that the principal strain of this continuous effort fell. These were liable to be operating in combat over enemy territory almost daily for months on end, with but short respites every few weeks for re-equipping at an advance base.

To counter the inevitable fall in efficiency after being engaged for a certain period of time in this type of operation, the Americans adopted a system of changing their combat carrier air groups at the end of four or six months. A relatively untrained air group without close union with its ship, was found to give better results than a highly trained group suffering from operational fatigue. The scale of the operation was immense, even for the Americans who were accustomed to fling across oceans great forces of men, ships, and aircraft. From staging areas at Leyte Gulf, distant 900 miles, and Saipan and Ulithi, both distant 1,200 miles, a force of 548,000 men with 318 fighting ships and 1,139 auxiliary vessels – exclusive of personnel landing craft – was to converge on the objective, Okinawa. Preparatory operations were unusually thorough, consisting of preliminary air strikes over a wide area, and, at the objective, prolonged preliminary bombardment, minesweeping, beach reconnaissance and obstacle demolition.

6. Short Account of the Operation

COMMAND

The U.S. Fifth Fleet, under the command of Admiral R.A. Spruance, was directed by the Commander-in-Chief. U.S. Pacific Fleet and Pacific Ocean Areas, to carry out the principal tasks entailed, while all other major task forces in the Pacific Ocean Areas were directed to support the operation. The original intention was to capture Okinawa Shima, and the outlying satellite islands of Kerama Retto, Keise Shima, Ie Shima, and the islands of the south-east coast in the approaches to Chim Wan and Nakagusuku Wan, in two phases designated Phase I and Phase II, subject to changes which conditions might later impose.

Under Phase I the capture of the Kerama Retto, Keise Shima, and the main island of Okinawa south of the Ishikawa Isthmus together with the Eastern Islands was to be executed. Under Phase II the capture of Ie Shima and the Motobu Peninsula simultaneously, followed by the capture of the remainder of Okinawa north of the Ishikawa Isthmus, was to be effected. It was further foreseen that if during Phase I adequate airfields had not been captured at an early date, the capture of Ie Shima might have to take place during Phase I.

Phase II actually became amalgamated with Phase I and was completed prior to the conclusion of Phase I. During the Phase I period, too, orders were given to take certain additional minor islands for the purpose of enlarging the air warning net for Okinawa Gunto. These islands, and the dates of their seizure by elements of the Tenth Army were:

Tori Shima – 12th May 1945
Iheya Shima – 4th June 1945
Aguni Shima – 9th June 1945
Kume Shima – 26th June 1945

The Joint Staff Study amplified from time-to-time certain objectives for Phase III. Those were:

IIIa Okino Shima[6]
IIIb Kume Shima
IIIc Miyako Shima
IIId Kikai (Kikaga) Shima
IIIe Tokuno Shima

Plans were drawn up for the capture and development of each of these objectives. However, before the completion of Phase I of the operation all Phase III directives and plans were either cancelled or indefinitely postponed by direction of higher authority, the sole exception being IIIb Kume Shima.

Four divisions were to be landed abreast on the chosen beaches on the south-west side of Okinawa, directly across the island to the east coast, whilst the left and right flank divisions pivoted towards the north and south respectively. The Japanese forces isolated in the southern part of the island by these manoeuvres, were then to be overcome by attack from the north. Coincident with the main landing, a demonstration on the south-east coast was planned, with an actual landing if necessary.

ASSEMBLY AND SAILING

The dispersion of troops and shipping allocated to the Joint Expeditionary Force for the operation, from the Philippines to the west coast of the U.S.A. and in the south Pacific, precluded a joint rehearsal of all units. Cargo and troops were lifted from places as far apart as the west coast of the United States, the Hawaiian Islands, south-west Pacific, Marshall Islands Caroline Islands and Leyte.

The various elements proceeded to assemble afloat at Ulithi, Guadalcanal, Saipan. After rehearsals, the various forces sailed for the objective, except the Expeditionary Force Floating Reserve (Task Group 51.3) which remained at Ulithi on call, and the Expeditionary Troop Area Reserve (Task Force 51.4) which stood by at Numea (New

6 Presumably Okino Oagari Shima, or Rasa Island.

Caledonia) to await orders to load. The Area Reserve was not called forward to the objective.

Movement of all forces to the objective was carried out without enemy interference.

OPERATIONS OF THE FAST CARRIERS

The American Fast Carrier Force (Task Force 58) struck Japan, Formosa, the Sakishima Gunto, and the Okinawa Gunto previous to L-Day to destroy enemy aircraft and air installations and to soften up enemy defences which might interfere with the Okinawa operation. This force later provided air cover and direct support at Okinawa and covered the front and flanks against hostile and potential surface attack by strikes on Japan, and by destruction of a hostile surface task force in the Battle of the East China Sea, 7th April.

A British Carrier Task Force (Task Force 57, a self-sufficient unit with its logistic task force – Task Force 112) operating under the Commander 5th Fleet and in conjunction with the 5th Fleet, assisted in the neutralization of Formosa and the Sakishima Gunto and covered the western flank against hostile surface vessels and aircraft.

For a period of nearly three months the fast carriers and their escorts of Task Forces 58 and 57 operated in support of the operation. In the course of this duty, they lost 599 aircraft. They destroyed 2,008 enemy aircraft and caused widespread damage to shore installations in Japan, the Nansei Shoto and other enemy-held areas, and detracted considerably from the ability of the enemy to oppose the landing forces on Okinawa, thereby contributing notably to the final success. This was not achieved without loss, however. At the outset of the operation the strength of Task Force 58 was built around ten fleet carriers and six light carriers divided into four Task Groups. By the 11th May, five of the Fleet carriers had been put out of action, though two more fleet carriers and one light carrier had joined; and the Fast Carrier Force had been re-organized into three Task Groups. The British carriers were more fortunate: four of them were hit by suicide aircraft, but all were saved by their armoured decks and remained in operation.

OPERATIONS OF THE INDEPENDENT AIR FORCES

The Strategic Air Forces, Pacific Ocean Area, operating from bases in the Marianas struck Okinawa Gunto from time to time previous to L-Day (1st April) for the purpose of softening up the enemy, destroying his aircraft, neutralizing his airfields, and destroying his shipping. It further engaged in photographic reconnaissance and air-sea rescue work. With the capture of Iwo Jima in March 1945, aircraft based on that island carried out strikes on Japan itself in accordance with the general softening up plan, and provided cover and protection against hostile surface and aircraft on the eastern flank.

The 21st Bomber Command of the 20th Air Force, operating from bases in the Marianas, contributed to the general softening up plan by strikes on Japan, co-ordinating them with those of the fast carriers. It increased the frequency and strength of its strikes on the airfields and installations on Kyushu to neutralize the airfields and destroy the installations in order to minimize the employment of hostile aircraft against the American forces at Okinawa.

SUBMARINES

The Submarine Force, Pacific Fleet, carried out reconnaissance, attacked enemy shipping, engaged in lifeguard service, conducted photographic missions, and provided weather reports.

OPERATIONS AT OKINAWA PREVIOUS TO MAIN LANDING

On L-8 Day battleships of the Fast Carrier Force bombarded Okinawa, and minesweepers (Task Group 52.2) which were part of the Amphibious Support Force (Task Force 52) commenced work off the islands to ensure the safe approach of the advancing units. Next day, the bombarding vessels of the Amphibious Support Force, and the Gunfire and Covering Force (Task Force 54) arrived at the objective area and began to carry out their missions of surface and air bombardment, underwater demolitions, providing at the same time cover for the Expeditionary Force.

The Western Islands Attack Group (Task Group 51.1) arrived on L-6 Day (20th March) and commenced landing assault troops for the capture of Kerama Retto and Keise Shima. These islands were secured, a repair and seaplane base was established at Keramo Retto, and field artillery landed on Keise Shima by L-1 Day. Reconnaissance aircraft (Search and Reconnaissance Group – Task Group 50.5) based at Kerama Retto and Okinawa Shima supported the subsequent operations through searches of the East China Sea and attacked hostile shipping and aircraft, whilst other aircraft conducted anti-submarine patrols, air-rescue, and photographic reconnaissance.

MAIN LANDING

On L-Day, 1st April, the Northern Attack Force (Task Force 53) and Southern Attack Force (Task Force 55) arrived, disembarked and landed assault troops over the Hagushi beaches on the south-west shore of Okinawa.

DEMONSTRATION

The Demonstration Group (Task Group 51.2) also arrived on L-Day and executed a diversionary feint at landing on south-eastern Okinawa; the feint was repeated next day, and after landing the Army Reserve over the Hagushi beaches the Demonstration Group retired to the rear area.

CAPTURE OF SATELLITE ISLANDS

The unloading of ships immediately followed the disembarkation of assault troops. The Expeditionary Force Floating Reserve was called forward and using one Regimental Combat Team (the equivalent of a British Brigade Group) supported by surface craft and air forces, landed and captured the Eastern Islands on L+9 Day while the remainder of the Force was landed over the Hagushi beaches.

The Western Islands Landing Force, after embarking at Kerama Retto, landed on L+15 Day (16th April) at Ie Shima and captured the island by L+20 Day (21st April). The operation was supported by naval gunfire, air bombardment, and by artillery previously emplaced on Menna Shima, small island four miles south of Ie Shima; and after its completion the force was withdrawn and landed over the Hagushi beaches.

A detachment of Garrison Troops supported by light surface elements landed on Tori Shima without opposition, and on L+41 Day (12th May) established an Air Warning and Fighter-Director Station.

CHARACTERISTICS OF THE FIGHTING

In general, opposition to the landings was weak. U.S. held territory on Okinawa was rapidly enlarged. The advance northward was relatively fast against scattered resistance, resulting in the conclusion of Phase II of the operation on L+20 Day, against fortified positions. The Allied forces were under constant attack by bombing, torpedo, and suicide aircraft, and guided bombs, which sank 28 ships and damaged about 227, and caused many personnel casualties.

Defence was by combat air patrol and ships' gunfire. Fighter-Directors and Air Warning Service, in which radar picket ships and shore stations were employed, did valuable work. Smoke was used extensively at night with good results. Suicide boats and other small craft were active but were effectively kept in check by illumination and ships' gunfire.

BATTLE OF THE EAST CHINA SEA

An enemy force consisting of the fast battleship *Yamato*, one cruiser and eight destroyers, which made a sortie from the Inland Sea passing south of Kyushu into the East China Sea was engaged by aircraft of Task Force 58 on L+6 Day (7th April), and only four destroyers escaped destruction.

SHIP DAMAGE REPAIRS

The repair of battle damage and the upkeep of ships during the Okinawa operation constituted a difficult problem. The necessity for carrying out repairs to the greatest possible extent at the objective had been foreseen, and it was for this purpose that the formation of a repair base at Kerama Retto was envisaged. But the prolonged period during which the naval forces had to be retained at the objective placed a very heavy load upon repair facilities, which had to be considerably increased over those originally provided.

PERSONNEL FATIGUE

Personnel fatigue, particularly in ships on radar picket stations, became marked, and material deficiencies increased appreciably during the latter part of the operation.

CHANGE OF COMMAND

At 2400 on 27th May, Admiral W.F. Halsey, Jr., Commander Third Fleet, succeeded Admiral R.A. Spruance in command of the operation.

COMMANDER TENTH ARMY KILLED

Lieut.-General S.B. Buckner, Jr., commanding the troops which carried out the operation (Tenth Army), was killed in action on 18th June.

END OF RESISTANCE

On 21st June 1945, after 82 days of fighting, organized enemy resistance was declared at an end.

Chapter II

THE OBJECTIVE – OKINAWA GUNTO

The Okinawa Gunto, northern of the two groups composing the Ryuku Islands, is a densely populated group of rugged islands situated at the approximate centre of the Nansei Shoto.

7. General Description of the Group

It consists of Okinawa Shima, the largest and most important island of the Nansei Shoto chain, and numerous smaller islands, the whole covering an area roughly 90 miles east and west, and 65 miles north and south. The distances from Okinawa Shima to the most important adjacent enemy bases are:

Kiirun (Formosa) 330 nautical miles
Shanghai 450 nautical miles
Kagonhima (Kyushu) 360 nautical miles

The principal of the smaller islands and islets composing the group were from an operational point of view, the Kerama Retto, Keise Shima, Ie Shima, and the South-Eastern Islands.

8. Okinawa Shima

The island of Okinawa lies north-east and south-west, and is about 60 miles long and from three to ten miles wide. The south-western and north-eastern parts of the island differ greatly in character. The north-eastern is rugged, mountainous, and wooded, with few inhabitants, and very little cultivated land. Roads and trails are few and generally confined to the coast, which is precipitous and rocky and broken only by small beaches, with narrow alluvial flats at the stream mouths.

On the other hand, the south-western part is populous, and consists of hills and plateaux, the latter highly cultivated except where a sparse growth of trees occurs. Nearly all the low ground is commanded by heights. This rolling country is broken by numerous steep limestone scarps, ridges and steep-sided ravines. The largest flat areas are around the shores of Nakagusuku Bay (renamed by the Americans Buckner Bay) on the east, and from about ten miles north of Chiyamu (Cham) Saki (Cape Yakimu), the south-western extremity of Okinawa Shima, to Machinato. Elsewhere, the shores are formed by cliffs or steep slopes, with but few significant beaches.

There was a large population on Okinawa, numbering in 1935 about 451,620. Naha, the principal town, had in 1933 about 65,200 inhabitants, whilst the ancient capital, Shuri, two miles to the eastwards, had a population of about 19,300.

Okinawa Shima affords two fleet anchorages, in Nakagusuku Wan and Chim Wan respectively, on the east coast, the only substantial fleet anchorages south of Kyushu. Naha harbour in the south-west, which in peace time was an "open port" in which vessels were free to anchor, will accommodate destroyers in the outer harbour. It is somewhat exposed to westerly gales. During the year 1935 steam vessels to the number of 2,816, with an aggregate tonnage of 461,708 tons, entered the port. Usual weather conditions in Okinawa are cool, refreshing. and stimulating from September to June.

9. The Assault Beaches on Okinawa

The beaches chosen for the landing extended over some 10,000 yards on the south-western side of Okinawa, between Zampa Misaki on the north and Chatan, halfway between Zampa Misaki and Naha Ko, on the south. The beaches were not continuous but were interrupted by bluffs which dropped almost vertically to the sea. Other factors limiting landing were sea walls, reefs, and a shortage of exits from the beaches. Nevertheless, this stretch of coast was chosen not only on account of being sheltered from the easterly winds of the spring transition period, between the winter and summer monsoons, but also because the conditions of reef, gradient, and surf were comparatively good, the terrain behind the beaches gave space for manoeuvring a large assault force and afforded immediate access for the capture of the airfields Yontan and Katena.

A shallow fringing reef, with scattered coral heads, borders the entire coast. The average depth of water over the reef at low tide is three feet. Along much of its extent the fringing reef approaches the character of a barrier reef, with deeper water between the lip of the reef and the shore. At the north end of the assault beaches the distance from the shore to the outer edge of the reef is about 1,300 yards, narrowing to 200 yards about one mile south, and widening again to approximately 900 yards at the southern end.

The width of the beaches, which are composed largely of coral sand, ranges from 3 to 30 yards. The gradient is moderate to gentle in the southern beaches and moderate to steep in the northern beaches. Maximum spring tides average about 5.5 ft.

More than half the length of the beaches is backed by a very narrow fringe of trees and brush. Immediately behind the beach is an uplifted terrace which rises from 20 to 70 feet, abruptly in places, especially in the north; in other places it slopes gradually, particularly in the south.

Most of the beaches had at least one road exit. The roads varied in width from 6 to 12 feet, and some of them had coral surfacing. There were no first-class roads in the area. The southern beaches had fewer roads, but had larger expanses of beaches of cleared land adjacent to the beach, while the northern beaches had sufficient roads for adequate dispersal.

10. Enemy Defences on Okinawa

Of the one or two infantry divisions, one mixed brigade and supporting troops, which intelligence reports indicated as the garrison of Okinawa, it was assumed that the greater concentration would be in the southern half of the island. The northern, more mountainous half of Okinawa contained few vital installations; while the southern half of the island appeared to have prepared positions at and behind the beaches on both the east and west coasts. Defence positions on the west coast did not appear to be as heavily concentrated as those on the east, but it was believed that a mobile plan of defence had been prepared against landings on the west.

The defences, frequently located in almost inaccessible places, consisted in general of the usual mutually supporting system of trenches, anti-tank ditches, caves, under-ground installations and revetted areas. Cave warfare was extensively adopted, despite its weaknesses, in an attempt to avoid the tremendous fire power which the American ships could bring to bear, and to gain delay, in the hope of exacting such toll that the will to win would be weakened. A marked advance of this type of warfare was shown by the Japanese at Okinawa.

The sea walls were, in part, formidable obstacles. Strongly built of rubble and cement, rising sometimes to a height of nine feet, with almost vertical faces, they formed efficient tank traps. In places, blockhouses and posts sited for crossfire control of the beaches, were built into them. The sea walls were not, however, continuous along the length of the beaches.

Coast defence batteries, as far as the American knowledge of them extended, were concentrated in three areas:

- (i) South of Nakagusuku Wan, just north of Chinen Misaki:
- (ii) On the southern end of Tsuken Shima (one of the Eastern Islands, at the entrance to Nakagusuku Wan);
- (iii) South of Naha Ko, in the neighbourhood of Naha Airfield.

These coast defence gun positions and their supporting positions were found to be well sited, in concrete and steel casemates. They were excellently camouflaged and extremely hard to identify.

Underwater obstacles consisting of three or four lines of timber posts, probably strung with barbed wire and possibly mined, were known to exist off the northern half of the proposed landing beaches and on the Machinato-Yonabaru area, approximately 200 yards offshore.

Okinawa Gunto had many small coves that could be used as possible hiding places for enemy suicide boats.

The five airfields on Okinawa, *viz.*: Yontan, Katena, Machinato, Yonabaru, and Naha, were all situated in the southern part of the island.

11. The Satellite Islands

(A) KERAMA RETTO

The Kerama Retto is a group of small islands lying from 10 to 20 nautical miles west of Okinawa. The population in 1935 was about 3,500. The islands are very rough and hilly, maximum elevations 400 to 800 feet, and the summits are covered with dense forests and pine trees. The few small valley flats are well watered. The largest island of the group, Tokashiki Shima, is five miles long. The coasts are very steep and irregular, with narrow beaches of coral rock in many places. Coral reefs are common on parts of islands which are exposed to currents along the north-west and south-west side. Precipitous rock cliffs form the coastline except for occasional coral sand beaches. These beaches have a moderate slope and vary from 150 yards to 600 yards in length. In peacetime, the group afforded harbours of refuge.

(B) KEISE SHIMA

Keise Shima (Reef Islands) is a group of three sand and pebble islets lying between Kerama Retto and Okinawa. In peacetime the islets were uninhabited, except during the fishing season, when temporary rush huts were erected on them. Nagannu (Nagandu) Shima, the largest islet, measures about 4,500 by 1,000 feet, and on it are some trees. It is surrounded by wide fringing and barrier reefs. The other islands are much smaller.

The value of the islands to the Americans for operational purposes, was that they provided gun sites for the support of the main landings on the Okinawa beaches, 20,000 yards distant.

(C) THE EASTERN ISLANDS

Nakagusuku Wan and Chim Wan, the two great anchorages on the east side of Okinawa, are protected by a fringe of reefs and islands. One of the latter, Tsuken Shima, commands the entrance to Nakagusuku Wan, and was defended by the Japanese.

(D) IE SHIMA

Ie Shima, four miles north-west of the tip of the Motobu Peninsula, is a flat, slightly elevated plateau, with a pointed rocky hill, Ikosuku Yama or Sugarloaf Hill, 555 feet high, towards the eastern end of the island, where there was also a village. The island is lozenge shaped, some 4½ by 1½ nautical miles in extent. The southern and eastern shores have four firm beaches of coral and sand, from 9 to 35 yards wide and 125 to 900 yards long. The remainder of the island is bounded by rocky sea-cliffs. A fringing reef 360 to 720 yards wide, with scattered coral heads, and without channels, borders the island. Moderate slopes lead inland from all beaches. The Japanese had three airstrips on the island, each one approximately 5,000 feet long.

(E) TORI SHIMA

This rocky islet lies about 55 miles west of Okinawa and is some 300 yards long and 50 yards wide, and 77 feet high. It was used by the Americans during the latter part of the Ryukus operation, as an air and search and fighter director station.

(F) IHEYA SHIMA

Iheya Shima, 20 miles north-west of Okinawa, appears from a distance like a row of islets, for its surface consists of hills separated by deep valleys. The Americans established on it air warning and fighter director stations, though not until a late stage in the operation.

(G) AGUNI SHIMA

Warning and fighter director stations were established late on the island of Aguni, which lies nearly midway between Tori Shima and Okinawa.

(H) KUME SHIMA

Kume Shima is the westernmost island in Okinawa Gunto and the largest of the satellites. It was occupied by the Americans subsequent to the ending of organized resistance on Okinawa.

Chapter III

ORGANIZATION OF THE ALLIED FORCES

Shortly after the commencement of the Ryukus operation, a new U.S. command organization for the Pacific Theatre was announced.

12. Command Organization in the Pacific

There had previously been two independent commanders, each responsible only to the Joint Chiefs of Staff at Washington. General of the Army Douglas MacArthur commanded all forces in the South-West Pacific Area, and Fleet Admiral C.W. Nimitz was Commander-in-Chief of the Pacific Fleet (Cincpac) and in command of all forces in the Pacific Ocean Areas (Cincpoa) – that is, roughly, the Central Pacific. On 5th April, 1945, the United States Chiefs of Staff released an announcement modifying the command organization for the war against Japan. The directive pointed out that rapid advances in the South-West Pacific and in Pacific Ocean Areas had brought the Allies into close proximity with the Japanese homeland and the China coast and thus changed the character of the operations against Japan.

The Joint Chiefs of Staff appointed General MacArthur Commander-in-Chief, U.S. Amy Forces, Pacific (Cincafpac), and gave him command of all army forces and resources in the Pacific Theatre (less the South-East Pacific Area, and the resources under the command of the Commanding General, Alaska Department) though the Commander-in-Chief, U.S. Fleet and Chief of Naval Operations (Fleet Admiral E. J. King), retained for himself the right to re-allocate naval forces within the Central and South-West Pacific Areas. No Supreme Commander was appointed: the Joint Chiefs of Staff retained the direction of the Pacific war, and announced that they would "charge either General

MacArthur or Admiral Nimitz with the overall responsibility for conducting specific operations or campaigns".

The attempt to amalgamate the two previously independent Area Commanders, without appointing a Supreme or Theatre Commander over them, resulted in a confused state of higher command within the Pacific. The intention of the Joint Chiefs of Staff was that both commanders should retain their areas until passed to the other command by mutual agreement or by direction of the Joint Chiefs of Staff. Throughout the operation, however, both commanders continued to retain their areas and to rely for logistic support on a separate chain of bases.

The Twentieth Air Force in India, under the command of General of the Army H.A. Arnold, although it operated in the Central and South-West Pacific, was not brought under either General MacArthur or Admiral Nimitz.

The four principal commands under the Joint Chiefs of Staff, and their functions in the Okinawa operation, were as follows:[7]

(i) XX Air Force (General of the Army H.A. Arnold).

XX Bomber Command. All available sorties against enemy installations in northern Formosa.

XXI Bomber Command, Okinawa (L-30 Day to L-10 Day), Kyushu (L-9 Day to L-5 Day), and Tokyo area (L-4 Day onwards).

(ii) China-based Forces (Lieut.-General A.C. Wedemeyer). Aerial reconnaissance and strikes over Chinese coastal area.

(iii) Pacific Fleet and Pacific Ocean Areas Forces (Fleet Admiral C.W. Nimitz). Establish and maintain control of the approaches to the East China Sea by the capture and defence of positions in the Nansei Shoto in order to provide facilities for further advances towards Japan.

(iv) South-West Pacific Forces (General of the Army D. MacArthur). Air attacks from Luzon on enemy bases in Formosa and neutralization of airfields in Formosa. Searches over the China Sea, Strait of Formosa, and the sea areas east of Formosa.

13. The Pacific Fleet and Pacific Ocean Areas Forces (Cinepac-Cincpoa Forces)

The Joint Chiefs of Staff charged Admiral Nimitz with the task of carrying out the Ryukus operation. His net was flung wide, and under

[7] The four principal commands are shown as before the directive of 5th April 1945. The functions of the commanders remained as shown.

his command were a number of forces, all of which were directly or indirectly to become engaged in the operation. Some, such as the Marshalls-Gilberts Force under Rear-Admiral W.K. Harrill, guarded the lines of communication by holding positions needed for security. A force under Vice-Admiral F.J. Fletcher contained the enemy in the North Pacific. The South Pacific Force (Vice-Admiral W.L. Calhoun) provided logistic support as directed, as did also Admiral R.E. Ingersoll, Commander Western Sea Frontier (United States), and the Army Forces of the Pacific Ocean Areas under Lieut.-General R.C. Richardson, Jr.

The Service Force Pacific Fleet under Vice-Admiral W.W. Smith and the Commander Air Force, Pacific Fleet, Vice-Admiral G.E. Murray, provided logistic support for the Commander Logistic Support Group (TG 50.8) who furnished direct logistic support to the units in and near the combat zone, Vice-Admiral Murray being responsible for the supply of replacement air crews and pilots, aircraft and aircraft spares to forward area bases. The Submarine Force under Vice-Admiral C.A. Lockwood, Jr. was widely disposed to provide intelligence of movements of enemy naval units, interdict the sea approaches to Okinawa from Japan and Formosa, and for lifesaving services.

The Forward Area Central Pacific, to which ships returned for rest and replenishment, was under Vice-Admiral J.H. Horner, who had in his command naval and air forces for anti-submarine cover, the neutralization of enemy bases by aircraft, air-sea rescue services and evacuation transport service. The Strategic Air Forces, Pacific Ocean Areas (Major-General W. H. Hale) had the duties of neutralizing enemy bases in the Carolines and Nanpo Shoto, attacking the airfields and air installations in the Nansei Shoto and Japan, and providing fighter cover for XX Air Force strikes on Japan.

The plan called for a series of operations to confuse and deceive the enemy, and to systematically reduce the defended island group. The actual landing and necessary supporting and covering operations were to be carried out by the Central Pacific Task Forces under Admiral R.A. Spruance, Commander 5th Fleet, who on 3rd January issued his Operation Plan No.1-45 to implement Admiral Nimitz's directive (Operation Plan No.14-44).

14. Forces Which Carried out the Operation (Central Pacific Task Forces)

The Central Pacific Task Forces were organized for the operation in two forces: (a) The Covering Force – Task Force 50 – (under Admiral

Spruance's own command); (b) The Joint Expeditionary Force – Task Force 51 – (Vice-Admiral R.K. Turner, succeeded by Vice-Admiral H.H. Hill on 17th May when the command of forces ashore passed to the Army).

At 2400 on 27th May a re-organization was effected of a nature which, so far as is known, was peculiar to the American forces. At that moment operational control of all naval forces then attached to the Fifth Fleet passed from Admiral Spruance to Admiral W.F. Halsey, Jr., Commander Third Fleet, and in consequence all component units, such as task forces, task groups, and task units, changed their designations by the substitution of the number '3' for '5', e.g., Task Group 52.1 became Task Group 32.1.

15. The Covering Force

The covering forces consisted of the fast carrier task forces. These were two in number, one American and one British. The American force, Task Force 58, was under the command of Vice-Admiral M.A. Mitscher (succeeded on 28th May by Vice-Admiral J.S. McCain) until the 17th April when heavy losses and damage compelled Task Group 58.2 to be dissolved in order to reinforce the remainder.

Task Force 58 comprised four groups of carriers, protected by heavy ships and screen, each group constituting a balanced force. From this task force, if necessity arose, a Striking Force, Task Force 9, could be formed under Vice-Admiral W.A. Lee, Jr., to destroy any enemy surface force which might attempt to interfere with the operation. On the fast carriers themselves there devolved the exacting task of neutralizing Japanese air power prior to the landings, and thereafter preventing enemy air interference with the operation. The battleships, in addition to protecting the carriers, had also a bombardment role. The force carried 919 aircraft, in the proportion of 70 per cent fighters to 30 per cent bombers.[8]

The British Carrier Force (Task Force 57), under Vice-Admiral H.B. Rawlings, although treated on the status of a Task Force, approximated in size to but a single group of the American fast carrier force, the aircraft load, at the commencement of the operation, being 218.[9] Its task was to protect the left flank of the operation, by neutralizing the

---

8 *The Campaigns of the Pacific War*, p.324. This was presumably the average load. The figure decreased considerably consequent on losses as the operation proceeded. The load, before the withdrawal of the *Wasp* and *Franklin*, damaged on 19th March off Kyushu, was about 1,300 aircraft.

9 *The Campaigns of the Pacific War* gives the figure as 244, but no authority for this statement has been found.

airfields in the Sakishima Gunto. It was formed from the British Pacific Fleet (Commander-in-Chief, Admiral Sir Bruce Fraser), based on Australia, and was in every respect self-sufficient, having its own fleet train, Task Force 112 (Rear-Admiral D.B. Fisher, C.B., C.B.E., R.N.).

Although operating in Admiral Nimitz's area, the Central Pacific, its advanced bases were in General MacArthur's area at Leyte and Manus, whilst its only shore base was in Australia. The Force was subject to withdrawal from the operation and transfer to the south-west Pacific at 7 days' notice by the C.-in-C. U.S. Fleet.

16. Joint Expeditionary Force

The Joint Expeditionary Force included all elements directly engaged in the landings. Vice-Admiral R.K. Turner, Commander Amphibious Forces, U.S. Pacific Fleet, in his capacity of Commander Joint Expeditionary Force (Task Force 51) was charged with the task of capturing, occupying, and defending positions in the Okinawa Gunto, and of commencing the development of advanced naval and air bases.

The Expeditionary Troops (Task Force 56) under Lieut.-General S.B. Buckner, Jr., U.S.A., Commanding Tenth Army, were initially under the command of the Commander Joint Expeditionary Force. They included the Assault troops and assigned Garrison Troops required for the capture, occupation, defence, and development of the objective. The Assault forces were the Northern Landing Force (Task Group 56.2) (III Amphibious Corps consisting of 1st and 6th Marine Divisions) under Major-General R.S. Geiger, U.S.M.C., and the Southern Landing Force (Task Group 56.3) (XXIV Corps consisting of the 7th and 90th Infantry Divisions) under Major-General J.R. Hodge, U.S.A., who were to be landed respectively by the Northern Attack Force (Task Force 53) under Rear-Admiral L.F. Reifsnider and the Southern Attack Force (Task Force 55) under Rear-Admiral J.L. Hall, Jr.: the Western Islands Landing Force (Task Group 66.4) (Major-General A.D. Bruce, U.S.A.), to be landed by Rear-Admiral I.N. Kiland, Commanding the Western Islands Attack Group (Task Group 51.1) , who was under the direct command of Rear-Admiral W.H.P. Blandy, commander of the Amphibious Support Force (Task Force 52); the Demonstration Landing Force (Task Group 56.5) under Major-General Watson, U.S.M.C., consisting of the 2nd Marine Division who were to be landed by the Demonstration Group (Task Group 51.2) under Rear-Admiral J. Wright; the Expeditionary Force Floating Reserve (Task Group 56.6) under Major-General G.W. Griner, Jr. U.S.A., and consisting of the 8lst Infantry Division, which was to be assigned to the Tenth Army by the Commander Pacific Ocean Areas if required.

Thus, the forces under the operational direction of the Commander-in-Chief, Pacific Fleet and Pacific Ocean Areas (Admiral Nimitz), included Army, Navy, and Marine units, organized not only for combat but also for base operation and development. At such time as the Commander 5th Fleet considered that the Amphibious Phase of each part of the operation had been completed, he was directed to turn over command of all forces ashore at the objective to the Commanding General, Tenth Army, who would then be responsible directly to Admiral Nimitz.

The composition and functions of the Gunfire and Covering Force (Task Force 54) under Rear-Admiral M.L. Deyo,[10] who took the place at the last moment of Vice-Admiral Oldendorf, injured in a small boat accident on 11th March, were a new feature. The force comprised the fire support ships detailed, viz., the ten old battleships and the other covering vessels not with the fast carriers, organized in five units of battleships, cruisers, and destroyers, and a sixth unit of escort vessels. Ships once detailed to T.F. 54 remained assigned and did not take their turn in screening or other duties, though periodic readjustments were made to reconcile the composition of the force with other requirements. for the ground forces throughout the operation, and ensured cover for the task force in the neighbourhood of the objective against hostile surface attack, including that of small boats.

The Amphibious Support Force (Task Force 52) under Rear-Admiral W.H.P. Blandy consisted of fire support ships assigned from the Gunfire and Covering Force; a Support Carrier Group of 14 escort carriers with Screen whose primary task was to furnish air support at Okinawa;[11] an Air Support Control Unit; a Mine Flotilla; Underwater Demolition Flotilla; Gunboat Support Flotilla and Mortar Support Flotilla. It carried out gunfire and air support, minesweeping and underwater demolitions in support of the operation. It provided continuous fire support. On arrival at the objective on L-Day, Vice-Admiral R. K. Turner, C.T.F. 51, took command of the Amphibious Support Force. Rear-Admiral Blandy then assumed command of Fire Support and Air Units in the south-eastern area of Okinawa as C.T.G. 51.19 until relieved by Rear-Admiral Fahrion who assumed additional duties as S.O.P.A. Eastern Okinawa at L+17 Day.

The command relationship between C.T.F. 54 and C.T.F. 52 as planned was that the latter would be responsible for the execution of all operations at the objective, whilst C.T.F. 54 would be responsible

---

[10] Succeeded on 4th May by Rear-Admiral A.E. Smith.

[11] The escort carriers had 564 aircraft. This figure probably includes the 2 ships of the Anti-Submarine Warfare Group (T.G. 50.7) and the 6 in the Logistic Support Group (T.G. 50.8).

for the movement and approach to the objective of T.F. 54 and ships of T.F. 32 moving with T.F. 34, for fighting surface actions should there be any, for night deployments and for acting as S.O.P.A. in the objective area.

17. Logistic and Special Groups

Service Squadron 10 (Task Group 50.9) was responsible for replenishing the fleet at forward area bases, and routeing and sailing supply ships for the forces in the combat area. The Commander of the Logistic Support Group, Service Squadron 6 (C.T.G. 50.8), Rear-Admiral D.B. Beary, commanding fleet supply ships in the combat area, co-ordinated fuelling schedules for the fast carrier task forces and amphibious forces, and exercised direct command of replenishment activities at sea. One unit of the Anti-Submarine Warfare Group (Task Group 50.7) comprising four destroyer escorts, operated in the neighbourhood of the replenishment groups of the Logistic Support Group whose escort carriers provided the necessary aircraft. The other two units, each of which included an escort carrier, were assigned to the operational control of the Commander Joint Expeditionary Force whose duty it was to protect shipping along routes and in the objective area.

In all, a total of 1,213 ships were employed by Task Force 51, including assault shipping and ships of the first garrison echelon, but excluding ships from other forces which operated temporarily under Senior Officers Present Afloat at the objective.

SUMMARY OF SHIPS EMPLOYED IN THE JOINT EXPEDITIONARY FORCE[12]

Type	*No.*	*Type*	*No.*
Old battleships	18	H.Q. ships	8
Heavy cruisers	8	Assault Transports	126
Light cruisers	4	High speed destroyer transports	36
Escort carriers	18	Transport vessels	3
Destroyers	82	Evacuation transports	2
Destroyer escorts	54	Transports, attack	3
Minelayers	3	Cargo ships	65

12 Figures in this summary are those given by the Commander of the Joint Expeditionary Force. *Operations in the Pacific Ocean Areas*, May, 1945, p. 42, says that there were approximately 1,400 ships and landing craft of all types but this presumably includes landing craft, etc., carried aboard ships.

Light minelayers	14	Repair ships	5
High speed minesweepers	13	Tugs	8
Minesweepers	42	Salvage vessels	1
Motor minesweepers	40	Landing ships	303
Patrol craft	40	Landing ships, dock	6
M.G.Bs.	39	Landing craft	249
Seaplane tenders	10	Netlayers	12
		Unclassified	1
Total	285	*Total*	828

Expeditionary personnel employed during Phases I and II of the operation, including the 2nd Marine Division which was at the objective but not land, were as follows:

	Army	*Marine*	*Navy*
Landing Force	98,567	81,165	2,380
Garrison Force	182,137	8,310	79,307
Total			451,866

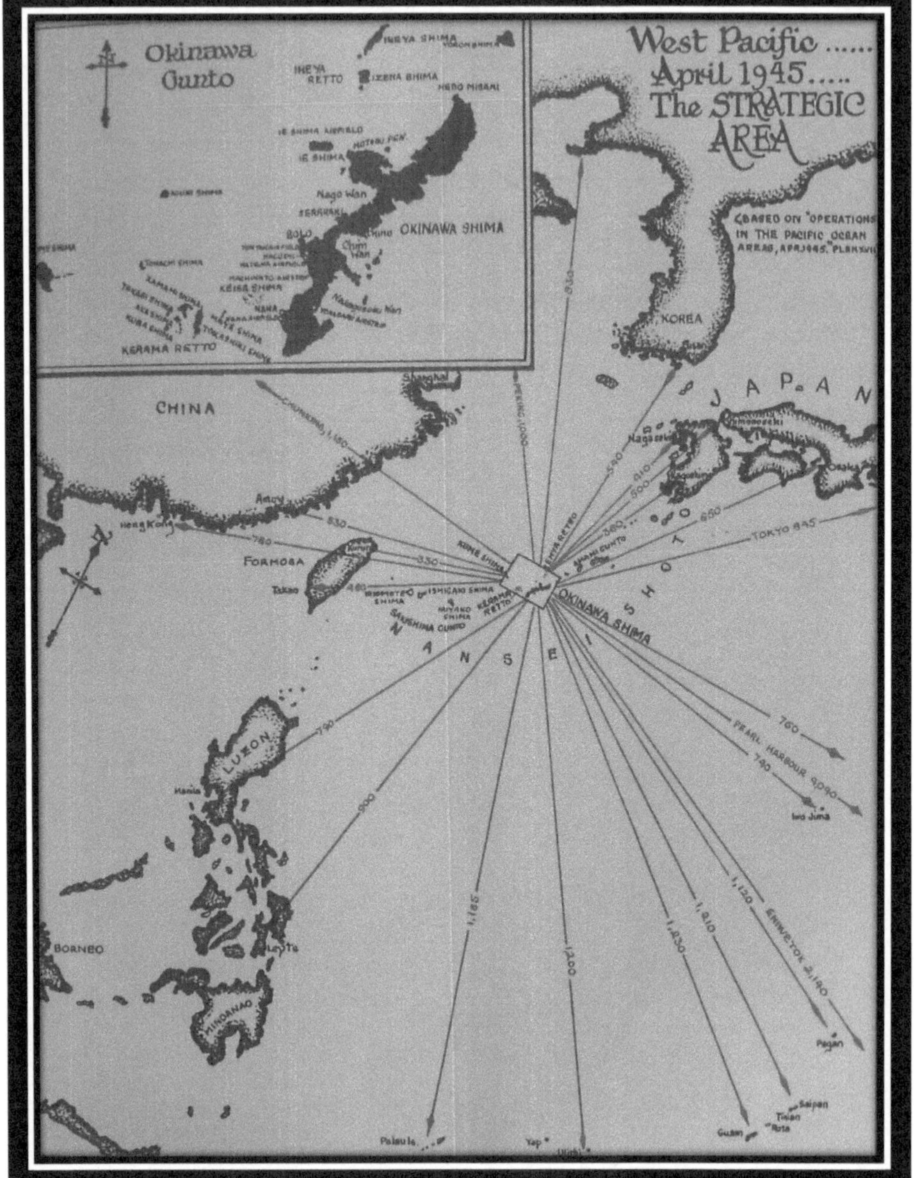
West Pacific ......
April 1945.....
The STRATEGIC AREA
(BASED ON "OPERATIONS IN THE PACIFIC OCEAN AREAS, APR 1945." PLAN XVII
Okinawa Gunto
INEYA SHIMA
IHEYA RETTO
IZENA SHIMA
HEDO MISAKI
IE SHIMA AIRFIELD
IE SHIMA
Nago Wan
OKINAWA SHIMA
Chim Wan
KEISE SHIMA
NAHA
KERAMA RETTO
CHINA
Shanghai
KOREA
JAPAN
Nagasaki
Amoy
Hong Kong
FORMOSA
Takao
OKINAWA SHIMA
NANSEI SHOTO
TOKYO 845
PEARL HARBOUR 4,090
Iwo Jima
LUZON
Manila
BORNEO
Leyte
MINDANAO
ENIWETOK 2,140
Pagan
Saipan
Tinian
Rota
Guam
Yap
Palau Is.

Chapter IV

PREPARATORY OPERATIONS

The preparatory operations included preliminary air reconnaissance, rehearsal exercises, mounting of the amphibious forces, movement of various groups of vessels to the combat area, preliminary air strikes by carrier-based aircraft on targets in the Empire area, shore bombardment of Okinawa by surface ships, minesweeping in the objective area, reconnaissance of approaches to the landing beaches at Kerama Retto and Okinawa, and demolition of underwater obstructions and mines found thereon.

18. Photographic Reconnaissance

Okinawa Gunto was a prefecture of Japan. Isolated from the world by the Japanese as it was, information of military value was difficult to obtain. However, captured Japanese charts furnished hydrographic data; and captured documents, interrogation of former residents of the islands, and old publications furnished limited basic intelligence. The greater part of the intelligence used by the Expeditionary Force for the Ryukus Operation had to be obtained from photographic coverage. The distance of the nearest Allied airfield, 1,200 miles at this time, necessitated the use of B.20s or carrier-based aircraft for photographic missions.

Adequate small scale air coverage of Okinawa Gunto for mapping purposes was obtained on 2nd September, 1944, by B.29s of the U.S. XXI Bomber Command. The photographs from this flight covered the entire island and partially covered off-lying islands. Unfortunately, some cloud obscured part of the northern area. From then on until the conclusion of the operation, additional photographing was done at frequent intervals by Army aircraft and aircraft of the Fast Carrier Force. The prompt developing, printing, and interpreting of these photographs, and the early and wide distribution of the prints and of the information gleaned from them, was an important feature of the operation.

The relatively large land masses involved, the frequent cloud cover encountered, the distance from American bases, and the restriction imposed by the scheduling of strikes on Okinawa, made it difficult for carrier aircraft to obtain the necessary large-scale photographs for detailed study of installations. Photographs taken by Fast Carrier Force aircraft on l0th October, 1944, however, covered 30 per cent, of Okinawa Gunto, and provided large scale vertical and oblique photographs that could be used for detailed study.

The XXI Bomber Command flew further missions on 29th November, 1944, 3rd January, and 28th February, 1945; the fast carriers of Task Force 58 flew photographic missions over the objective on 22nd January, 1st March and 22nd March, 1945, two of the carriers, the *Bunker Hill* and the *Hornet*, alone supplying over 14,000 photographs each. The coverage on most of these missions was good, and permitted a continuous study of changing enemy installations. The small-scale coverage by long-range B.29s, although not always suitable for detailed study, served as an excellent means of detecting changes made in the more important enemy installations. This coverage effectively closed the gaps in those obtained by aircraft from the fast carriers.

From L-7 Day (25th March), when the Amphibious Support Force (Task Force 52) arrived at the objective, the photographic missions of the fast carriers as well as of the Support Carrier Group (Task Group 52.1) were coordinated by the Commander Amphibious Support Force.

19. Assembly, Mounting and Rehearsals

The dispersion entailed in lifting cargo and troops for the Ryukus operatian on the west coast of the United States, in the Hawaiian Islands, south Pacific, south Pacific, Marshalls, Carolines and Leyte Gulf precluded a joint rehearsal of all units, and the various elements proceeded to assemble and conduct training and individual rehearsals as follows:

Gunfire and Covering Force (TF 54) – Ulithi – 21st March.
Amphibious Support Force (T.F. 52) – Ulithi – 11th-21st March.
Northern Attack Force (T.F. 53) – Guadalcanal – 1st-8th March.[13]
Southern Attack Force (T.F. 55) – Leyte Gulf – 14th-21st March.
Western Islands Attack Group (T.G. 51.1) – Leyte Gulf – 9th-16th March.

13 Staged from Ulithi.

Demonstration Group (T.G. 51.2) – Saipan – 16th-21st March.
Floating Reserve (T.G. 51.3)[14] – Espiritu Santo – 12th-25th March.
Area Reserve (T.G. 51.4) – Numea – After 18th March.

Plans originally envisaged ships of Task Forces 52 and 54 would assemble at Ulithi on 5th March and that the period from then until 21st March would be available for upkeep, replenishment, training, and rehearsal. Actually, ships continued to arrive up to the day of departure. Many late arrivals came directly from Iwo Jima and badly needed upkeep and replenishing, and rest for their crews, and, moreover, they had received no plans at all previous to arrival. Training was affected by the necessity for manning radar picket stations around Ulithi, which was subject to enemy air attacks.

The fast carriers also assembled at Ulithi to prepare for the forthcoming operation, and on 11th March the carrier *Randolph* was damaged here by air attack and was unable to re-join her group until the 8th April.

When the various forces comprising the Joint Expeditionary Force sailed for the combat area after rehearsals and final replenishment most of them had one or more carrier units of the Amphibious Support Force (T.F. 52), consisting of escort carriers and screen, detailed to provide cover on passage. The various forces proceeded direct to their objective areas, the Western Islands Attack Group (T.G. 51.1) to Kerama Retto, the Northern Attack Force) (T.F. 53) and Southern Attack Force (TF 55) to an area off the main landing beaches on the western side of Okinawa, and the Demonstration Group (T.G. 51.2) to the eastern side of the island.

These movements were carried out without enemy interference, though two successful attacks on Japanese submarines were made. At 2333 on 22nd March, whilst screening 12 miles ahead of a task group nearing Okinawa, the destroyer *Haggard* attacked a radar contact with depth charges and at 0028 on the 23rd in 22° 57′ N., 132° 10′ E, brought to the surface a submarine which she rammed. Her bow cut into the submarine just abaft the conning tower. The Japanese craft *I-371* rolled to port, blew up and sank. *Haggard*, badly damaged by the explosions of her own depth charges and by ramming, was escorted back to Ulithi by the *Uhlmann*.

At 2330 on the 30th March the destroyer *Stockton* in the Logistic Support Group screening a convoy approaching Okinawa, attacked about 65 miles south-cast of the island the large Japanese submarine *I-8*.

14 Conducted amphibious training but no rehearsals.

With the assistance of the destroyer *Morrison* of the Transport Screen, and illumination by aircraft A.S.P. 14-V-461, the enemy vessel was eventually sunk at 0412 on 31st in approximately 25° 29′ N., 128° 35′ E., a single survivor and some mangled bodies were recovered.

Operational breakdowns en route to the objective were insignificant.

20. Pre-Assault Fast Carrier Strikes, 18th-31st March

Once more, as in all the operations of the previous three years which had carried the American flag from Hawaii right across the Pacific to the Philippines, the fast carriers (Task Force 58) opened the ball. From the support of the expedition against Iwo Jima, Vice-Admiral Mitscher proceeded to Ulithi for a ten days' period of regrouping and replenishment, carrying out, on the way, a photographic reconnaissance of the Nansei Shoto on 1st March and a bombardment, largely for purposes of experience, by his cruisers next day of Okino Oagari Shima, a small island some 215 miles south-east of Okinawa, containing a phosphate plant.[15] He sailed from Ulithi after replenishment on 14th March to attack airfields in order to eliminate airborne resistance to the forthcoming assault on Okinawa.

Vice-Admiral Mitscher considered his first task to be air strikes against Japan itself. It was believed that fighter sweeps would eliminate enemy airborne opposition and destroy dispersed aircraft on the ground, whilst bombing attacks would destroy the facilities at the principal airfields. It was hoped that as the result of these raids the enemy would be unable to mount an air attack of any size against the American forces in Okinawa. Target areas were selected on the basis of the number of primary airfields in Kyushu, Shikoku and southern Honshu, and four Task Group Commanders were each assigned a target area. Airfields were designated as the primary targets of all fighter air sweeps. Bomber strikes from all task groups, however, could be concentrated on a single target, or on targets in the same general area, in order to provide a maximum concentration of bombs and mutual protection.

There were to be two days of strikes, 18th and 19th March. The Fast Carrier Force which Vice-Admiral Mitscher led against Japan still consisted at this date of the five groups which had supported the operations against Iwo Jima. The force fuelled on 16th March, and at dawn on the 18th commenced flying off fighter sweeps and combat air patrols from a position approximately 100 miles to the east of

[15] Referred to in the American reports by its former name Okino Diato Jima. Also known as Rasa Island.

the southern tip of Kyushu. Almost simultaneously a heavy enemy air attack was made on the carriers, resulting in some damage to the *Intrepid, Yorktown* and *Enterprise*. However, all three ships were able to continue operating, though the *Enterprise* was subsequently put out of flight operations by friendly gunfire. In general, the schedule for air attacks on the Kyushu airfields which had been arranged for the first day's operations was carried out. The results were excellent, and the Japanese were unable to mount any strong air attack against the Okinawa invasion forces until nearly a week after the landing.

Next day, 19th March, Vice-Admiral Mitscher was instructed to move north-east with Task Force 58, in order to launch attacks against units of the Japanese fleet which had been located at Kure and Kobe by reconnaissance flights on the previous day. A good deal of damage was caused ashore, but apart from heavy damage to the light carrier *Ryuho* at Kure the strikes against fleet units were only moderately successful, principally on account of the extremely heavy anti-aircraft fire encountered.

Whilst flying off the first heavy strike that morning the carrier *Franklin* was hit by a bomb and badly damaged, losing no less than 852 of her crew; and she was only saved by damage control of a very high standard. The enemy air attacks continued, and the carriers *Wasp* and *Yorktown* were both hit by bombs, the former badly, but both continued operating. The *Franklin* was taken in tow by the heavy cruiser *Pittsburgh*, and during the afternoon Task Force 58 retired, covering the disabled carrier by launching fighter sweeps against the Kyushu airfields, thus preventing any organized attacks against the force as it moved slowly southward. Later next afternoon 15 Japanese aircraft came in low and fast; fourteen were destroyed, seven by fighters and seven by ships' gunfire, but one of the falling machines damaged the destroyer *Halsey Powell*, slowing her to ten knots and causing further delay in the retirement southward.

On the afternoon of the 21st another air attack on the crippled force was beaten off, a group of 48 enemy aircraft being intercepted 60 miles from the force by 24 fighters from Task Group 58.1, who shot down every one, only two American fighters being lost. This ended the troubles of the Task Force. Next morning the Logistic Support Group was met, and Vice-Admiral Mitscher set about fuelling, provisioning, replenishing ammunition, and re- organizing for the operations against Okinawa. The number of task groups was now (21st March) reduced from five to four, by dissolving Task Group 58.5.

In all, 328 enemy aircraft were destroyed between the 18th and 22nd March: 108 American aircraft were lost, including 52 in the *Franklin*.

On the 23rd March, Task Force 58 began launching daily strikes against Okinawa Shima and the adjacent islands. All known enemy installations were extensively bombed, in order to prepare the area for minesweeping operations and for the landing on Kerama Retto which was to precede the main assault. There was practically no enemy air opposition, and it became increasingly apparent, as L-Day approached, that the strikes of 18th-19th March on the Kyushu airfields had interfered with Japanese air operations to a greater extent than had been estimated; and although the extent of the damage done was not easy to access, it undoubtedly hampered the enemy's subsequent efforts to launch strikes from their airfields in the Nansei Shoto against the invading forces.

In the forenoon of the 28th March there were indications that a sortie in strength of the Japanese fleet from the Bungo Suido might take place. Admiral Spruance at 0933 informed C.T.G. 58.1 (Rear-Admiral J.J. Clark) that a reduction in the strikes and sweeps against Okinawa in which he was engaged, could be accepted if his carriers could get within striking distance of the Japanese units to the south and west of Kyushu. Rear-Admiral Clark at once headed north at high speed, and at 1430[16] launched a strike against the Japanese fleet reported to be 225 miles away, supporting it with a fighter sweep against Kanoya and the Southern Kyushu airfields; but the enemy fleet was not to be found.

On the morning of the 20th, Task Groups 58.3 and 58.4, which had been fuelling to the south-eastward, moved north to meet Task Group 58.1 at a launching point in 29° 15′ N., 131° 15′ E., south of Kyushu. Search aircraft were launched at dawn, but found no sign of the Japanese fleet in an area extending from Sasebo on the West to the Inland Sea on the East. The strike aircraft, which had been launched in expectation of attacking the Japanese fleet, bombed airfields in the Kagoshima Bay area of Kyushu on their way back to the carriers, in the course of which seaplanes made a spectacular rescue of two pilots who had parachuted into the Bay under the guns of the enemy.

Task Group 58.3 also found and attacked so many miscellaneous ships' units that according to her Commander "on no other single day were so many shipping targets presented, or was so much shipping damage inflicted by this Task Group."[17] Enemy shipping remained a high priority target for the carrier-based aircraft until it practically disappeared from the area. Whilst the American fast carriers were engaged in these preliminary strikes the carriers of the British Pacific Fleet (Task Force 57) on 26th March commenced to play their part in

16 There is internal evidence that the time 1630 given in his report is in error.

17 C.T.G. 58.3, *Action Report 14th March-1st June, 1945.*

guarding the left flank of the invasion against the attacks of Japanese air forces from Formosa and the Sakishima Gunto.

21. Principal Strategic Features of the Amphibious Support Force Operations

On 19th March the Amphibious Support Force (Task Force 52) under Rear-Admiral Blandy in the Headquarters Ship *Estes*, commenced to sail for the objective in echelons from Ulithi where it had assembled. This force had three duties to perform in the preparations for the assault, namely:

(a) to neutralize or destroy enemy installations in the Okinawa Gunto which threatened the approach and security of the Joint Expeditionary Force and to effect the maximum possible destruction of enemy forces and defences of Okinawa Shima by aircraft and surface ship bombardment, minesweeping, and underwater demolition, in order to facilitate the capture of Okinawa Shima south of the Ishikawa Isthmus;
(b) to capture and defend Kerama Retto, and begin the development of an Advanced Fleet Base in the Group;
(c) to capture and defend Keise Shima and establish artillery on the island.

The components of the Amphibious Support Force were as follows:

(a) Air Support Control Unit (T.G. 52.10);
(b) Fire Support Group (T.G. 54.1) consisting of heavy fire support ships assigned from the Gunfire and Covering Force (T.F. 54);
(c) Support Carrier Group (T.G. 52.1) consisting of 14 escort carriers and screen;
(d) Mine Flotilla (T.G. 52.2), comprising 15 Sweep Units and an Investigation and Disposal Unit, 75 sweepers in all;
(e) Net and Buoy Group (T.G. 52.8);
(f) Underwater Demolition Flotilla (T.G. 52.11) containing 10 Underwater Demolition Teams organized in two groups;
(g) Advanced Support Craft (T.G. 52.25). Four Gunboat Support Divisions, 3 Mortar Support Divisions, and a Rocket Landing Ship Group;
(h) Western Islands Attack Group (TG 51.1) which included the Western Islands Landing Force (TG 56.4), transports, landing ships, and a screen of destroyers and escorts;

(i) S.O.P.A. Kerama Retto (T.G. 51.15), Rear-Admiral Kiland, who commanded the Kerama Retto Screen, ammunition ships and oilers and all vessels whilst engaged in replenishment, maintenance or repairs;
(j) Seaplane Base Group (T.G. 51.20).

22. Bombardment by Fast Battleships, 24th March

At daylight on 24th March the fast battleships of Task Force 58 were temporarily detached, and with three divisions of destroyers formed into Task Group 59.7. The group proceeded towards the south-eastern coast of Okinawa to bombard coast defences and protect the minesweepers which commenced work in the area on this day. This was a diversionary move to deceive the enemy as to the real landing beaches which were to be used later in the assault on the island.

The force was organized as follows:

Task Force 59 (Vice-Admiral WA Lee, Jr.).
Task Group 59.7 (C.T.F. 59, O.T.C.)

	Battleships		Destroyer Division
T.U. 59.7.1 (Rear-Adm. O.C. Badger)	*New Jersey*		*Black*
	Wisconsin	96	*Bullard*
	Missouri		*Kidd*
			Chauncey

T.U. 59.7.2	*Washington*		*Cushing*
(Rear-Adm. T.R. Cooley)	*North Carolina*	*105*	*Benham*
	South Dakota (flagship of C.T.F. 59)		*Colahan*
			Franks

T.U. 59.7.3	*Massachusetts*		*Sigsbee*
Rear-Adm. J. F Shafroth)	*Indiana*	50	*Murray*
			Hailey

The Commander 5th Fleet, Admiral R.A. Spruance, was present in his flagship, the cruiser *Indianapolis*.

A target area was assigned to each group. The battleships opened fire at 0022, with the destroyers as a screen to seaward. No opposition was encountered, and the battleships, which opened fire at extreme range, gradually closed to approximately 14,000 yards as minesweeping progressed. A total of 1,375 16-inch projectiles had been fired when firing ceased at 1400 and the bombardment units formed up as a task group and proceeded to rendezvous with the fast carriers, Task Force 58.

The action reports described the action variously, from "reasonably accurate" to "effectiveness of fire not considered great". Apparently, the defences were less extensive than expected and damage was largely confined to buildings in the small villages. The diversionary purpose of the bombardment was, however, probably achieved.[18] On the 28th the two large cruisers *Guam* and *Alaska* were formed with the light cruisers *Flint* and *San Diego* and 6 destroyers[19] into Task Unit 58.4.9 which during the night 28th-29th carried out a bombardment of Minami Oagari Shima[20] in the Borodino Islands, with both 5-inch and 12-inch batteries.

23. Minesweeping

The minesweeping operations were planned to provide for the approach of the fast battleships of Task Force 59 within bombardment ranges off south-east of Okinawa outside the 100 fathom line; to clear the approaches to the Kerama Retto and the passage between Kerama Retto and Tonachi Shima; to find the northern limits of the minefield between Okinawa Gunto and Sakishima Gunto, including the clearance of the shoal in 26° 14′ N. 127° 31′ E.; to clear the water to the shore line for the attack force landings and close fire support, and to clear the approaches for the Attack Forces. In addition to sweeping all waters surrounding Okinawa and adjacent islands according to plan, daily clearance sweeps were maintained of transport areas and approach channels.

The first echelon of the Amphibious Support Force, Mine Group One (Task Group 52.3) arrived at the objective on 24th March and commenced minesweeping operations. The first day's minesweeping was carried out under the protection of bombardment by the fast

[18] *Operations in the Pacific Areas, April, 1945*, p.61.

[19] *Franks, Trathen, Mc Cord, Hailey, Hazelwood, Heermann.*

[20] Referred to in the American reports by its former name, Minami Daito Shima.

battleships of Task Group 59.7. When, however, the remaining echelons of Task Force 52 arrived at the objective on the following day, the Gunfire Support Group (54.1) and the Advance Support Craft Group (52.25) took over the duty of providing covering fire. Air cover was provided on the first day by the Fast Carrier Force (T.F. 58), though subsequently the duty devolved also on the escort carriers of the Support Carrier Group (52.1) and the Tactical Air Force ashore.

During L-8 and L-7 (24th and 25th March) minesweeping and underwater demolition operations were carried out without interference, and no mines or obstacles were found. Minesweeping progressed according to plan until L-5 Day, when the schedule was delayed because the minefield found off Hagushi (Area C.2) on the west coast of Okinawa Shima extended further westward than had been anticipated. Failure to complete clearance of this area necessitated postponement of underwater demolition reconnaissance of the Hagushi beaches from L-4 to L-3 Day.

Each morning during this period, there was evidence that the enemy had laid additional drifting or moored mines during the night, for it was the practice of the Minesweeping Force and Fire Support ships to withdraw from the sweeping area during the hours of darkness without leaving any night patrols to impede enemy minelaying operations, though the Japanese did not take full advantage of this practice. On the 28th March (L-4 Day) the minesweeper *Skylark* hit two mines and sank. The dangerous and very difficult task of clearing this minefield of considerable nuisance value in the approaches to the Hagushi beaches was completed on L-3 Day.

The clearance opened the way for close range bombardment, and the lesson was learnt that where large areas must be swept, the areas off the fire support and U.D.T. beaches should be cleared first to permit fire support ships to close the beaches to effective ranges.[21] The planting of radar reflector buoys for the approach of the attack forces began on L-2 Day. By next day all buoys had been established and all sweeping for the assault had been accomplished.

All these operations were carried out with no greater loss or damage to the minesweepers than the sinking of the *Skylark* and damage by air attack to four other vessels. On 26th March, however, the destroyer *Halligan*, screening Fire Support Unit 2 (54.1.2) off south-west Okinawa in 20° 10′ N., 127° 30.5′ E., sustained an underwater explosion, probably a mine, which completely destroyed the fore part of the ship, and she became a total loss.

21 *Commander, Gunfire Support Group, Action Report*, p. 40.

The Americans considered that the minesweeping preparation for this amphibious operation was probably the largest assault sweep operation ever executed. In all, 76 sweepers were engaged in the work. It was estimated that over 3,000 square miles were swept and declared safe prior to L-Day, including the entire coastal perimeter of southern Okinawa, the sweeping necessary for the capture of Kerama Retto and for the possible early capture of Ie Shima, including re-sweeping. The number of mines swept previous to the main landing on 1st April was 177, and approximately 80 floating mines were destroyed. The immunity with which great numbers of bombardment and assault ships closed the assault beaches without significant loss was evidence of the thoroughness with which the minesweepers carried out their task.

24. Underwater Demolition Operations

The ten teams of the Underwater Demolition Flotilla (T.G. 52.11) were divided into two groups, Group A (4 teams), Group B (6 teams) carried in 6 and 8 high speed destroyer transports respectively. Group A assembled at Ulithi and proceeded to the objective in company with the Gunfire and Covering Force (T.F. 54). Group B assembled at Leyte and sailed with the Western Islands Attack Group (T.G. 51.1)

The work which the flotilla had to carry out was as follows:

(a) Reconnoitre and prepare beaches in the Kerama Retto for the landing of the 77th Infantry Division.
(b) Reconnoitre and prepare beaches in Keise Shima for the landing of artillery and radar equipment.
(c) Reconnoitre and prepare the Hagushi beaches for the landing of the assault divisions.
(d) Make a diversionary feint reconnaissance and demolition on designated beaches in southern Okinawa.
(e) Compile and chart the information thus obtained and deliver it to the Attack Forces (at sea) on L-6 and L-1 Day.
(f) On L-Day furnish guides for the initial waves of all assault battalions.
(g) Subsequent to the assault – carry out demolitions to increase serviceability of beaches.
(h) Provide reconnaissance and demolition services on Ie Shima, the Eastern Islands, and such other beaches as might be selected.

The responsibility of the Underwater Demolition Teams stopped at high-water mark, and ceased as soon as harbour engineers were available to take over port and beach development.

Group A commenced work on L-7 Day, Group B on L-4 Day: the work of the latter group previous to L-Day was entirely confined to the Hagushi beaches, all other tasks being carried out by Group A.

Three teams of Group A conducted the operations at landing beaches in Keramo Retto. No man-made obstacles were encountered, though light intermittent enemy fire of small calibre was received, but caused no casualties. Individual charts and reports on each beach to be used by the landing force were prepared and delivered to the Attack Force Commander and Transport Division Commanders within 24 hours, namely at daylight on L-6 Day, and in the case of certain beaches immediate information which was required, was despatched already at 1300 on L-7 Day. Operations on Keise Shima beaches were carried out by two teams of Group A.

The work was postponed for a day, until 28th March, owing to insufficient progress of minesweeping. Sniper fire was experienced, but did not interfere with the progress of the work, which was completed on L-2 Day, two days' demolition work having been found to be necessary. Reconnaissance of the Hagushi beaches on Okinawa commenced on L-3 Day by the six teams of Group B. Light resistance in the form of machine-gun, rifle and mortar fire was encountered on the northern beaches but was quickly silenced by the covering forces. Simultaneous demolitions on all beaches were carried out on the morning of L-2 Day by the same teams which had done the reconnaissance, to destroy the obstacles, consisting of approximately 2,000 large timber posts inserted at six of the beaches, in some places in as many as four rows.

On two of the beaches the demolition charges failed to explode. After a delay of 20 minutes for rechecking fuses, the charges were blown again, but at one beach they still did not go off. On the following morning a further attempt was made, and all but some 200 of the posts were demolished. It was decided that the demolition teams should guide the assault waves past the remaining unexploded charges. Reconnaissance charts and information were transferred to the Attack Force Commanders at sea before noon on L-1 Day. The teams continued to work up to and including L+4 day, blasting channels and trimming the reef edge.

The diversionary feint reconnaissance of the south-eastern beaches was carried out on L-Day, with the same thoroughness as at the main landing beaches, two teams from Group A being employed.

On the following day demolition charges were exploded, to give the impression that the ragged reef edge was being prepared for beaching of landing craft, even though no obstacles were found. That evening. Tokyo Radio broadcast indicated that landings would be made on the south-eastern as well as the western beaches, from which it might be inferred that the feint was successful.

The total casualties in all the pre-assault work of the Underwater Demolition Teams amounted to no more than one man killed and two wounded. Two high speed destroyer transports of Group A received minor damage from air attack.

25. Pre-Landing Bombardment and Support

The pre-landing bombardment and support for the minesweepers and underwater demolition units were controlled by the Commander Amphibious Support Force (C.T.F. 52) and were provided by units of the Gunfire and Covering Force (T.F. 54) and of the Advance Support Craft Group (T.G. 52.25), the latter consisting of gun and rocket landing craft and rocket ships. Whilst the fire support ships of Task Force 54 were under the command of C.T.F. 52 (Rear-Admiral W.H.P. Blandy) during fire support missions, they were under their own Task Force Commander during the movement to the assault area and when acting as a covering force for that area or preparing to engage enemy surface forces. They commenced operations on 25th March.

The fire support ships (Gunfire Support Group 54.1) were organized in five major fire support units under Rear-Admiral B.J. Rodgers, Commander Unit 3 (54.1.3) who operated under the direction of Rear-Admiral Blandy. Fire Support Unit One was detailed for bombardment of the south-east coast of Okinawa; Unit Two the bombardment of the Naha area and support of the landing on Kerama Retto; and Units Three, Four and Five for the pre-landing preparation of the Hagushi area and the support of early ground operations from Zampa Misaki southward and extending about two miles inland. The two cruisers of Unit Five were detailed for various operations in support of minesweepers.

The gun landing craft and destroyers were under the command of Commander Underwater Demolition Flotilla (C.T.G. 52.11) during the preliminary operations off the Hagushi beaches, and the heavy ships under C.T.F. 52. On the demonstration beaches the senior destroyer commander was in command of destroyers and gun landing craft, the Commander Fire Support Unit No. 1 (C.T.U. 54.1.1.). Rear-Admiral P.K. Fischer, being in overall command.

These assignments were based upon the fact that since the size of the objective prevented destruction of all possible targets, the principal efforts of the fire support ships had to be focussed on definite tasks, including the destruction of defences opposing the landing; the destruction of weapons threatening ships and aircraft, with emphasis on the Naha airfield area underwater demolition work, support of the demolition landings; and the support of minesweeping and underwater demolition work.

The fire support plan followed the trend established as a result of experience at Iwo Jima. Three lines of ships were provided, each increasing in fire-power from the beach seaward. Gun landing craft formed the first line, at approximately 1,200 yards from the beach, covering the underwater demolition work as closely as possible with 40-mm. fire. Next a line of destroyers at 2,700 yards range covered the L.C.I. (Gs.) with 40-mm. and 5-inch fire as far inland as 300 yards. Finally, about 1,000 yards farther to seaward cruisers and battleships used their secondary and A.A. batteries to neutralize all ground from 300 yards to 1,000 yards inland.

The heavy ships were stationed in such positions that they could continue scheduled main armament bombardment on specific targets inland, and were ready with all batteries for instant counter-battery fire.

The programme was carried out according to plan, but it was not until L-8 Day when the minesweeping and underwater demolition operations ended, that the battleships were able to close the range and engage coast defences by direct fire.[22] The Japanese camouflage was good and the fire support ships experienced difficulty in locating worthwhile targets, but all known coast defence guns in the area were destroyed or heavily damaged either by air or ship bombardment. Beach defence weapons and positions were not numerous. There were a few heavy pillbox-type installations along the beaches and farther inland, and some open emplacements, but most of them were empty.

There was extensive firing into cliffs and rocky points overlooking and flanking the beaches, to disclose defensive positions such as the enemy had frequently used in the past, but few were found. No return fire was received during the bombardment, except the slight small-arms fire experienced by the underwater demolition teams. By the afternoon of L-1 Day, after 48 hours of close-range bombardment, the preparation was sufficient for a successful landing, with the exception

---

22 *British Combined Observers' Report*, p. 14, states that interrogations of prisoners and civilians revealed that the Japanese 32nd Army H.Q. moved its location from the south-east coastal sector after the bombardment on L-2 day, to a point further south, as a landing in that area was considered probable.

of certain potentially dangerous batteries that were still to be found in the Naha area.

The number of rounds of 5-inch to 16-inch ammunition fired at the shore during the preparatory period was 27,226, totalling 5,162 tons. Anti-aircraft action accounted for a further 4,098 rounds of 5-inch.

As its name implied, the Gunfire and Covering Force (T.F. 54) had the further duty of protecting the ships operating off Okinawa in the event of a raid by Japanese fleet units, for which purpose the ships engaged on fire support would concentrate to form a surface covering group. At night, for strategic reasons, two groups were formed, to the north-west and north-east of Okinawa respectively. As rapidly as the progress of mineweeping permitted, ships were placed on night patrol around Kerama Retto and off eastern, southern, and western Okinawa, to prevent the escape or reinforcement of the enemy garrison.

26. Air Support

During the preparatory period the operations of the support aircraft were controlled by the Advance Commander Air Support Control Unit, C.T.G. 52.10, embarked in Rear-Admiral Blandy's (C.T.F. 52) ship, the *Estes*. Air support during this period was furnished by aircraft from the Fast Carrier Task Force (T.F. 58) and from the Support Carrier Group (T.G. 52.1).

After study of the available intelligence material, including photograph interpretation, the following target priority was set up for air:

Priority 1 – Enemy aircraft;
Priority 2 – Amphibious tanks and small boats (the "amphibious tanks" were later found to be suicide attack boats fitted with depth charges);
Priority 3 – Island installations:
(a) Coast defence guns and field artillery,
(b) Anti-aircraft guns,
(c) Floating mines,
(d) Communication system,
(e) Barracks area.

The target priority list "was dependent on the assessment of damage to targets. On L-7 the advanced C.A.S.C.U.[23] was considerably handicapped in his selection of targets as the Fast Carrier Force had

23 Commander Air Support Control Units.

not informed him of the results which it had achieved in its strikes against Okinawa; moreover the photographic coverage flown by the carriers had not been delivered on L-8 nor was it received until late on L-7".[24]

Both the Fast Carrier Task Force and the Support Carrier Group furnished aircraft for Combat Air Patrols and Target Combat Air Patrols.[25] Until L-3 Day, the morning C.A.P.[26] arrived 45 minutes after first light and left the area 45 minutes before last light. Whether or not the Japanese knew this, up to L-3 Day the suicide air attacks were invariably completed before the morning C.A.P. had come on station.[27]

The fast carriers operated during this period principally against targets which could not be reached by naval gunfire. The Support Carrier Group consisted at the commencement of the operation of 14 escort carriers and screen. Their aircraft were used not only against the targets listed above, but for bombardment and artillery spotting on photographic, hydrographic, and smoke missions, and on anti-submarine patrol; the later duty was taken over on L-3 Day by four seaplane squadrons based on Kerama Retto.

The following sorties were flown, exclusive of those against enemy air attack, and anti-submarine missions:

L-7 Day (25th March)	The primary duty was the support by escort carrier aircraft of the underwater demolition work off the Kerama Retto beaches. Aircraft from the Fast Carrier Task Force attacked airfield installations and suicide boat positions on Okinawa Shima. Sorties flown were 388.
L-6 Day (26th March)	A total of 424 sorties was flown. Fast carrier aircraft continued to search out and destroy enemy suicide and midget submarine bases, airfields and heavy gun batteries on Okinawa; while the escort carrier aircraft operated, for

24 *British Combined Observers' Report of Operations against Okinawa Gunto*, p.21.

25 *Operations in the Pacific Area* April, 1945, p.37. *The British Combined Operations Observers' Report*, p. 22, says the C.A.P. was provided by the Fast Carrier Force except for a short period during one day when they were refuelling, but other reports mention specific dates on which the escort carriers provided C.A.P.

26 Combat Air Patrol.

27 *British Combined Observers' Report of Operations*, p.23.

	the most part, under control of the Commander Western Islands Attack Group (C.T.G. 51.1) in support of the landings on Kerama Retto.
L-5 Day (27th March)	Attacks were continued against suicide boats, revetments, airfields, and gun batteries on Okinawa. Important barrack areas, requested by H.Q. 10th Army, were worked over with bombs, napalm, and rockets.
L-4 Day (28th March)	The principal targets were heavy A.A, coast defence and dual-purpose guns around the airfields and on the Eastern Islands. Sorties totalled 347.
L-3 Day (20th March)	The fast carriers were attacking Japan and part of the escort carriers were absent from the objective area. The number of sorties dropped to 251, and those were largely in support of underwater demolition operations on the Hagushi beaches.
L-2 and L-I Days (30th, 31st March)	Support of underwater demolition activities on the Hagushi beaches continued. At the request of the 10th Army, certain bridges on Okinawa Shima were attacked. Fast carrier and support carrier aircraft flew 1,176 sorties during the two days.

On L-Day, the control of aircraft at the objective area was undertaken by Commander Air Support Control Unit (C.T.F. 51) in the Headquarters ship *Eldorado*.

27. Japanese Reaction to the Preliminary Operations

Prior to the landing, no Japanese battery opened fire on any of the American ships; even minesweepers were left unmolested whilst engaged in clearing minefields within range of enemy guns which had not at that time been knocked out. If the Japanese hoped to keep their skilfully camouflaged coast defence guns intact to aid in repelling a landing by prohibiting them from engaging in pre-landing duels with fire support ships they did not succeed, for most of the coast defences which could oppose the landing were located and heavily damaged or destroyed before effective use could be made of them.

A number of attacks by midget submarines and suicide boats occurred. On the 27th March the destroyers *Callaghan* and *Porterfield* whilst screening Fire Support Unit 5 attacked a midget submarine in 26° 20′ N., 127° 30′ E. and brought up debris containing Japanese markings; and on the same day the cruiser *Portland* had an inconclusive encounter with a similar vessel off Zampa Misaki in 26° 29′ N., 127° 45′ E. On the following day, the light minelayer *Tolman* was unsuccessfully attacked in the early hours off Nago Wan by about eight motor torpedo boats, of which she destroyed two and probably severely damaged others.

Suicide boats made several attacks during the early morning of 29th March, and at least 8 were destroyed, the only damage suffered by the American ships being minor damage to one L.C.I.[28] Another ineffective night attack by M.T.B, believed to be from Nago Wan, was de on 30th. On the 3lst March, shortly before midnight, the destroyer *Barton* of the screen of Fire Support Unit 3 (54.1.3) made sound contact west of Okinawa in 26° 20′ N., 127° 41′ E. with a submarine, which was believed, though incorrectly, to have been sunk by her second depth charge attack.

Within 48 hours of the commencement of preliminary operations at the objective the Japanese gave evidence that they were aware the Americans were preparing the stage for assault on an area vital to the safety of the Empire. On L-6 Day, 20th March, the enemy launched the first and one of the most damaging of a number of uncoordinated air attacks which took place during the preliminary operations. During morning twilight that day,[29] about 8 enemy aircraft attacked ships near Kerama Retto, where the first landing was due to take place at 0800.

Seven of the enemy were destroyed by ships' gunfire and C.A.P., or destroyed themselves by suicide attack, but the high-speed destroyer transports *Gilmer* and *Knudson* of Demolition Group A, the light minelayer *R.H. Smith* and minesweeper *Skirmish* received minor damage, and the destroyer *Kimberly* in the screen of the Western Islands Attack Group was severely damaged and had to proceed later for Navy Yard repairs. The destroyer *Hickox* in the Fast Carrier Group 58.2 also received minor damage.

During the night of 26th-27th the ships were attacked by a total of about 15 enemy aircraft. The largest attack was made in the early

28 Variously given as *L.C.I (G)* 558, and *L.C.I (G)* 588.

29 Radar pickets were stationed that day to the north-west , west, and south-west of Okinawa, but it is not known whether they had come on station.

morning when Task Force 54 was attacked by three raids, which made attacks singly, their numbers being rendered uncertain through the use of *window*.[30] Two were shot down and three crash dived. The destroyer *Porterfield* and the light cruiser *Biloxi,* both in Fire Support Unit 4 (54.1.4) received minor damage from suicide hits, and the destroyer escort *Foreman* in Fire Support Unit 6 (54.1.6) was severely damaged. The battleship *Nevada* in Fire Support Unit 3 (54.1.3) was crash-dived but damage was negligible. The high speed minesweeper *Dorsey* and the destroyer *Murray* in Fast Carrier Task Group 58.1 off Okinawa received major damage from aerial torpedoes, though the attack on the latter task group was not well timed; it arrived after daylight and was effectively dealt with by Combat Air Patrols.

No further air attacks occurred until the early morning of the 29th March. Between 0055 and daylight the ships shot down no less than 13 enemy attackers, and the Combat Air Patrol accounted for three. The *Preston* underwent four attacks, the *Wiley* five, the *M. F. Bauer* six, and the *Twiggs* seven. None of these ships were damaged, but *L.C.I.* 550 was crash-dived and dismasted, *L.S.M. (R)* 188 was considerably damaged by a suicider which dived into her, and the attack cargo ship *Wyandot* had several holds flooded from a near miss.

In the early morning of the 31st March, Admiral Spruance's flagship, the cruiser *Indianapolis,* was crashed by a suicider, which caused major material damage and many casualties, and the light minelayer *Adams* was damaged. On 5th April, Admiral Spruance shifted his flag to the battleship *New Mexico,* whilst the *Indianapolis* remained at Kerama Retto, where already at this early date the institution of a repair base had begun.

28. Capture of Kerama Retto, 26th March

The seizure of the Islands of the Kerama Retto was dictated by the necessity for establishing a replenishment and naval repair base and a seaplane base. The necessity for a supply base arose from the great distances from the nearest Allied advanced and permanent bases; and for a repair base from the heavy casualties to shipping anticipated in an assault on the inner ring of the enemy's homeland defences involving a landing operation within 350 miles of industrial Kyushu. Events fully justified the seizure of the islands, for a major repair and upkeep problem did in fact arise, for perhaps the first time in Pacific Operations. The large number of ships damaged in action, and the unexpectedly prolonged requirement for large naval forces off Okinawa created a

30 Anti-radar device.

very heavy load on repair facilities, which had to be increased greatly over that initially proposed; in fact, it was not until four docks were brought into the area, and not until the scale of Japanese air effort was reduced, that an appreciable decrease could be made in the number of battle-damaged ships at Kerama. As the operation against Okinawa continued Kerama Retto assumed a progressively more important role. It became the principal haven for damaged ships, both for complete and emergency repairs; and ships of all types were replenished and rearmed there.

The strength of the enemy garrison of Kerama Retto was not known, but was thought not to exceed 400 men. Strong opposition was not expected, for air photographs showed that only two of the islands possessed fixed defences, limited in each case to machine guns and light artillery.

The minesweepers swept through the islands of the Kerama Retto supported by one Fire Support Unit. Simultaneously the Underwater Demolition Teams were reconnoitring the beaches of the various islands for landing conditions and obstacles, with L.C.I. (Gs.), and aircraft in close support.

The capture of Kerama Retto was entrusted to the 77th Infantry Division (TG 56.4) (Major-General A.D. Bruce, U.S.A.), under the Commander Western Islands Attack Group (Rear-Admiral I.N. Kiland, C.T.G. 51.1), who was under the immediate command of Rear-Admiral W.H.P. Blandy, Commander Amphibious Support Force (Task Force 52). The Western Islands Attack Group consisted of one transport squadron, with sufficient landing ships to lift a reinforced infantry division. The Amphibious Support Force provided 2 cruisers, 4 destroyers, 12 L.C.I. (M) (R.Č.M.), 24 L.C.I. (G), and 12 L.S.M. (R) to provide for independent movement and an amphibious assault on a one-division scale.

The major tasks assigned to the Western Islands Attack Group were:

(a) the capture of Kerama Retto;
(b) establishment in the Kerama Retto of an anchorage for the logistic support of fleet units;
(e) the landing of two battalions of 155-mm. guns, on Keise Shima, for the support of the main landing on Okinawa Shima.

The group sailed from Leyte in three major sub-divisions; the first leaving Leyte on 19th March and arriving off Kerama Retto early on the morning of 26th March.

By the evening of the 25th March preparations for the capture of the islands were complete. A slight alteration was made in the plan of attack after beach reconnaissance had shown the two beaches designated for assault by L.C.V.P.[31] to be unsuitable for these craft. This made it necessary for LV.T.[32] (Amphibians) which had been used in the initial assaults, to be employed again.

The enemy air attack which took place during the morning twilight on the 26th caused no disarrangement of the plan. At 0804 landings commenced, with gunfire and air support provided by units of the Amphibious Support Force. Gunfire support was given by the battleship *Arkansas*,[33] heavy cruisers *San Francisco* (flagship) and *Minneapolis*, with five destroyers, 18 L.C.L (G), 12 L.C.I. (M) and 12 L.S.M. (R). The aircraft detailed for the assault included fighters, bombers, hydrographic and air observers, and spotters. L.4 (Piper Cub) aircraft operating from special gear installed on an L.S.T. were used successfully for artillery spotting and local reconnaissance, though carrier-borne aircraft were available in case L.4s were unable to operate. Actually, during the time that the L.4s operated the weather was particularly good and there was little swell.

The first landing was made by a battalion landing team on Aka Shima against sporadic rifle and mortar fire; and by 1600 on 27th all organized resistance had been overcome. Among the items of enemy equipment destroyed were 38 suicide boats located in caves along the north-west coast. It was estimated that Aka Shima was defended by 200 Japanese soldiers with an equal number of Korean labourers.

In the course of the 26th four further landings were made: one at 0825 on Keruma Shima,[34] where enemy resistance was light and the island was over-run and declared secured in three hours; and at 0000 on Zamami Jima, where also resistance was light and the estimated 300 enemy soldiers and an equal number of Korean labourers took to the hills and were mopped up by 1600 next day, after a further battalion landing team had been landed as a garrison force. Fukasi Jima[35] was found to be undefended and was occupied at 0021 on 20th. On Yakan Jima,[36] also, where a landing took place on the same day, no enemy troops were encountered although sporadic rifle fire was received at first.

---

31 Landing Craft, Vehicle, Personnel.

32 Landing Vehicle, Tanks.

33 *ComPhibForPac, Action Report, 17th Feb-17th May*, 1945, *Okinawa*, p.317, says there were two battleships.

34 Called Geruma Shima in the U.S. reports.

35 Called Hokaji Shima in the U.S. reports.

36 Called Yakabi Shima in the U.S. reports.

Commencing at 0011 on 27th March a regimental combat team landed over Orange Beach on Tokashiki Shima, encountering no resistance. A battalion landing team encountered slight resistance at Beach Purple a few minutes later, but no serious opposition was met anywhere on the island. There were no enemy on the islet of Fukase Shima. Numerous suicide boats were found in caves along the eastern beaches of Tokashiki Shima, and mopping up and searches for suicide boats continued until the 31st March.

Amuro Shima and Koba Jima[37] were both taken on 7th March, by shore movements from Zamami Jima and Yakan Jima respectively, with little enemy resistance.

Bases for three Japanese Sea Raiding Squadrons were found in Kerama Retto, on Zamami Jima, Aka Shima, and Tokashiki Shima respectively. Each squadron was equipped with 100 suicide boats. These squadrons were under the 5th Amphibious (Sea) Raiding Base, the headquarters of which was located at Naha on Okinawa. The Base appeared to be organized for ten squadrons, though the location of the other seven is not known. By the 31st March, approximately 310 suicide boats had been captured or destroyed, a total which later reached 359.

Casualties in the landing force during the period to 31st March were 31 killed and 88 wounded. It was estimated that 516 of the enemy were killed; 106 prisoners were taken.

Immediately after the capture of Kerama Retto the work of establishing the logistic and seaplane base and anchorage began. All nets (more than 22,000 feet) were installed by 2300 on 28th March. Replenishment of ships of the Amphibious Support Force began that day, according to schedule; thus, in no more than three days a base where ships could replenish fuel and ammunition and carry out battle damage repairs, was established.

The seaplane base was established in sheltered waters in Aka Kaikyo on the 29th March. The Seaplane Base Group (T.G. 51.20) arrived early that day and commenced operating at once. Thirty flying boats (patrol bombers) were brought in from Saipan, and more arrived later. All facilities were afloat, 11 seaplane tenders being employed. The flying boats provided block patrols, and long-range offensive reconnaissance and offensive anti-shipping sweeps from Samosa to Korea, along the coast of China and Kyushu as far north as Tsushima Strait. Navy Liberators (patrol bombers) from Yontan augmented this armed reconnaissance from 25th April. In addition, a six-sector A.S.P.[38] about

---

37 The time of the landing is given by *Cincpac, April* 1945, p.39, as noon, but *C.T.F.* 52, *C.T.G.* 51.19, *Action Report* p.50 gives the time as 1341.

38 Anti-submarine patrol.

Okinawa was flown day and night, and air-sea rescue missions were flown from Formosa to Kyushu; rescues were made under the most difficult conditions, at times in heavy seas and during foul weather, and also under enemy fire.

29. Occupation of Keise Shima, 31st March

Keise Shima (Reef Islands), Aware Saki[39]and Maikirima[40] were found to be unoccupied. On the 31st March the 420th Field Artillery Group (two battalions of 155-mm. guns) was landed on Keise Shima according to plan, and all guns were emplaced and ready for action against Okinawa by 0600 on 1st April, L-Day.

During the early hours of L-Day unloading was stopped owing to heavy enemy artillery fire, which, however, caused no damage. By 1600 on the 1st all units, equipment and supplies of the Keise Shima force had been landed, except 30 per cent of the bulk cargo of the 420th Field Artillery Group. An airstrip was made on the island from which 24 aircraft commenced operating on the afternoon of L-Day for artillery spotting and local reconnaissance.

39 At the south tip of Tokashiki Shima.

40 Called Mae Shima in the U.S. reports.

Chapter V

THE LANDING

Although lack of opposition during minesweeping, U.D.T.[41] operations and pre-assault bombardment had made it extremely difficult to estimate the enemy strength in the neighbourhood of the Hagushi landing beaches, by the afternoon of L-I Day (1st March) Rear-Admiral Blandy, Commander Amphibious Support Force (T.F. 52) was able to report to the Commander Joint Expeditionary Force, Vice-Admiral R.K. Turner (C.T.F. 51) that all preparations for the assault were complete. It was considered that the prospective weather conditions would permit a successful landing on Okinawa on 1st April in accordance with the Preferred Plan.

30. The Plan

In this plan, the southern half of Okinawa Shima, viz., that part south of a general line from Shirachi in the south part of Nago Wan to Chimu on the heights above Chim Zaki, including the small islands off the east coast, was selected as the objective of the first assault. The plan was designed to isolate the southern half of the island by seizing the Ishikawi Isthmus in order to prevent enemy reinforcements from the north. Simultaneously, the assault forces were to seize and occupy a general east-west line from Kuba Saki (at the head of Nakagusuku Wan) in order to prevent enemy reinforcement from the south.

After the capture of the northern half of Okinawa, the attack was to be continued in order to capture and occupy the remainder of the island. Early important objectives were Yontan and Katena airfields, which were required in order to provide operating facilities for shore-based aircraft, and the Katchin Hanto (peninsula) on the north side of Nakagusuku Wan, to assist in securing the latter as a naval

41 Underwater Demolition Teams.

anchorage and unloading port. Other important objectives were Machinato and Yonabaru airfields to provide fields for additional land-based aircraft for control of the air in this, the first combined operation undertaken within staging distance of fighter aircraft from Japan; and the port of Naha to expedite the unloading of base development equipment.

The Preferred Plan called for simultaneous landings on beaches north and south of Hagushi by the Tenth Army, with two corps abreast, each corps landing on a two-division front; the XXIV Corps with the Southern Attack Force (Task Force 55) on the right flank: and the III Amphibious Corps with the Northern Attack Force (Task Force 53) on the left.

The alternative plan called for the main landings to be made on the eastern and south-eastern beaches of Okinawa Shima, also with four divisions abreast.

At 0600 on 1st April, two hours and a half before the scheduled landing, the Commander Joint Expeditionary Force (C.T.F. 51), Vice-Admiral R.K. Turmer, took command of Task Force 52 (Amphibious Support Force) and Rear-Admiral W.H.P. Blandy assumed command of Task Group 51.19, the Eastern Fire Support Group.

31. The Demonstration Landings

It was the immediate task of the Eastern Fire Support Group to cover with air and fire support the feint landings which were made on the south-eastern side of Okinawa Shima, near Sakibaru Saki.

This operation was under the command of C.T.G. 51.2, Rear-Admiral J. Wright. The Demonstration Group (51.2) consisted of one transport squadron with the 2nd Marine Division under Major-General Watson embarked, together with one tractor flotilla and the necessary control and screening vessels.

The operation simulated an actual assault in every respect. The waters adjacent to the beaches had already been swept to enable ships to approach; real, but unnecessary, charges were exploded by the Underwater Demolition Teams to simulate preparations of the reef for landing. The troops of the 2nd Marine Division were combat-loaded and actually embarked in landing craft. The demonstration was planned to be as realistic as possible, in order to deceive the enemy into believing that landings were to be made on the south-eastern beaches as well as the Hagushi beaches.

In the event of the alternative plan for the main landing being put into effect, the 2nd Marine Division was prepared to land on the eastern islands Tsuken Shima, Kutaka Shima, Bamahi-ga-Banare,[42] and Ichi Banare, on 30th March, or to land on the Hagushi beaches in support of the main beaches if needed.

The main body of transports of the Demonstration Group arrived in the Transport Area[43] off the demonstration beaches early in the morning of L-Day, 1st April. As the group entered the Transport Area, T.G. 51.2 was attacked by enemy aircraft which were undetected by radar or visually, until they were close aboard. At 0546 a suicide aircraft crashed into and flooded the main engine-room of the assault transport *Hinsdale,* and another hit *L.S.T.* 884, causing heavy fires and temporary abandonment; and both ships had to be towed to Kerama Retto.

Three battleships, the *Texas, Arkansas,* and *Maryland,* the 8-inch cruiser *Tuscaloosa,* and eight destroyers, the *Laws, Longshaw, Morrison, Laffey,* Pritchett, *Isherwood, Zellars,* and *Bryant* were assigned to C.T.G. 51.19 (Rear-Admiral Blandy) to give fire support to the feint landings. They commenced pre-landing bombardment on time, and at 0600 a bombing and rocket attack was completed on the beaches by support aircraft.

The demonstration consisted of despatching close in to the beaches seven waves of boats, each composed of 24 L.C.V.Ps., from the line of departure at five-minute intervals. The L.C.V.P. waves were preceded by two divisions of L.C.I. (Gs) and flanked by two divisions of L.C.I. (Ms) on the left and two divisions of L.C.1. (Ls) on the right. No return fire was experienced from the beaches. Davit boats were lowered and disembarkation of troops was simulated. When the fourth wave crossed the line of departure at H-Hour (0830) for the main assault on the Hagushi beaches, all boat waves reversed course and returned to their ships. At H-10 minutes aircraft controlled by C.T.G. 51.19 laid a heavy smoke screen along the entire length the demonstration beaches, which was augmented at H-4 minutes by all L.C.Is. to cover the reversal of course and the retirement.

During the approach and withdrawal, C.T.G. 51.19 maintained neutralizing fire on the southern end of Okinawa on both sides of the demonstration beaches. All boats were recovered by 1500, and T.G. 51.2 retired from the demonstration area at 1530. Rear-Admiral Blandy's ship, the *Estes,* and screen remained off the demonstration beaches overnight. The only enemy reaction to the demonstration was one salvo of four rounds, which landed close to the *Gregory,* one

42 Cincpac, p.42 calls it Harahika Banare and his plan terms it Hamahika Shima.

43 The American term Transport Area corresponds to the British Lowering Position.

of the screening destroyers; whilst the battleship *Arkansas* reported being fired on by a coast defence gun just south of Naha Airfield, and as she was outranged, the *Maryland* with her longer firing range silenced the gun.

The demonstration was repeated in its entirety, with similar timing, on L+1 Day. No enemy opposition was encountered, either from shore or from the air.

The 2nd Marine Division was released from the target area on 14th April and returned to Saipan.

The degree to which the demonstration succeeded in containing enemy forces in southern Okinawa is uncertain. It certainly drew the attack of suicide aircraft which completely ignored the imposing array of ships lying off the western shore until the evening of L-Day. A Japanese news broadcast 2nd April declared that "an enemy landing attempt on the eastern coast of Okinawa on Sunday morning (L-Day) was completely foiled, with heavy losses to the enemy".

32. The Weather on 1st April

A special submarine was placed in the Yellow Sea in about 34° N., 124° E, for the express purpose of providing weather reports twice daily in direct support of the Okinawa landings. These reports started six days before the actual landings. Other submarines furnished reports once daily from the Tokyo area, Shikoku area, East of Kyushu, West of Kyushu, Amami O Shima area, twice daily from the Okinawa area, and special reports whenever storm conditions were encountered. There was no single failure to report.

The preparatory operations had been conducted under unusually favourable conditions. For several days before L-Day the prevailing wind was from the north-east so that no swell was produced on the landing beaches.

At H-Hour (0830) skies were clear with three-tenths of stratocumulus at 3,000 ft. Visibility at this time was reduced to 6-8 miles[44] by haze and pre-invasion gunfire.[45] The wind was east, 13 knots. Sea was slight with a chop, but no waves or swell over two feet.

The remainder of the day was substantially the same. Cloud increased through the morning and afternoon, and averaged six to seven tenths from 1400 to 1800. Since the wind direction was E.N.E.,

---

44 *British Combined Observers' Report*, p.14.

45 ibid, p.13. *Cincpac Report*, p.43 says there was a slight surface haze which reduced early morning visibility in the transport area to 6,000 yards. *C.T.G.* 52 *C.T.G.* 51.19, *Action Report*, pp.11-12 says visibility was unlimited but the evidence is against this.

and consequently off-shore, there was no objectionable surf or swell on the reef. Visibility increased to over ten miles during the afternoon.

After 1800 cloud decreased, and by midnight the sky was clear. The related statistical data for 1st April were as follows:

Sunrise 0021

Sunset 1845

Moonrise 2146

Moonset 0829.

High water	0850, height 5.9 feet.
	2208, height 5.3 feet.
Low water	0247, height 2.1 feet.
	1520, height 0.2 feet.

33. The Main Landing on L-Day

The main landing over the Hagushi beaches was preceded by a naval bombardment by eleven battleships, eight cruisers, 15 destroyers[46] and 177 gunboats[47] and by closely co-ordinated air strikes, by escort carriers of Task Group 52.1 and fast carriers of Task Groups 58.1, 58.3, and 58.4, who flew a total of 1,027 sorties. The new rocket ships, firing 3-inch rockets, were used with "stupendous" success, although they were merely of hasty interim design. The first support ships were required on station at sunrise. The programme provided continuous cover on L-Day for the landing forces until H + 60 (2030 on 3rd April), after which time call fire became available.

The Americans had anticipated that the provision of gunfire support for the landing would present a considerable problem. The contiguousness of units rendered rigid control necessary immediately before and after the landing. With one or two minor exceptions, all fire support ships were supplied with air spotting. Numerous sea walls along a large section of the beach had to be breached in order to afford exits for tanks and amphibians; but the length of the landing beaches, almost 10,000 yards, and the navigational hazards off them limited the density of fire that could be provided. There were, too, large numbers of enemy troops on Okinawa which could reach the landing area in

46 24th Army Corps – Battleships *Nevada, Tennessee, Colorado*; heavy cruisers *Wichita, Minneapolis*; light cruisers *Birmingham, St. Louis*; destroyers *Daly, P. Hamilton, Twiggs, Barton, Anthony, Hall, M. L. Abele*. 3rd Phib Corps – Battleships *West Virginia, Idaho, New Mexico, New York*; heavy cruisers *Salt Lake City, Portland, Pensacola*; light cruiser *Biloxi*; destroyers *H.L. Edwards, R. P. Leary, Preston, Newcomb, Rooks, Irwin, Callaghan, Porterfield*.

47 This figure probably includes those supporting the Demonstration Landings.

a few hours unless continuous interdiction fire was maintained on a number of roads. Actually, however, little need was found on L-Day for naval gunfire support after the preparatory bombardments.

All direct fire support of troops was under the command of the respective attack force commanders. C.T.F. 51 was responsible for detailing the fire support ships; and the Commanders of the Northern and Southern Attack Forces, C.T.F. 53 and 55, were in command of direct support for the III Amphibious Corps on the northern beaches, and the XXIV Corps on the southern front respectively. C.T.G. 51.19 (Commander Eastern Islands Fire Support and Attack Group) commanded the fire support ships on the east side of Okinawa, and in addition delivered fire for both C.T.F. 53 and 55 on request.

"The gunfire plan of the Okinawa operation was better than previous gunfire plans in that it was more flexible. Gunfire communications were better than formerly."[48]

Air support for the landing was under the control of Air Support Unit 51.10 in the *Eldorado*. A.S.C.U. 53.10 in the *Panamint* directed the air support of the III Amphibious Corps, and A.S.C.U. 55.10 in the *Teton* that of the XXIV Corps.

"One of the most dramatic developments of the entire war in the Pacific has been the development of air support of landing operations ... This support depends entirely upon communications."[49]

Up to H-hour (0830), and shortly thereafter, air support was carried out as planned, targets attacked being supposed blockhouses, AA, positions, ammunition dumps, and targets of opportunity on and near the landing beaches, with strafing attacks of the beaches from 0823. The rapid advance of the American troops and lack of ground opposition posed a problem for air support, and consequently Direct Support Group and Roving Patrols were used inland, far ahead of the troops.

Under cover of the pre-arranged bombardment and air strikes, the Tenth Army was launched to the attack on the western beaches; the XXIV Army Corps on the right (southern) flank, and the III Amphibious (Marine) Corps on the left. The Northern Attack Force (T.F. 53) with the 1st and 6th Marine Divisions, and the Southern Attack Force (T.F. 55) with the 96th and 7th Infantry Divisions, landed the assault waves. The distance from the line of departure to the shore was 4,000 yards, but the leading waves in amphibians were up to 10 minutes late in landing on both corps fronts.[50] The timing of direct gunfire support

48 Com. Fifth Fleet *Action Report, Ryukus Operation through 27th May* 1945, p.VI-I-5.

49 ibid, p.VI-I-6.

50 *British Combined Operation Observers' Report*, p. 13. C.C.O.R./81, p.5 says the first wave of LVTs. landed at 0840 (ten minutes late).

was, however, related to the position of the first assault wave and not to a rigid time-table.[51]

Opposition was very light. Most of the defences had been destroyed by the bombardment or abandoned by the enemy. Intermittent mortar and artillery fire fell on the beaches, but caused no damage and few casualties. The landing craft encountered very little enemy fire, the ships none, and no mines were found on the beaches. Many of the infantry left their amphibians on the beaches and continued to advance on foot, their craft being required at once to bring supplies ashore across the reef. The armoured amphibian battalions which had preceded the assault waves went straight inland for a distance of about 4,000 yards, where they waited for the infantry to join them before reverting to their assigned role of artillery.

These armoured amphibian battalions were being used in an artillery role for the first time. They were under the command of the Divisional Artillery Regiment and were linked to the forward observing officers of the Division, who had landed early. Tanks of both Corps were landed by noon:[52] they were fitted with detachable pontoon floats, and on the XXIV Corps front they were carried to the reef in landing ships and craft before launching, whilst those of the III Corps were apparently launched from about 5,000 to 8,000 yards out to sea.

On both Corps fronts the advance continued eastwards all day, with negligible opposition in the north and only slight resistance in the south. By noon both Yontan airfield and the airstrip at Katena were captured. They were found to be little damaged, and were reported ready for emergency landing next day, when OY (artillery spotting) aircraft were sent to Yontan for operations. A number of undamaged Japanese aircraft were captured near Yontan airfield. But although the actual occupation of the airfields was far ahead of schedule, and all unloading was subordinated to that of aviation,[53] the landing schedule could not be adjusted to take full advantage of this by getting the necessary personnel ashore and expediting the off-loading of engineering equipment;[54] and it was not until the 7th April that the first garrison aircraft flew from their ferry escort carriers to Yontan field.

---

51 C.T.F. 51 Report, p.V-G-6.

52 C.T.F. 51, *Action Report*, p. III-9 and *Cincpac Report*, p. 43. *Combined Operations Observers' Report*, p. 15, says the tanks in the assault waves were landed between H+20 and H+30.

53 PhibForPac Action Report, 17th Feb.-17th May, 1945, p.37.

54 *British Combined Operation Observers 'Report* and Com. Fifth Fleet, Action Report.

Before dark on L-Day the Tenth Army had some 50,000 troops ashore. It had gained a beachhead of 4,000 to 5,000 yards in depth, secure from small arms fire. This represented approximately the line it had been hoped to reach by L+3 Day.[55] Vessels not required at the objective retired at 1815 for the night, 20 being left to furnish direct support.[56]

Three ships received enemy damage on L-Day. During the evening twilight at 1910 the transport *Alpine* off the western beaches was hit by suicide aircraft and a hole 30 feet x 30 feet was torn in her side from main deck to water line; and five minutes later the battleship *West Virginia* in the Gunfire and Covering Force was crashed but remained fully operational. At 2200 the destroyer *Vammen* in the Transport Screen (T.G. 51.5) struck a booby-trapped group of planks and about 15 seconds later an underwater explosion occurred similar to a 300-lb. depth charge, causing slight damage to one shaft.

34. Progress of Unloading, L-Day to L+2 Day

(A) NORTHERN SECTOR

The Northern Assault Beaches (III Amphibious Corps) were Green 1 and 2, Red 1, 2 and 3, Blue 1 and 2, Yellow 1 and 2. The Black beaches were not used at all; and Yellow 3, which was in the mouth of the Bishi-gawa river, was not used until it had been reconnoitred on the afternoon of L-Day. It was functioning by 1200 on L+1 Day.

The Underwater Demolition Teams made continual efforts to blast channels through the reef fronting the beaches but were frustrated by the nature of the coral. Consequently, the only craft which could cross, and these only for some two hours on each side of high water, were L.C.V.Ps. and some L.C.Ms. This necessitated transfer points being established there for work during low water periods, and these required cranes on barges which were not available in sufficient numbers until 3rd April. Further factors which delayed the unloading programme were a lack of suitable exits from the beaches, and (apparently) of engineering equipment to make them; and the delay in turn-round

55 *British Combined Observers' Report*, p.14, states that interrogation of prisoners and civilians revealed that the beach defences had been abandoned on L-2 day and indicated that one division may have been sent to Formosa before its expected replacement could arrive from Japan.

56 Direct Support: 24th Army Corps – Battleship *Nevada*; heavy cruiser *Minneapolis*; light cruisers *St. Louis, Birmingham*; destroyers *Daly, P. Hamilton, Twiggs, Barton, Anthony*. 3rd Phib Corps – Battleships *Idaho, West Virginia*; *Portland* heavy cruiser; *Biloxi* light cruiser; destroyers *Irwin, Callaghan, W.D. Porter, Preston*. General Support: 3rd Phib Corps – Destroyer *Porterfield*. 10th Army – Heavy cruisers *San Francisco, Pensacola*.

of L.V.T.s and D.U.K.W.s which resulted from the extremely rapid advance of the Corps in the early stages before their vehicles could be landed.

General unloading was ordered on 2nd April, and the Corps Commander reported euphemistically by signal that "unloading was proceeding with the minimum satisfactory progress". In an attempt to make the most of the high water period, work continued all night with the aid of lights from 2nd April onwards, and transports whose discharge was incomplete remained in the anchorage instead of joining in the general night retirement plan. The situation improved next day (3rd April), and although the organization was scarcely flexible enough to cope with the unexpected military situation, after 2nd April no serious criticism of the unloading progress was made by the Corps Commander.

(B) SOUTHERN SECTOR

In the southern sector the assault was made over 11 beaches stretching from Purple 1 to Brown 4. On account of the very irregular contours of the fringing reef, the Brown beaches were abandoned after the assault waves had been landed and efforts to improve the reef by blasting had failed. Notwithstanding the alteration in the plan necessitated by the unsuitability of the Brown beaches for landing vehicles and cargo, the southern beaches were rapidly and smoothly organized.

The fringing reef which fronted all the beaches dried out at low water, so that vehicles could be landed from all types of landing ships and craft at or near low water. But the depths were insufficient to allow landing craft to cross the reef even at high water, and accordingly the continuous operation of a transfer line for landing craft was necessary.

The in the northern sector one pontoon causeway was constructed, in the XXIV Corps sector causeways were rapidly formed by bulldozing from the beach to the edge of the reef, by which means the delay in arrival of the crane lighters for use on the transfer line was offset.

Delay in unloading occurred, however, from the following cause. Wheeled transport had been combat-loaded in the transports in anticipation of comparatively short haul from the beaches during the first few days, after which more transport became available. On account, however, of the rapid advance, the turn-round time of lorries was unduly prolonged, which led to an acute shortage of transport for clearing stores from the beach areas. This in turn necessitated amphibians being used for taking stores and ammunition all the way to the dumps inland, to the detriment of their primary function of running a shuttle service between the transfer line and the beaches.

However, by L+3 Day the whole organization was working "like clock-work". The garrison beach parties were established ashore this day and as the majority of the transports had completed unloading, the Naval Beach Parties were re-embarked at 1600, and the control vessels on the line of departure withdrew.

(C) SALVAGE OF LANDING CRAFT OFF THE REEF

Many landing craft which had beached on the edge of the reef found themselves unable to retract under their own power and were in danger of being left high and dry on the falling tide. This had been foreseen, and measures for dealing with it were well organised. An L.C.M. fitted with additional towing gear, and with a Salvage Officer embarked, was stationed continuously off each beach. The Assistant Boat Group Commander for each beach, embarked in a L.C.P.L.,[57] was also charged with the conduct of salvage operations off the reef, and was given authority to commandeer any unladen landing craft off his own beach to assist in towing off stranded craft.

[57] Landing Craft Personnel (Large).

Chapter VI

DEFENCE OF THE INVASION SHIPPING

35. The Screening Plan

The operation was now well launched. In the Transport Area off Okinawa a mass of shipping such as had seldom in history been assembled off an enemy coast. It was expected that the Japanese would attempt by every means in their power to expel the invaders; and the defence of the Transport Area consequently called for measures to combat practically every type of hostile interference which ingenuity could invent.

The Screening Plan accordingly provided for the following measures:

(a) Action against enemy aircraft, surface ships, submarines, midget submarines, and coastal craft;
(b) Prevention of enemy barge movement along the coast of Okinawa;
(c) Prevention of enemy movements between the islands of the group, and between Okinawa Shima and the offshore islands;
(d) Action against swimmers carrying limpet mines or similar explosive charges, human torpedoes, explosive motorboats or other types of fast small boats carrying explosives.

The means employed to implement this plan were as follows:

(i) Surface Covering Group;
(ii) Radar pickets;
(iii) Outer anti-submarine screen;
(iv) Hunter-killer groups;
(v) Inner anti-submarine screen;

(vi) Anti-small craft screen and patrols ("flycatchers");
(vi) Radar counter-measures screen;
(viii) Boat patrols (a) Within the Transport Area.
(b) Off the beaches;
(ix) Night Retirement;
(x) Smoke.

Detailed screening plans, showing the position of all screening stations and patrol lines, were issued. A general signal was made daily, indicating which screening plan was to be effective for the following 24 hours and which positions were to be occupied.

36. Surface Cover; Night Retirement and Smoke

(A) SURFACE COVERING GROUP

In view of the disastrous losses inflicted on the Japanese Fleet in the autumn of 1944 at the Battle for Leyte Gulf, it was considered that the enemy would not commit his major naval surface units in the defence of the Ryukus, though a raid on the amphibious forces was held to be a distinct possibility. Vice Admiral Mitscher's fast carrier force, Task Force 58, operating to the east of Okinawa, was in a position to intercept any Japanese surface force approaching the objective from Japan by the route east of Naisei Shoto, whilst the British Pacific Fleet, Task Force 57, guarded he western flank.[58] Responsibility for detecting the approach of surface forces to the west of the chain, and preventing any attempt either to reinforce or evacuate Okinawa by means of fast vessels, was assigned to the Support Carrier Group of escort carriers (Task Group 52.1).

Late afternoon and early morning aircraft searches were carried out in the sectors to the north and north-west of Okinawa until the search seaplanes of the Search and Reconnaissance Group (T.G. 50.5) arrived and assumed this task. During the day, fire support ships, while engaged in covering minesweeping, underwater demolitions, and bombardment, were in sufficiently close proximity to concentrate rapidly for surface action, if necessary. If intelligence of the approach of enemy fleet units were received a formation termed the Surface Covering Group was to be formed from the Gunfire and Covering Force of old battleships and cruisers (Task Force 54), together with destroyers from the Transport Screen, and was to drive off the enemy.

---

58 Although this role of the British Pacific Fleet is not mentioned by either Adm. Fraser, Vice Adm. Rawlings, or the Cdr. Fifth Fleet, the Comdr. Joint Expeditionary Force regarded the British Pacific Fleet as securing his western flank. (*Report on Okinawa Gunto Operation 17th Feb. to 17th May*, 1945, p(1) 6.)

Supporting and covering aircraft for the Surface Covering Group were to be furnished by the Support Carrier Group.

It was recognized, however, that at night the entire surface fighting force would probably be unable to concentrate. The fire support ships stationed off south-eastern and eastern Okinawa were few in number, and many valuable hours of destructive bombardment and fire cover for minesweeping in these areas would have been lost in moving them to join the ships operating at night off the west coast. This particularly applied during the first few nights of the operation, when the existence of unswept waters west of Naha would have necessitated the Eastern Fire Support Group passing westward of the Keramo Retto both whilst going to and returning from the western area.

Accordingly, about 80 per cent of the fire support ships deployed nightly to the north-west of Okinawa and about 20 per cent to the north-east. Their cruising area at night, known as the Retirement Area, was within 40 miles, or three hours' steaming of the Transport Area and beaches which the force had to protect. The north-western group was powerful enough to engage successfully any fleet which the enemy could bring against it. The group to the north-east was probably capable of dealing with any attempt at reinforcement from islands to the north, and in the event of attack by an enemy surface force on this side, it could count on the rapid support of Task Force 58, which took station at night close east of Okinawa. In grave emergency the Task Force Commander was willing to run the risk of passing his ships through the unswept but mineable waters to the north of Okinawa, which intelligence indicated, correctly, as subsequent events showed, were not mined.

(B) NIGHT RETIREMENT

Retirement from the Transport Area at night and return at daylight next day, by transports, and by L.S.Ts. which were not at the time beached on the reef, does not appear to have been the practice after the fourth night. Any ships of the Gunfire and Covering Force not on night assignment continued, however, to withdraw to their northerly stations for defence of the expedition's shipping against surface attack and for their own protection against enemy air or submarine attacks. Three considerations – readiness to deploy for surface action, defence against air attack and submarines – governed the disposition of the force in night retirement.

Towards the middle of April, when the shortage of destroyers became acute and losses mounted, heavy ships sometimes outnumbered destroyers during night retirement. After the destruction of the Japanese battleship *Yamato* in the attempted raid of 7th April (see Chapter IX) further surface raids were considered unlikely. Accordingly, the battleships remained in the Assault Area at night, under smoke when necessary, and only relatively few cruisers and destroyers withdrew. Later on, all retirement ceased, and all the support ships not engaged in night firings remained in or near the Transport Area.

(C) SMOKE

The Smoke Plan made provision for covering the anchorages with smoke during enemy air attacks at night; it was used only during darkness, and except during air attacks only to a very limited extent during minesweeping and U.D.T. operations, feint landings and the landing at Ie Shima.

The plan used at Okinawa consisted basically of stationing all available landing ships and craft equipped with fog generators on a line across the windward side of the anchorage area. In addition, each transport stationed two L.C.V.Ps. equipped with fog generators or smoke pots to windward of her. Smoke boats were provided for heavy combatant ships, and for large ships loaded with troops or important cargo if not equipped with them. Each heavy ship suitably equipped also made smoke. In addition, 45 fog generators were set up ashore to assist in covering the anchorage.

Smoke was commenced on orders of the S.O.P.A. in sufficient time to form good cover when there were indications, usually by radar, of impending air attack. The use of smoke more or less approximated to red alerts; and during the period 1st April to 16th May it was used on 38 out of 46 nights, for an aggregate of 98 hours, an average of just over two hours per night. From 17th May to 21st June it was used 72 times, for a total of 52 hours, an average of nearly one hour and 27 minutes per night. The times varied from no smoke to as much as eight hours during a single night.

Despite the large number of air attacks and the practice of the enemy of dropping bombs through the smoke cover, which became more prevalent during the later stages of the operation, only minor damage was suffered by ships covered by smoke in the transport anchorage.

Oil-laden smoke from smoke generators gave considerable trouble owing to the fact that the oil reduced insulation resistance in cables, motors, generators and so forth to the point where rewiring was often necessary. Admiral Spruance reported that the supply of fog oil at Okinawa was inadequate and was in a continual state of crisis.

37. Radar Pickets and Radar Counter Measures Screen

(A) RADAR PICKETS

The bulk of the defence of Okinawa amphibious operations centred around the reporting and fighter direction exercised by the exposed Fighter Ships and their supporting elements in the Radar Pícket Stations.

Six Headquarters ships, each carrying a Group Fighter Director, and 19 Fighter Director Ships (16 destroyers and three minelayers) were used in the operation. After employment on passage to the objective and in the preliminary operations, the Fighter Director ships were assigned duty in Radar Picket stations and in the screen, and as escorts for various retirement groups.

Fifteen Radar Picket stations, to which a sixteenth was added later, were established at distances varying from 50 to 70 miles from the Transport Area to cover all points of the compass. In the early stages Radar Picket Numbers 3, 4, 7, 10, 12 and 14, were filled, with No. 9 added subsequently, as nine stations were required for full cover. With the completion of shore-based radar installations on Hedo Saki, the northern extremity of Okinawa Shima, on 21st April, and on Ie Shima two days later, only five ship stations were needed and a revised picket arrangement was drawn up, under which only Nos.5, 7, 9. 15 and a new No.16 were filled, the remainder being left vacant.

The fighter director-fitted destroyers on picket duty manoeuvred at 15 knots within a 5,000-yard circle. They maintained continuous radar and visual air and surface searches, and also carried out asdic sweeping from beam to beam. Vice-Admiral Turner, C.T.F. 51, until 17th May, laid down as their primary function the early detection of approaching enemy aircraft, particularly low-flying, in order to facilitate interceptions at as great a distance as possible from the Transport Area. Besides the normal fighter director procedure depending entirely on radar, each destroyer had a "Visual Controller" to direct fighters on to low-flying enemy aircraft. The picket line normally controlled two to four divisions of fighter aircraft, with four aircraft to a division. Vice-Admiral Hill, who on 17th May succeeded Vice-Admiral Turner as C.T.F. 51, considered the first duty of the radar picket stations was to destroy or turn back enemy air attacks, and that long-range warning of impending attacks was secondary.

These radar pickets stopped a high proportion of the attackers, though the tactics of the enemy in concentrating on the more distant pickets, in particular, resulted in extremely heavy losses from enemy air attacks being suffered at first because the stations were too remote from the Combat Air Patrol and the number of vessels in each was too few for protection against multiple attacks. Of the 19 ships originally provided with fighter direction equipment, one was sunk by a mine, and four by suicide aircraft, eight were seriously and three slightly damaged by suicide attacks. Of the 14 replacement ships, one was sunk, five were seriously and two slightly damaged through the same form of attack. Nevertheless, it was considered by Admiral Spruance that the enemy committed a serious error in concentrating upon the pickets instead of attacking the transports.

Anti-aircraft fire power of the stations was augmented as practicable. In addition to the picket destroyers' own gunfire, which was entirely unrestricted against hostile or unidentified aircraft, it was soon found necessary to augment the fire power of the picket destroyers and assist them in covering the space between stations by groups of L.C.S.(Ls), termed Radar Supports. Fire power was finally standardized at three destroyers and four L.C.Ss. in each station, and additional destroyers were detailed when air attack was expected. After the raids of the 12th April, a special Picket Combat Air Patrol was furnished by Tactical Air Force for each station, solely as local picket protection. These measures eventually resulted in reducing the Japanese concentration on picket ships.

(B) RADAR COUNTER-MEASURE SCREEN

The Radar Counter-Measures (R.C.M.) Screen comprised stations for twenty L.C.I. (R) (R.C.M.) spread over the Transport Area, each station covering a square of 50 yards in which the landing craft lay to. Large ships equipped with R.C.M. co-operated in the screen but did not shift from their normal berths. The screen maintained continuous intercept watch on Japanese radar frequencies, but only carried out R.C.M. on order from the Force Commander.

The Japanese airborne radar was observed intermittently early in the operation but after about one night of R.C.M. the enemy stopped using it, and it is doubtful whether they made any subsequent use of it.

38. Anti-Submarine Measures

Two anti-submarine screens were maintained. The outer consisted of a continuous line of A/S vessels – destroyers, destroyer escorts, high speed destroyer transports, minesweepers, etc. – from a point south-east of Nakagusuku. This line was divided into seven sectors, each occupied by five ships which patrolled screening stations 700 yards in length at a speed of 15 knots. The average distance of this screen from the shore or from the Transport Area was 10 miles.

The function of the screen was to detect submarines by sight or sound contact and carry out A/S operations under the Sector Commander until relieved by a Hunter-Killer Group.

In addition to the outer screen, a close semi-circular screen of A/S vessels was stationed round the Transport Area from shore to shore. It comprised two sectors, each consisting of five ships which patrolled screening stations 5,000 yards in length at a speed of 10 knots and carried out duties similar to the outer A/S screen.

Four Hunter-Killer Groups were formed, each composed of two ships of the anti-submarine screen and one or two aircraft detailed by Commander Air Support Control Unit. Four Hunter-Killer stations were established, three just inside the outer A/S screen to the north, west and south of the Transport Area, and the fourth at Kerama Retto. Their purpose was to take over A/S operations from vessels on the screens as soon as a contact had been made.

When sufficient A/S vessels were available the Hunter-Killer Groups remained concentrated at their stations; otherwise ships in screening stations nearby were detailed as Hunter-Killer Groups. Aircraft were kept in the "standby" condition on board a carrier.

39. Submarine Attacks on the Transport Routes

Continuous day and night air Anti-Submarine Patrols were also maintained, consisting of six patrol aircraft from the Seaplane Base Group (51.20) at Kerama Retto. One torpedo bomber was supplied for special search over the Transport Area. Intensive day and night searches were also carried out along the shipping lanes to the south-east of Okinawa by the escort carriers *Anzio* and *Tulagi* of the Anti-Submarine Warfare Group (50.7).[59] The area 200 to 300 miles to the south and south-east of Okinawa was one of the two where the greatest concentration of Japanese submarines attempting to intercept American convoys was to be found. The other area, chiefly infested by midget submarines, was close to and in the Okinawa Gunto.

At 1453 on 29th April a torpedo bomber from the *Tulagi* surprised the Japanese submarine *R-109* on the surface in 24° 15′ N., 131° 16′ E., 13 miles S.S.E. of Okino Oagari Shima (Rasa Island), and sank it by depth charges.

On 31st May, an aircraft from the *Tulagi*'s sister ship, the *Anzio,* attacked an enemy submarine on the surface in 22° 22′ N., 134° 9′ E.

---

[59] On 5th June, T.G. 30.7 (as it had become when Com. Third Fleet relieved Com. Fifth Fleet) was relieved by T.G. 30.6 (*Anzio* (Escort Carrier) and five Destroyer Escorts under Capt. G. C. Montgomery).

whilst on a sweep between Okinawa and the Marianas, but although it is now known that the submarine, *I-12*, was sunk there was at the time no conclusive evidence of destruction.

Although several attacks on Japanese submarines took place on the transport route south-east of Okinawa where normal A/S screens were employed by Task Groups, no certain kill occurred subsequent to that of *I-8* by the destroyers *Stockton* and *Morrison* on the night 30th-31st March, until 10th April. On that day the destroyer escort *Fieberling* in the screen of Task Unit 51.29.11 en route from Okinawa to Saipan, made a contact at 1651 south-east of Okino Oagari Shima. Assisted by the destroyer *Haworth* and the high speed destroyer transport *Barr*, the *Fieberling* made eight attacks between 1651 and 1912. Heavy underwater explosions were heard after the sixth and seventh attacks, with large bubbles and craters of air rising to the surface of the water. Contact was completely lost after the last attack, but although no debris was recovered, it is now known that the submarine, *I-44*, was sunk.

On the 27th April the high speed destroyer transport *Ringness*, in the screen of a convoy from Saipan to Okinawa, possibly destroyed a midget submarine; and the destroyer escort *Hemminger* probably damaged a submarine during the night 24th-25th May, 60 miles south-east of Okinawa.

At 1400 on the 14th May in the fuelling and replenishing area south-east of Minami Oagari Shima in the Borodino Islands, Service Squadron 6 (Task Group 50.8) sighted inside the formation an abandoned one-man midget submarine and sank it by gunfire. Although the fast carriers were confined for much of their time to flying off areas close to Okinawa, they were singularly free from hostile submarine attack, and at least one Task Group (58.1) discarded anti-submarine air patrols early in the operation, in order that their elimination should help to clear up the radar picture.

On the 9th April the destroyers *Mertz* and *Monssen* in the screen of Task Group 58.5, each made five attacks on a contact in 26° 09′ N., 130° 21 ′E., south-east of Okinawa. There was no evidence of destruction at the time, but it is now known that the enemy submarine, *R.O.-46*, was sunk. The *Mertz* was also concerned in the destruction of *I-56* on the 18th April: at 1312 that day, after 24 attacks extending over some 14 hours by the destroyers *Heerman, Uhlmann, McCord, Collett* and *Mertz*, assisted by bomber aircraft from the light carrier *Bataan*, *I-56* was finally destroyed in 26° 42′ N., 130° 38′ E., east of Okinawa.

In all, a total of eight Japanese submarines, apart from midgets, were sunk during the Ryukus operation.

40. Midget Submarine and Air Attack on 20th May

On the whole, the Japanese made very little use of their submarines in an offensive capacity at Okinawa, and although there were numerous reports of midget submarine activity in the area and some unconfirmed reports of sinkings, no damage was done to any combatant vessel and very little to auxiliaries throughout the operation.[60] The submarine pens in the Unten Ko, in the north-west part of Okinawa Shima, were found to be empty when captured on 10th April.

On several occasions, torpedoes were reported to have been fired by hostile submarines and attacks were made by American A.S.W. vessels, but only one certain kill resulted. At 0230 on 5th April *L.C.S. 115* detected a large submarine near Kume Shima in 266° Zampa Misaki 68 miles (26° 22′ N., 126° 30′ E.). The destroyer *Hudson* was called to the scene and sank the enemy, now known to be *R.O.41*, though at the time it was thought the submarine was merely damaged. On the same day, a midget submarine was hemmed in against the reef around Zampa Misaki by the *Hyman*, *Starling*, *Impeccable*, *Fieberling*, and *P.C.* 855, and was heavily depth charged and believed sunk.

On the evening of the 20th May the Japanese made what appeared to be a co-ordinated air and midget submarine attack, the only occasion when such co-ordination was evident.[61] The apparent intention was to create a gap in the A/S screen to allow midget submarines to penetrate into the Transport Area.

Action commenced with suicide aircraft concentrating on ships in the A/S screen to the north-west of the Transport Area and to the northward of Ie Shima. At 1844 the minesweeper *Buller* on screen five miles north-east of Ie Shima was attacked and hit twice by suicide aircraft; she was not seriously damaged though her radar was put out of action.

At 1920, the high speed destroyer escort *Chase* in screening station B.11 bearing 255° distance 25 miles from Zampa Misaki was hit and put out of action by a suicide aircraft. Simultaneously, the high-speed destroyer transport *Register* in screening station B.13 bearing 265° distance 20 miles from Zampa Misaki was hit by a suicide aircraft, causing underwater damage to shaft and propeller and to one 40-mm. gun. At 1923 the destroyer *Thatcher* in screen station A.39A bearing 300° distance 14 miles from Zampa Misaki was hit and put out of action by a suicide aircraft. These actions left an appreciable temporary gap in

60 *Cincpac, April*, 1945, p.11, but no single instance of damage has been found amongst the available reports.

61 *C.T.F.* 51 and *C.T.F.* 31 *Action Report*, p.51.

the A/S screen to the west and north-west of the Transport Area and to the north of Ie Shima.

About an hour later submarine contacts began to be established. At 2022 the destroyer *Badger* sighted a possible midget submarine near Nago Wan but was unable to develop the contact. The destroyer escort *Finnegan,* working with her, subsequently had good sound contact and made two attacks the second of which caused heavy explosions and was believed to be a kill. At 2030 the destroyer escort *Fieberling* in Screen station A.37A made a sonar contact in 350°, 14 miles from Zampa Misaki and made three depth charge and two hedgehog attacks over a period of two hours.

The contact, evaluated as a midget submarine, disappeared after seven hours in water over 100 fathoms and was believed to have been sunk or damaged. Other contacts, which, however, produced no results, were made N. of Sesoko Chima (on the N.W. side of Nago Wan) and in position 270° Zampa Misaki 20 miles. At 2125 *L.C.S. 58* sighted two wakes on course 020° at 800 yards distance about 2,000 yards west of Machinato airstrip, south of Hagushi anchorage area; and at 2148 *L.C.S. 68* sighted three wakes in the same area which were thought to be midget submarines. Fire was opened.

After alternately sighting and losing the targets *L.C.S. 68* reported that the remaining target appeared to submerge. Further targets were picked up south of the Hagushi anchorage area by radar before midnight, but none were actually sighted.

41. Measures Against Suicide Boats and Barges

Scarcely greater success attended the operations of enemy suicide boats. It was known that the Japanese had assembled a number of fast, small explosive boats at Okinawa, for use in counter-landings and attacks against ships. About 1,000 were accounted for, in all. Large numbers were destroyed by the bombardment of Kerama Retto and Okinawa Shima, 330 were captured at their base in Kerama Retto, and over 300 were destroyed on or near Okinawa up to the middle of May. Special photographic missions were flown to find the caves in which these boats were concealed, and both naval gunfire and air strikes were employed to destroy them.

The standard design was a plywood boat 18 feet long, decked, driven by a Chevrolet engine of about 70-80 h.p., giving a speed range reported to be from 6 to 35 knots. Depth charges with an effective distance of 30 feet were carried in a rack in the stern, abaft the pilot: but there was also accommodation in the bow for an explosive charge: and a wheel-locking device was fitted for ramming.

The planned tactics of the Okinawa force were to approach in groups of three from astern of the target and drop the depth charges three feet from the ship's side, at a vital point. Captured instructions specified a full-power approach and withdrawal. It is obvious, however, that these tactics would have to be varied in the case of boats fitted with bow charge, or if, as sometimes occurred, men with "limpets" for affixing to ships' keels were carried. The majority of the boats discovered at Okinawa were non-powered. These would steal along in the shadow of the land as close as possible to the ship to be attacked, before closing.

The most effective methods of dealing with these pests were found to be co-ordinated air and surface search and attacks on the areas from which they were suspected to operate.

An Anti-small Craft Screen was formed, primarily for night duty, though it could be used in daylight if required. The patrol line was from the flanks of the Transport area northward as far as Ie Shima, and south round the tip of Okinawa Shima and up the south-east coast to Chim Wan. Each station covered an area three miles long by two miles wide, the line of stations being about one mile off shore.

Each station was occupied by an L.C.I.-type gunboat, fitted with radar if possible; and each group of five or six gunboats was allotted a cruiser and a destroyer, which patrolled to seaward in support of the line of gunboats, the group being termed a "flycatcher" team. The screening stations were designed to cover the large bays and indentations on the coast which might harbour small craft.

The functions of the screen were to prevent the effective night operations of enemy barges, M.T.Bs. and other small craft by bombardment and illumination of suspected small boat bases, in which heavy ships operating to seaward of the small craft shared, and by running to earth those which were able to venture forth. After 8th June, only one destroyer and assigned small craft conducted "flycatcher" operations, as the limited operating area did not warrant the use of both the cruiser and destroyer for the purpose.

The "flycatcher" ships also performed the additional tasks of dusk to dawn harassment of Naha, Itoman, and Yonabaru airfields, to prevent enemy aircraft from taking off and landing.

Each large ship remaining in the Transport Area after dark provided a landing craft (L.C.V.P. or L.C.P.L.) which patrolled round the parent ship at a distance of 300 yards. These craft were equipped with machine guns, rifles, 5-lb. charges and hand grenades with which to destroy swimmers and suicide boats.

There were further boat patrols off the beaches. At night two groups of 12 L.C.V.Ps. each, were stationed close inshore on the northern and southern flanks respectively of the main assault beaches. Co-operating with these landing craft were two groups of six amphibious and six armoured amphibians respectively, which occupied similar stations on the flanks, but took up positions on the reef inshore of the landing craft.

The purpose of these patrols was to protect the Transport Area and the beachheads from midget submarines, suicide boats, swimmers, "limpeteers" and the like, and generally to fill the gap between the inshore ends of the close A/S screen and the beaches. The amphibians were responsible for repelling infiltration along the beaches or over the reef, and for destroying small boats or swimmers attempting to reach the beach.

In addition to counter-landing attempts and attacks on shipping the Japanese, both military and civilians, made use of small boats in efforts to escape to outlying islands. Gunboat types proved themselves to be most valuable in frustrating these efforts.

Taking into account the large numbers of attacks by suicide boats, and the numbers of these pests discovered and destroyed, the success achieved was exceedingly small. After the attacks of 29th and 30th March no further damage to shipping occurred until the morning of 3rd April, when *L.C.I. 82*, in the Nakagusuku Wan anti-small boat screen, was so heavily damaged by an enemy M.T.B. attack that she sank next day whilst under tow. This was the only Allied vessel sunk by a suicide boat during the operation. The enemy boat was sunk, and the Zamami (Kerama Retto) patrol sank four boats the next day.

During the night 8th-9th April considerable enemy suicide and small boat activity occurred. C.T.G. 51.15 reported that 12 to 15 boats in all were sighted in Kerama Retto area, of which five were destroyed by gunfire. At least 15 swimmers, some with hand grenades, were killed. Between 0830 and 0430, suicide boats of the 3-man skimmer type, apparently from Naha, attacked shipping in the southern transport area. *C.J. Badger*[62] was holed on the starboard side and seriously damaged, and the cargo ship *Starr* was slightly damaged, being saved by an L.S.M. alongside, which was struck by the attacking boat.

The destroyer *Hutchins* was seriously damaged whilst delivering fire support to the 7th Division from Nakagusuku Wan during the night 26th-27th April. A 16-ft. skimmer type enemy boat came in on her port quarter at high speed, and an explosion occurred 30 seconds after the boat turned away. Twenty or more boats were observed that night in Yonabaru Wan, and about 12 were destroyed. On the following night, the cruiser *St. Louis* destroyed nine off the south-west coast and other

---

62 Not to be confused with the *Badger* (see Section 40).

ships a further ten; at 0240 on 28th April *L.C.S. 37* was damaged in Nakagusuku Wan by a depth charge dropped by an enemy boat which she destroyed; several of the enemy boats penetrated the screen and headed for the transport area, where some were destroyed and the cargo ship *Bozeman Victory* was hit and damaged.

With one exception this was the sum total of the enemy's success. An attack on the cargo ship *Carina* which occurred on the 4th May was the last occasion on which any ship was damaged by suicide boats or swimmers. Although enemy suicide boats of standard design were reported on several occasions, and many were destroyed, from 17th May at least, it was not positively established that any attack was attempted on any ship of the Amphibious Force.[63]

Mines of booby trap and other types, launched from the shore by the enemy, were encountered in considerable numbers, but achieved little success. The destroyer *Vamnen* was damaged on L-Day and on 8th the motor minesweeper *Y.M.S. 92* was damaged and *Y.M.S.* 103 was destroyed in Nakagusuku Wan, and a motor gunboat was also sunk.

42. Loss of the *Longshaw*, 18th May

It was in the course of flycatcher operations that the destroyer *Longshaw* was lost. She was one of the few ships sunk other than by air attack and the only one sunk by enemy gunfire from shore.

On the morning of the 18th May the *Longshaw* and the heavy cruiser *Salt Lake City* were conducting flycatcher operations along the south-west shore of Okinawa, illuminating the coast, bombarding likely hiding places for suicide boats and barges, and providing harassing fire as directed by C.T.G. 51.2. At 0739 the *Longshaw* reported herself aground on a reef 2,600 yards from Omine Saki south-west of Naha air strip, which was held by the enemy. Her hull was intact, and the destroyer *Picking* attempted to tow her off, without success. An attempt at 1050 by the ocean tug *Arikara* also failed.

About 1100 enemy shore batteries opened fire on the *Longshaw*, and obtained four or more direct hits with a large mortar which caused several fires throughout the ship. One salvo hit the forward magazine, and blew off the ship's bow as far aft as the foremost funnel. The *Salt Lake City* and destroyers *Picking* and *H. L. Edwards* laid down a smothering counter-fire and the enemy ceased fire. But the damage had already been done.

The *Longshaw* was practically engulfed in a heavy oil fire, and after further explosions the ship was abandoned. Her casualties were heavy:

---

63 *C.T.F.* 51 *and C.T.F.* 31, *Action Report*, p. IV-1.

13 officers and 76 men killed or missing, and four officers and 61 men wounded. Amongst those lost were her captain and executive officer. The hulk was destroyed by the Americans, salvage being impracticable.

43. Communications

The anti-suicide boat and swimmer measures provided for in the plans of operations, became an important part of the Okinawa campaign. But co-ordinated support between the small craft patrols and the cruisers and destroyers on flycatcher operations had not been provided for; and owing to the limitations of communications it was some time before the requisite standard was reached. Communications in the Okinawa operation were generally good, though there was a lack of communication personnel. On relinquishing command of the Fifth Fleet on 28th May, Admiral Spruance wrote:

> Commander Fifth Fleet is well aware that we must win the war with the men and material available; however, it is believed that there is a wide-spread ignorance of the expansion of Naval communications. And the enormous burden that expansion has put upon the inadequate allowance of officers and men.
>
> The radio operators on the staff of Commander Joint Expeditionary Force stood watch and watch for 46 days. The radio operators on the small ships, the L.C.Is., the L.S.Ts., the DEs and the like have been on watch and watch since they came aboard or since they left Pearl Harbor.[64]

The efficient functioning of the voice circuits was somewhat affected by two causes, one technical, the other shortcomings on the part of the operators (unauthorized transmissions and lack of proper procedure). There were certain deficiencies of radio equipment to be overcome both during the assembly period and at the objective itself, partly due to the many different types of vessels used and because of the losses of portable radio material in the Iwo Jima operation which had barely concluded before Operation "Iceberg" commenced.

For the first time during a combined operation more than one T.B.S. (V.H/F radio (voice)) channel was used, necessitating many last-minute installations. It had been hoped to use eight such channels. This hope was not realized, and it was only through temporary transfers of material from ships not making use of it at the time, that it was possible to use three different T.B.S. frequencies. On the 4th May, date of the great Japanese counter-attack, a peak load of 1095 messages was cleared on these three frequencies. There were numerous requirements

---

64 *Action Report through 27th May*, 1945, p. VI-I-5.

for special radio facilities to meet unforeseen needs in establishing and augmenting communications.

Deliberate enemy jamming was not effective, and Allied communications were not interrupted by enemy interference at any time.

44. Enemy Counter-Landing Attempts

The enemy barges and small craft had very little success in counter-landings. Many were attempted, principally it would seem for sabotage, but few succeeded. The most important of these operations was that carried out on the 4th May, co-ordinated with sea, air and land attacks, in an attempt to effect landings behind the American lines on both sides of Okinawa Shima. At 2540 on the 3rd May small enemy craft were observed in Nakagusuku Wan, of which at least one was destroyed by naval gunfire. In all, 15 suicide boats were destroyed in or near the transport area during the night, though only one ship, the cargo ship *Carina,* received damage.

The first air attacks began at 0130 on the 4th and lasted until 0145, but caused no damage to ships. At 0200 enemy troops, estimated to number from 500 to 600, were landed from two large and four small barges west of Machinato Airfield. Some 20 were killed on the beach, but many got into the town carrying knee mortars, small arms, demolition charges and food for one week. On the east coast the enemy intended to land some 300 troops, embarked in nine boats. The attempt was completely defeated, three of the boats were destroyed by American troops and five or six by naval gunfire. The enemy shore forces counter-attacked both flanks of the 1st Marine Division prior to the landings but were successfully repulsed.

A second series of 14 air raids by about 70 aircraft took place from 0745 to 0915 and caused great damage. The destroyers *Luce* and *Morrison* and two L.S.Ms., all on radar picket stations, were sunk by suicide attacks, and the light cruiser *Birmingham,* the destroyer *Ingraham,* and the light minelayer *Shea,* both the latter also on picket duty, were seriously damaged, the last named by Baka bomb.[65] Many other light craft were slightly damaged.

In the evening, a third air attack damaged the escort carrier *Sangamon* and the light minelayer *Gwin,* the latter only slightly, however, and she remained on her picket station. In all, 137 enemy aircraft were destroyed during the day, including 12 by suicide hits. Task Force 58 fighters assisted in the defence of Okinawa against the air attacks

[65] A Japanese rocket-propelled bomb-carrying aircraft guided by a suicide pilot.

and shot down 98 of the enemy destroyed, losing only five aircraft themselves.

A few further counter-landings were attempted during May, but on the 10th of the month the Commander Amphibious Forces was able to report that the intensified illumination and harassing of suspected small boat areas were producing satisfactory results. In any event, the menace of small craft and even of submarines, at its height, was small by comparison with that of the great Japanese air attacks.

Chapter VII

THE STRUGGLE FOR AIR SUPREMACY

The suicide ("Kamikaze") air attacks constituted the outstanding feature of the Japanese reaction to the invasion of Okinowa. The Americans were no strangers to this type of attack, which had first manifested itself in organised form on the 24th October, 1944, during the Battle for Leyte Gulf. At Okinawa, however, it reached its climax and the resulting loss and damage crated a serious problem of repair and replacement.

45. The Battle of Attrition

The attacks came from the flanks: from Formosa and the Sakishima Gunto on the left flank, and from Kyushu and Amami Gunto on the right flank. The Japanese air forces in Formosa were apparently supplemented by aircraft from South China and the South; while the whole of Japan, North China and Korea were drawn upon for aircraft which were staged through Kyushu and Amami Gunto.

Japanese air opposition had been expected, and it was as part of the preparatory operations that the fast carriers of the American Fifth Fleet had taken action towards neutralisation of the enemy's air power prior to the landings, by strikes on Kyushu and Kure on the 18th and 19th March. Simultaneously, XXI Bomber Command, operating from bases in the Marianas and from Iwo Jima after the capture of that island in March 1945, attacked airfields in Kyushu and areas in Honshu, whilst land-based air forces in the South-West Pacific Area attacked Formosa.

From the commencement of the amphibious operation against Okinawa the American Fast Carrier Force, and the British Pacific Fleet and American Escort Carrier Group, guarded the right and left flanks respectively, by constant attacks on enemy airfields. As the operation progressed, commencing on 16th April, XXI Bomber Command shifted part of the effort of its heavy bombers to Kyushu, at the request of Commander Fifth Fleet; and during April operations against the Kyushu airfields absorbed some 40 per cent of its strikes and were of undoubted assistance in reducing the scale of enemy air attack on Okinawa.[66]

Admiral Spruance recognized that airfields and air installations were not the best heavy bombing targets, but he believed that attacks upon the mounting and staging points of enemy air raids would be useful because of the known inflexibility of Japanese planning, their tendency to be put off balance easily, and their aircraft maintenance difficulties. A battle of attrition soon developed between American sea and air power and the Japanese Air Force. In the early stages of the operation the Japanese appeared capable of mounting a major attack every few days, in addition to daily raids.

Ten suicide attacks were carried out by the 6th Air Army and the Fifth Air Fleet during the operations as follows:

No.	Date	Navy Aircraft	Army Aircraft	Total
1	6-7 April	230	125	355
2	12-13 April	125	60	185
3	27-28 April	120	45	165
4	15-16 April	65	50	115
5	3-4 May	75	50	125
6	10-11 May	70	80	150
7	24-25 May	65	100	165
8	27-28 May	60	50	110
9	3-7 June	20	30	50
10	21-22 June	30	15	45
	Total	860	605	1,465

[66] *Com. Fifth Fleet Action Report*, p.VI-B-3. According to this report, the average number during the period 16th to 30th April was 120 on each of ten strike days. In May the average number dropped to about 40 and only five strikes were carried out, the last being on 10th May. *Operations in the Pacific Ocean Areas, April, 1945*, p.6, give different figures, the average for 17th to 30th April being 134 aircraft daily. *B.P.F.L.O. Com. Fifth Fleet Second Report*, p. 5, gives the commencing date as 17th April and states that the average attacking force numbered 50 aircraft.

These raids were termed by the Japanese "Kikusui attacks". Sporadic small suicide attacks were also carried out during this period by 140 Navy and 40 Army aircraft. From Formosa 250 suicide attacks were made, 50 by Navy and 200 by Army aircraft.

Greater in number, but less effective, were attacks of orthodox type by torpedo and dive bombers, Japanese Navy aircraft making some 3,700[67] sorties and the Army 1,110.[68]

The suicide attack was difficult to counter since any pilot who has decided to kill himself can hit a ship, unless killed first or knocked out of control. Although this type of attack, with its small penetrating power, failed to sink any capital ships or cruisers it caused a high rate of loss amongst smaller vessels. So many ships were severely damaged that before the landing was three weeks old five carriers and 37 destroyers, destroyer escorts, minesweepers, and the like had been put out of action for at least several weeks.

The Japanese were apparently aware of the limitations of the American air search radar and aircraft identification equipment, and developed a receiver which enabled them to make use of fade areas in making their approaches. They employed several types of search and attack, evolved since the Battle for Leyte Gulf in October 1944, which were difficult to counter. Dawn attacks proved most successful for the enemy, though fewer were made than had been anticipated.

The American carrier task groups were accustomed to launch combat air patrols, strikes and sweeps at morning twilight (sometimes before dawn). Within a few moments the ten-mile radius around the task group would become saturated with friendly aircraft, and it was comparatively simple for the enemy who about 30 minutes before first light had infested the area around the task group at all altitudes, to approach without detection by undiscriminating I.F.F.[69] and protected by cloud cover. Dawn attacks made it difficult for the Expeditionary Force shipping to judge whether or not to keep the Night Retirement Disposition intact whilst enemy aircraft were in the neighbourhood.

Dusk attacks were employed, both against the Expeditionary Force shipping, and against the carriers, to exploit the vulnerable period when the carriers were landing or had landed their aircraft. "The enemy," wrote the Commander, Gunfire and Covering Force, "could have inflicted more damage if he had concentrated more on evening

67 *The Campaigns of the Pacific War*, p.328

68 *viz.* 240 bomber, 750 cover and 120 reconnaissance. *Report on Operation "Olympic" and Japanese counter-measures*, p.27, where it is stated that the Naval effort was "slightly higher".

69 Identification Friend or Foe.

twilight attacks when night dispositions were being formed and just about the time the day's C.A.P. was landing."[70] Night attacks occurred, particularly as the moon waxed, but more frequent were small night-long nuisance raids. The ten large scale attacks which were made, proved very costly to the Japanese. Dispersed attacks were experienced throughout the entire operation.

46. Air Support

During the period which elapsed before the airfields in Okinawa Gunto were available direct air support of the operations was furnished by the fast carriers of Task Force 58 and by the escort carriers of Rear-Admiral Durgin's Support Carrier Group (Task Group 52.1).

As the result of enemy air attacks the number of fast carriers whose aircraft were available to protect and support the ground troops, gradually declined from 13 on 23rd March to eight on the 12th May; for replacements could not keep up with losses. Finally, when the enemy air effort had diminished as the result of his losses, only one task group was kept available for direct support missions. The escort carriers were more fortunate, and suffered little decline from their initial number of 14 vessels.[71]

C.T.G. 51.10 (Commander Air Support Control Units), in the flagship of C.T.F. 51 exercised control of all air support missions, but as the troops advanced and Landing Force Air Support Control Units became established the control of troop direct support missions was delegated to them, with C.A.S.C.U. Lanfor Headquarters, III and XXIV Corps respectively, directing the support aircraft.[72] The G.O.C. III Amphibious Corps reported that the average interval which elapsed from the time of request for air support to the time of commencing the attack was 55 minutes, whilst the average period from the time of request for a mission until its completion was 102 minutes. The reasons for these delays were partial failure of communications, enemy jamming activities, failure to include the necessary information in the request, and the necessity of requiring approval from the next senior echelon.

As the operations progressed, aircraft of the Tactical Air Force performed an increasing proportion of the direct air support missions,

70 *Task Force 54 Report*, p.17.

71 The escort carriers were stationed in a somewhat safer position to the southward of Okinawa.

72 Landing Force A.S.C.U. 1 (assigned to III Amphibious Corps) on L + 7 Day. Landing Force A.S.C.U. 3 (assigned to the Tenth Army) served as coordinating agency ashore for all for all air support operations.

but the primary duty of the Tactical Air Force, which consisted principally of fighter aircraft, remained that of providing Combat Air Patrols.

47. Combat Air Patrols

The problem of furnishing adequate air protection for the various separate units – the main Attack Force, the Demonstration Group, the Kerama Retto area, and the radar pickets – was not easy to solve. The original plan for the Target Combat Air Patrol called for one division of fighters[73] to be stationed in the south-west, six divisions in the objective area and five divisions to the north. However, on account, apparently, of the damage and losses suffered by the carriers this strength was not always available, and the scheme had to be modified.

For a few days after the landing approximately eight divisions were maintained on station, but from L+5 day onwards 56 to 76 aircraft were furnished on regular schedules by the fast carriers, escort carriers, and from L+7 day onwards, when their communication system was complete, by the Tactical Air Force as well.[74] This force, consisting primarily of Marine and Army fighters, ultimately relieved the carriers of responsibility for the air defence of Okinawa Gunto and direct air support of the ground troops. Latterly, when large scale raids were anticipated, an airborne C.A.P. of 84 aircraft was maintained with a further 36 aircraft on ground alert – this, in addition to the radar picket C.A.Ps.

On days when little enemy activity was expected, the C.A.P. was reduced to 60 aircraft with 24 on ground alert. The aircraft constituting the C.A.P., were stationed in accordance with the best estimate of the situation at the time. The approaches from Kyushu and Formosa were most heavily guarded, in that order. A small reserve was maintained, centrally located, and sectors of comparatively little activity were lightly covered.

The escort carriers, which were stationed to the south of Okinawa to co-operate with the British Pacific Fleet in keeping Sakishima neutralized, provided C.A.P. for patrol of the southern and south-western sectors. Most of the raids from Formosa, and the few from Sakishima, arrived in the late afternoon or night when the target C.A.P. from the escort carriers had left the area. Vice-Admiral Rawlings

---

73 Four fighters.

74 "The T.A.F. was slow in setting up adequate communications ashore. It was not until Commander Joint Expeditionary force made available to them equipment from his own supply that their communications became as reliable and complete as they should have been." Com. Fifth Fleet *Action Report*, p. VI-I-6.

co-operated by late afternoon strikes to lessen the weight and incidence of dusk and moonlight air attacks on the invasion shipping.

The C.A.P. could at any time be supplemented by the Advanced Commander Air Support Control Unit releasing fighters from the support groups of escort carriers, which was done on several occasions. The Fast Carriers provided two night fighters, one controlled through the Headquarters Ship of the Amphibious Support Group, the other by a battleship of the Gunfire and Covering Force. After L+13 Day the night C.A.P. was increased to between four and eight aircraft, furnished by the Tactical Air Force. The carriers also provided C.A.P. for their own ships.

The identification of friendly aircraft caused difficulty throughout the operation, and several were inadvertently shot down.

48. Build-up of Shore-Based Air Strength

The severe check to the Americans' advance about L+5 day, which kept them where they stood for a fortnight and was only resolved after a bloody frontal attack lasting several weeks, fortunately did not greatly delay the development of airfields in the Okinawa Gunto. Okinawa Gunto provided 26 potential airfields with an approximate capacity of five VLR[75] wings, two fighter wings, numerous heavy and medium bombers and other types of aircraft, and a depot field. Sufficient of these airfields, and potential airfields, to absorb the efforts of the construction units were captured in the first rush. These efforts were devoted at first, and for obvious reasons, to the rapid increase of fighter strength, at the expense where necessary of bomber development projects.

Major-General Mulcahy, U.S.M.C., Commanding General Tactical Air Force, assumed command of aircraft ashore on Okinawa on April 8th. For some weeks after the landing the excellent airfield at Yontan, which was all weather operational on 8th April, was the only one in full operation. The first fighters (100 Corsairs) were flown in from their transport escort carriers on L+6 Day, though it was three weeks before they were able to begin large scale operations. In addition to the group of Corsair fighters and a flight of photo-Lightnings, the transport and evacuation traffic was dealt with here.

There was a squadron of Avengers for local A/S work and tactical support of troops, and a flight of Liberator four-engine patrol bombers commenced offensive operations on 25th April, ranging as far afield as Chosen and Tsu Shima. A group of Corsairs operated from Katena airstrip at an early date, but although the strip was dry-weather

---

[75] Very Long Range.

operational on April 8th much work was required to render it fit for use in all weather and the accommodation of a second air group. Ie Shima, though potentially first class, was so heavily mined and deeply trenched that it was not until the 13th May that two strips were in operation there. On that day an Army Group totalling 100 Thunderbolt long-range fighters commenced to fly in from Saipan, and were followed later by further groups.

The partially complete Japanese airstrip at Machinato was not captured until the 20th April, Yonabaru a fortnight later, and Naha not until 6th June. These, like the various new airfields[76] could not be got ready before the Ryukus operation ended, though additional landing strips for artillery spotting aircraft were placed in commission on the 17th, 21st and 22nd April respectively.

In addition to Kerama Retto, the construction of flying boat bases in the east coast harbours of Chim Wan and Nakagusuku Wan was begun during May.

49. The First Heavy Japanese Air Attack, 6th April

It was not until the sixth day after the landing that the Japanese launched their first great air attack, both the Expeditionary and Covering Force being the targets. The attacks, which began about 1500 on April 6th, were mainly directed against patrol and picket stations. The destroyers *Bush* and *Colhoun,* and the high speed minesweeper *Emmons,* all on picket duty, were sunk.[77]

At Kerama Retto *L.S.T. 447* was sunk and two ammunition ships which had arrived only that day, were gutted by fire and became total losses. Twenty-two smaller vessels, many of them destroyers, were damaged. One, the high speed minesweeper *Rodman,* was attacked by at least 11 of the enemy, of which three hit the ship and eight were shot down. Several other co-ordinated or concentrated attacks occurred.

It was apparently such an attack which sank the *Bush* and *Colhoun.* The destroyer *Cassin Young,* assisted by *L.C.S. 110,* in Radar Picket Station 3, was under continuous attack from 0250 to 0600 by from one to three enemy aircraft at a time, an aircraft on a reciprocal bearing acting as a decoy to attract attention; the attacks were pressed to 4,000 yards and then broken off. The destroyer *Howorth* was attacked by five aircraft simultaneously, one of which hit the ship; and the destroyer escort *Witter* was subjected to a co-ordinated attack by an aircraft

76 Bolo, Chimu, Awase, Motobu, Futema, Tera.

77 The *Colhoun* started to break up and was sunk by gunfire about 0130 on the 7th April, and the *Emmons* at 0318 on the 7th.

diving from ahead, which was shot down, whilst a second came in low from the beam at the same time and hit the ship. Whilst the Night Retirement Group was forming, at 1610, sustained air attacks began and the destroyers *Leutze* and *Newcomb* in the screen were hit and severely damaged.

In addition to picket stations established to cover the objective area, Task Force 58, for their own protection, provided a radar picket group of destroyers, stationed 30 to 40 miles on the flanks of the task force to intercept suicide aircraft. These amply demonstrated their value on this day, 6th April. One destroyer alone shot down three suiciders.

In all, some 75 per cent of the 400 attacking enemy aircraft were destroyed, 248 of them by the two fast carrier task groups 58.1 and 58.3 participating in the action. The carrier *Essex*'s aircraft alone shot down 65. There were some apparent lacunae in the work of the Combat Air Patrol, for the latter was controlled by various fighter director ships and the circuits by which it was handled were not all manned aboard the fire support vessels. Four American ships were damaged by friendly A.A. fire.

50. First Use of Jet-Propelled Bombs, 12th April

On the 12th there was a report that enemy aircraft had landed at Naha, and the cruiser *Minneapolis* fired 100 rounds of 8-inch and 300 rounds of 3-inch into the airfield. All the portents pointed to another day of heavy air attacks. Accordingly, Task Force 58 cancelled all strikes and searches and placed fighters on station over the islands to the north of Okinawa; the Support Carrier Unit 52.1.3 was withdrawn from Sakishima which it was covering whilst the British Pacific Fleet struck Formosa; and fire support assignments were cut to a minimum so that Task Force 54 might cruise in compact A.A. formation.

About 1300 a very heavy air attack developed, the radar pickets again taking the brunt of it. For three hours the enemy came over in groups of ten or a dozen at heights between 18,000 and 20,000 feet. The fighters over the northern islands of Kikai, Tokuno and Amami met many of them and shot down 80. Nearly all the remainder came on to Okinawa, where the C.A.P averaged 72 fighters equally drawn from the fast carriers, the support carriers, and the Marine Air Group ashore.

This C.A.P. was stacked at heights between 2,000 and 20,000 feet over the various orbit points round the islands, control being carried out by radar pickets, C.T.G. 51.15 at Kerama, and C.T.F. 51. The C.A.P. accounted for about 80 of the enemy and only a single aircraft penetrated to the transport area.

On this day, as on the 6th April, the enemy concentrated his attacks on detached units and the radar pickets again suffered heavily, not only from jet-propelled bombs ("Baka" and "Viper") piloted, and launched usually from a twin-engine aircraft, which were used, apparently for the first time, by the Japanese. One sank the destroyer *M.L. Abele* which was subjected, in Radar Picket Station 14, to a co-ordinated low level attack by about 20 aircraft, not all of which actually attacked. The ship shot down two, then a suicide hit was followed almost at once by a jet-propelled bomb hit which caused the vessel to break in two and sink immediately. Two other light units were hit and damaged by jet-propelled bombs travelling at very high speed.

During a night attack at 2020 on Task Force 54 Retirement Group, Japanese aircraft used flares for the first time in the Okinawa operation. In this determined attack the battleships *Tennessee* and *Idaho* received serious damage from suiciders, though R.C.M. probably prevented more of the attackers from getting through to the Retirement Group. An enemy radar station was located on southern Okinawa, but caused little trouble. The Japanese had, however, a provoking mobile installation which had not been definitely destroyed by L+46 Day.

In all, 11 escort vessels and several smaller craft were damaged in varying degrees on this day 12th April, but the enemy again suffered severely, losing at least 208 aircraft.

51. Co-ordinated Attacks on 16th April

A few days later, during the night 15th-16th April, many enemy aircraft were over the assault area, which was put under smoke for six hours. Much wild shooting occurred despite explicit instructions from Vice-Admiral Turner that no ship was to fire without a good solution and, if in smoke, without his express permission. Friendly aircraft were taken under fire on at least two occasions, and shipping was endangered by wild firing.

At 2129 Vice Admiral Turner sent the following message to all ships: "The existing situation where ships were firing at nothing is scandalous. No ships will fire now except on personal orders of Captains, Captains enforce this order." On the following morning, 16th April, very heavy enemy air attacks commenced about 0730, both against the Expeditionary Force and the Covering Force, and against Yontan and Katena airfields. They were marked by coordination and by the usual Kamikaze feature of concentrating on isolated ships.

At 0745 the destroyer *Laffey* in R.P. 1 was subjected to a co-ordinated attack by about 30 aircraft. She was hit by four suiciders and two dropped bombs, and suffered 94 casualties; but the ship survived, shot down six of the enemy and proceeded under her own power to Kerama Retto at 20 knots.[78]

From 0845 to 1030 the high speed minesweeper *Hobson* and destroyer *Pringle*, in R.P. 14, a somewhat isolated station in about 27° 10′ N., 127° 15′ E., where the *M.L. Abele* had been sunk ten days previously, were attacked by 10 to 15 enemy aircraft, one of which apparently directed the operations. The *Pringle* was sunk by a suicide hit, apparently on her torpedo tubes, and the *Hobson* was badly damaged by a bomb from a suicide aircraft which was destroyed just before it would have hit.

As a general rule, destroyers and other small craft found that it paid to hold their fire until reasonably certain of a kill. Large ships, however, found it essential to effect their kill at longer ranges.

At 0051 the high speed minesweeper *Harding* came under co-ordinated attack by two enemy aircraft, whilst en route to relieve the somewhat isolated Station 14. One was shot down approaching from the stern, a favourite method of approach, but simultaneously the second aircraft came in on the starboard beam and hit the ship.

In the Covering Force, the fast carrier *Intrepid* was damaged a few hours later by a suicide hit. The Japanese losses were again severe, approximately 270 aircraft being destroyed. The Expeditionary Force ships shot down 62 of these and Combat Air Patrol 55.

52. First Heavy Night Suicide Attacks, 27th-28th April

On the evening of the 22nd April an attack was made by some 80 enemy aircraft, no single one of which, however, succeeded in penetrating to the Transport Area, though the minesweeper *Swallow* was sunk in the Area Screen. The radar pickets suffered again; the destroyer *Isherwood* was heavily damaged, and six other picket ships received lesser damage. No fresh feature characterized the attacks, in which 54 of the enemy were destroyed.

The 7th and 28th April were marked by the first large scale night suicide attacks. Raids began at 1910 on the 27th. Bombs were dropped in the Transport Area though it was under a smoke screen. No ship covered by the screen was hit. But the *Canada Victory*, loaded with troop ammunition, which was in a rift in the smoke cover, was hit and sunk at 2212 by a suicide aircraft. Two high speed destroyer escorts in the screen, the *Talbot* and the *Rathburne* were also hit and damaged by suiciders.

---

[78] These figures are all based on the report of C.T.F. 54 (in which the *Laffey* was serving). B.P.F.L.O. with T.F. 58 and C.T.F. 51 give different, and much higher figures, but these are presumed to be based on hearsay.

About 0400 on the 28th there was a lull until approximately 1400 when the attacks recommenced, and between that hour and 0200 on the 20th 44 raids were made by some 200 enemy aircraft, 118 of which were destroyed by ships and aircraft of the Expeditionary and Covering Forces. The destroyers *Daly* and *Twiggs* in R.P. 2 were damaged by suiciders, eight to ten of which were shot down with the assistance of the C.A.P. Many aircraft were over the Transport Area, and Yontan airfield was bombed; but no attacks were made on vessels covered by smoke in the transport area. The evacuation transport *Pinkney* was damaged at Kerama Retto, and at 2000 the hospital ship *Comfort* was hit by a suicide aircraft and badly damaged, 50 miles south-east of Okinawa.

This was not the first time the *Comfort* had been attacked, for she received minor damage from bombing in the forward area on the 7th April, and on the 9th one of the *Enterprise*'s night aircraft had mistakenly attempted to bomb her in 25° 06′ N., 127° 21′ E. (about 60 miles south of Okinawa) but fortunately without doing any damage.

The enemy night air raids increased in strength as the moon waxed. But even during the periods of the bright moon the Japanese aircraft were not interfered with except by a few night fighters, of which there was such a general shortage in the area that no effective night fighter Combat Air Patrol was developed.[79]

53. Three Flagships Put Out of Action, 11th-14th May

The night of the 3rd May and early hours of the 4th witnessed closely co-ordinated enemy air, sea and land attacks in an attempt to land behind the American lines on both sides of Okinawa.

For nearly a week thereafter Japanese air activity remained at a very low level. On 10th May, however, the American Tenth Army launched a co-ordinated attack on the entire front, and the occasion was marked by heavy enemy air attacks, undertaken simultaneously against shipping in the Okinawa area and against Task Force 58 which was supporting the operation from an area 80 miles east of Okinawa. During the night 10th-11th May the Fast Carrier Force was almost constantly shadowed by enemy aircraft.

Between 0100 and 0500 and 0800 and 0930 on 11th May approximately 110 enemy aircraft were in the Okinawa area. At Ie Shima, which had been captured on the 1st April, transports came under aerial torpedo attack about 0900. The *Panamint* avoided two torpedoes by swinging

79 *C.T.F. 54 Action Report, 5th-28th May, 1945*, p.3. As far as can be ascertained the maximum number of night fighters employed at Okinawa on any night was eight.

on her anchor, and the only ship damaged in the anchorage was the Dutch merchantman *Tjisadane*, which was hit by a suicider. In R.P. 15 the destroyer *Hadley* was both bombed and crashed, and had 92 casualties, and the destroyer *Evans* in the same station was also badly damaged by a suicide. But 93 enemy aircraft were destroyed in the two morning attacks in the Okinawa area, and Task Force 58, in which the carrier *Bunker Hill*, Vice-Admiral Mitscher's flagship, received serious damage from a suicide, shot down a further 35.

Admiral Spruance's flagship, the battleship *New Mexico*, was badly damaged by a suicide crash next evening, 12th May, when two enemy aircraft penetrated to the transport area. Two days later the carrier *Enterprise*, to which Commander Task Force 58 had shifted his flag when the *Bunker Hill* was hit, was seriously damaged by a suicide crash, and Vice-Admiral Mitscher had again to shift flag, to the *Randolph*. The Japanese mounted no further large air attack for nearly a fortnight, though small-scale attacks continued almost daily, the brunt being taken by the radar pickets and transport screen.

54. The Final Heavy Attacks, 25th-28th May

On the night of the 24th-25th May a heavy air attack was made on the invasion shipping; it was apparently co-ordinated with an attack on the objective area ashore (the Shuri line) which continued intermittently from dusk on the 24th until noon on the 25th and included the first attempt by the Japanese to employ airborne troops.

Attacks on the ships began later, about midnight on the 24th-25th, when some enemy aircraft penetrated to the anchorages. With the exception of the cargo ship *W. Allison*, which was badly damaged by an aerial torpedo at 0305 on the 2nd in Nakagusuku Wan, damage was confined almost exclusively to picket ships and screen. Nine ships were damaged and the high speed destroyer transport *Bates* and one L.S.M. were sunk by suicide crashes. A total of 195 enemy aircraft were destroyed, 11 of them in suicide crashes.

After morning raids on the 27th May, in which two ships were severely damaged, the last of the Japanese heavy air attacks commenced at 2000 on the 27th and continued until 0030 on the 28th, the anchorages at Ie Shima, Hagushi, and Nakagusuku Wan being involved. The destroyer *Drexler* and one L.C.S. were sunk, and upwards of 14 ships were damaged. The enemy lost 123 aircraft, 11 of them in suicide crashes.

From now onwards air attacks on Okinawa declined. Raids did not cease but during the remainder of the operation only eight ships were damaged and one sunk by aircraft.

The air attacks on the invaders of Okinawa between 1st April and 1st July cost the Japanese 6,810 aircraft. They succeeded, however, in damaging 227 ships and sinking 28 out of a total casualty list of 371 and 36 respectively. The contest between Allied and Japanese air power, which had now turned in favour of the former, was probably the most critical since Guadalcanal.[80]

The Japanese pilots in general were characterized by their lack of skill in combat, and it is reported that at Okinawa pilots with as little as 100 hours' flying experience were employed.[81] It was this, together with shortage of combat aircraft, which caused the Japanese authorities to encourage Kamikaze when it made a spontaneous appearance amongst their pilots in the autumn of 1944 and later decided them to set up a definite organization for suicide attacks; for this form of attack can be and was, carried out not only by combat aircraft but also by training machines.

A total of 1,900 aircraft were expended in suicide attacks, and they succeeded in sinking 27 and damaging 164 ships, a ratio of about one in ten. The Americans also reported a lack of aggressiveness on the part of the orthodox Japanese pilots, the result, no doubt, of lack of skill.

80 7th August, 1942-7th February 1943.

81 *Operations in the Pacific Ocean Areas, April, 1945*, p.65.

Chapter VIII

PROGRESS OF THE OPERATION

Whilst the struggle for supremacy in the air was in progress, a no less bitter struggle was taking place on shore in the south of Okinawa Shima.

55. Capture of Northern Okinawa, 22nd April

After the initial landing, the American Tenth Army plan called for the two corps abreast to drive eastward across the island. The XXIV Corps, on reaching the east coast, was to pivot on its right flank and seize a general east-west line from Kuba Saki (at the head of Nakagusuku Wan) in order to prevent reinforcement by the enemy from the south. The 96th Infantry Division on the right of the III Amphibious Corps was to drive to the east coast, while the left flank division (the 6th Marine) turned north to seize the Ishikawa Isthmus, in order to prevent enemy reinforcements from the Motobu Peninsula of the northern part of Okinawa, thus effectively blocking off the central portion of the island. The Tenth Army Reserve was to remain afloat until required.

The withdrawal of the enemy from his prepared positions on, and immediately in rear of, the Hagushi beaches, to make his first stand in the south, surprised the invaders. For a few days, the advance was rapid. By L+2 day the two inner divisions, the 7th Infantry and 1st Marine had already reached the east coast. One of the two outer divisions, the 6th Marine Division, turned north against little opposition; whilst the 96th Infantry Division turned south, where increasing opposition was met. The Commanding General, Major-General R.S. Geiger, moved his headquarters ashore on the 4th April.

The 6th Marine Division continued its drive north, and on the 8th April isolated the Motobu Peninsula by advancing across its base.

Strong opposition however was encountered in the mountainous terrain of the peninsula from well-organized enemy forces numbering about 1,500, supported by artillery and mortars and well dug in.

On the 16th April the 6th Division supported by air, artillery and naval gunfire bombardment, launched a full scale attack on the Japanese, and by the 20th the peninsula was secured.

In the meantime, the 1st Marine Division had been engaged in extensive patrol and mopping-up operations in the northern portion of Okinawa Shima, and by the 22nd April all organized enemy resistance in the northern two-thirds of the island had ceased.

56. Capture of Ie Shima, 16th-21st April

The capture of the Motobu Peninsula paved the way for attack on Ie Shima in order to secure its airfield. For the assault a gunfire support unit (T.U. 51.21.1) was formed under Rear-Admiral B.J. Rodgers, consisting of the battleship *Texas,* cruisers *Birmingham* (flagship) and *Mobile,* and destroyers *Porterfield, Hall, Irwin* and *Preston*. Underwater demolition teams prepared the landing beaches under cover of naval gunfire and air support, on 13th, 14th and 15th April; and on the 15th two field artillery battalions were landed on Menna Shima, south of Ie Shima, to support the main landing next day.

The assault on Ie Shima was carried out by the 77th Infantry Division, which after its assault on Kerama Retto, had been kept at sea in the neighbourhood of Okinawa pending further operations. The fire support ships that reinforced Task Unit 51.21.1 for the landing were the battleship *West Virginia,* heavy cruisers *Tuscaloosa* and *Portland,* and the destroyers *Twiggs* and *Isherwood.*

At 0830 on 16th April two Regimental Combat Teams landed, covered be artillery and naval gunfire and air support co-ordinated by Major-General D. Bruce, commanding 77th Division, one on Green Beaches and one on Red Reaches. Resistance on the beaches was light, but stiffened inland on 17th, and the reserve Regimental Combat Team was landed that day. Although the enemy fought with fanatical resistance to deny the Americans the use of Ie Shima as an air base, the island was secured at 1059 on the 21st April, and when the 77th Division moved to southern Okinawa on the 27th mopping up was completed.

By this date, 4,176 enemy dead had been counted, 208 prisoners of war captured, and 1,586 civilians interned; and several additional snipers and stragglers were estimated to be in hiding: a total of nearly 7,000 persons. Yet, in spite of excellent photographic coverage and reconnaissance by low-flying observation aircraft from 27th March to

15th April, only five people out of these 7,000 individuals had been seen on the small, relatively open island of Ie Shimara to such lengths were camouflage and concealment carried by the Japanese – and, it might perhaps be added, such are the limitations of air observation.

The entire inland area surrounding the airfield was found to be heavily mined. The airfield itself was mined and deeply trenched and required an immense amount of work to make it fit for use. An emergency landing strip became available on the 28th April, but it was not until 13th May that two air strips were in full operation.

The port facilities eventually provided at Ie Shima consisted of 64 anchoring berths with depths from ten to 52 fathoms. The estimated maximum daily port capacity on 30th June was 4,500 measurement tons.[82]

57. Advance Held up in the South, 9th April

Whilst the Marines in the north of Okinawa Shima were securing their objectives much in advance of schedule, the XXIV Corps in the south was conducting frontal attacks against well prepared and strongly held defensive positions. The 96th Division, on the right (south) flank, met increasing resistance in the hills overlooking the assault beaches. Major-General J.R. Hodge assumed command ashore on the 5th April. Then followed several days of increasing resistance against the drive of the Corps to the south. On the 9th April the advance had to be checked owing to severe shortage of artillery ammunition.[83]

The assault phase of the operation had called for the loading of 746,850 measurement tons of cargo into 433 assault transports and landing ships. C.T.F. 51 was responsible for the delivery of all supplies to the beaches, C.T.F. 55 for unloading on the beaches.[84] The Commanding General Expeditionary Troops, who provided working parties to discharge the cargo, was responsible for keeping the beaches clear and for moving cargo to dispersal dumps, and for providing working parties on board ships to assist in the discharge of vessels, either at piers or at anchor.

It was found that L.C.Ms. and L.C.V.Ps. could work over the reef at Hagushi for four or five hours at each high water. In order to enable

82 A measurement ton is 40 cubic feet.

83 Two of the 3 ammunition ships which arrived at Okinawa on 6th April were sunk by enemy action on the day of arrival. This is not, however, specifically mentioned in any report as a cause of ammunition shortage ashore.

84 After the capture of Ie Shima, and reconnaissance of Nago Wan, Nakagusuku Wan and Chim Wan, and as the character of the cargo unloaded changed from assault equipment and supplies to maintenance and garrison cargo, responsibilities were reassigned to local commanders concerned.

unloading to continue at low water, pontoon barges and causeways were put into operation. By the 4th April, 80 pontoon barges and four causeways were in use. By the 1st June, 54 causeway sets were launched and installed at 17 unloading piers. Over 110,000 deadweight tons of cargo were unloaded, and more than 64,000 troops were landed dry shod over pontoon causeways.

Pending the development of the beaches in this manner, however, speed of unloading was materially affected by the necessity for concurrent unloading over the same beaches of supplies required for both a large-scale land operation and for the early and rapid development of garrison facilities. The early possession of Yontan and Katena and the necessity for their rapid development, entailed the unloading of aviation engineers and ground echelons of fighter groups concurrently with assault cargo. For a long period, too, the craft unloading at the beaches were opposed to constant attacks by enemy aircraft and suicide boats, causing ever-present danger of loss of essential supplies.

To the supply difficulties caused through the troops outrunning their planned progress, bad weather was added soon after the landing. On L+3 Day the weather, which up to now had been ideal, began to deteriorate. By the evening a 20-knot wind was blowing from a northerly to north-north-easterly direction; surf increased to four to six feet by nightfall, and night unloading was discontinued.[85] Fifteen tank landing ships and some landing craft were damaged in varying degrees at the beaches next day, and unloading on all beaches was stopped until the 6th April. About midday on the 10th all ships and craft had again to retract from the reef of the Hagushi beaches and were unable to resume unloading until the 12th though unloading began over the Nago Wan beaches on the previous day. By the 18th, however, all assault shipping was unloaded, except for some 10th Army supplies loaded in one transport.

58. Occupation of the Eastern Islands, April 1945

The original plan called for the development of major naval facilities at Naha and in Nakagusuku Wan. The latter was commanded by one of the Eastern Islands, Tsuken Shima; and on the evening of the 9th April the high speed destroyer transport *Hopping*, on patrol east of Nakagusuku Wan, was hit six times by enemy guns mounted on this island. Reconnaissance of the Eastern Islands on the 5th and 7th April had revealed that all the islands were void of enemy troops and

[85] C.T.F. 51 had authorized the use of floodlights on all beaches at night beginning on 2nd April, and night unloading was authorized except during Red alerts.

defensive positions, with the exception of Tsuken Shima; and a landing on the latter in order to capture it, was arranged for the 10th April.

The assault was carried out by a regimental combat team of the 27th Infantry Division, landed by the Eastern Islands Attack Group under cover of naval and air bombardment. The amphibious tanks left the line of departure at 0828, followed by three waves by 0900. The landing itself met with little opposition, though resistance hardened in a strong point in Tsuken town as the troops moved inland. By nightfall on the 11th, mopping up had been completed and enemy resistance crushed. American casualties were 13 killed and 84 wounded. It was estimated that the enemy lost 284 killed. No prisoners of war were taken, and no civilians were found.

The largest of the Eastern Islands, Taka Banare, was occupied on the 21st April; the remainder were occupied or cleared on various dates during the month, Ichi Banare, Heanza Banare, Bamahi-ga-Banare on the 22nd April whilst Kutaka Shima had been occupied on the 8th. Sweeping of Nakagusuku Wan for mines had begun on the 5th April, and on the 2nd battleships rendered fire support from inside for the first time. Chim Wan was used as a night anchorage for landing ships and craft on the night 16th-17th April, and on 2nd May unloading on the beaches at Nakagusuku Wan was begun.

The development of Nakagusuku Wan had been timed to begin approximately on 5th May. The heavy fighting in the south caused delay and the work did not begin until the end of the campaign. The original plan was consequently changed, and naval bases were developed in central Okinawa, around Chimu, and, eventually, in Nakagusuku Wan.

59. The Advance Resumed, 19th April

On the 18th April, Task Forces 53 and 55 were dissolved and Lieut-General Buckner, Commanding General Tenth Army, established his headquarters on shore at Okinawa. All assault shipping was unloaded, with some trifling exceptions.

By the 19th April, all was in readiness for the XXIV Corps to resume the assault on the enemy defences on the Machinato Line in southern Okinawa. The Japanese defences, deep belts of heavily fortified positions, were ingenious and original. They included an unprecedented number of automatic weapons, together with 47 mm. guns which penetrated the armour of the American tanks at 500 yards range.

Various devices were successfully adopted by the Japanese to counter the deterioration in health and morale engendered by cave warfare, and it was not until near the end of the campaign that the American propaganda took effect. On the American side, although on the 14th April it was reported that constant enemy artillery and mortar fire had lowered the morale of some American units to a limited extent, as a whole this continued excellent throughout.

The fire support ships were reinforced for the resumed offensive by the battleships *Washington, South Dakota* and *North Carolina* of Task Group 58.3 which, with Destroyer Squadron 48, were formed into Task Group 58.7. Their task was to bombard the south-east coast of the island on the 19th and, in addition, it was planned that they would appear to be part of the Fire Support Group covering the demonstration feint landings on the beaches in this area. The results achieved seemed to be satisfactory, both in destroying military installations and in assisting to make feint landings appear authentic. The group re-joined Task Force 58 next day.

Before the attack, the 27th Division – the Tenth Army Reserve Afloat – was landed and attached to the XXIV Corps. The assault began with this division on the right (west) flank, the 96th in the centre, and the 7th on the left. Very heavy machine gun and mortar fire, reinforced by artillery and anti-tank guns covering all approaches, brought the attack to a temporary standstill after a limited advance, one of the costliest of the campaign.[86] With intense artillery and naval gunfire, the XXIV Corps line moved slowly forward, however, and by the 24th April the Japanese resistance had weakened and he began to disengage troops slowly to the southward without abandoning his positions. Nevertheless, the Americans were unable to make any real progress for a fortnight.

By the end of April XXIV Corps casualties amounted to 3,607 killed, 14,907 wounded, and 188 missing; and the 96th Division, weakened by front line casualties, particularly in the rifle companies, had to be relieved.

60. Naval Gunfire Support

By the end of April, the fire support ships had fired 214,00 rounds of all calibres – nearly 12,000 tons of steel – in support of the operation. The need for sustained co-ordination of naval gunfire and air support and artillery continued throughout the Ryukus Campaign. Co-ordination was for the most part accomplished at Corps level. Some targets located by naval units were referred to C.A.S.C.U. for attack and others reported by air were attacked by naval gunfire.

86 The XXIV Corps had 2,851 casualties between 19th-22th April.

Air furnished support for the ships when the latter were fired on. Fire from ships and bombing from the air were successful in removing the highly efficient Japanese camouflage which rendered the location of targets so difficult in this campaign. When the true positions and nature of the targets were disclosed, the artillery would destroy or neutralize them if unsuitable for attack by naval gunfire.

Two direct support ships were usually assigned to a regiment. In most cases this proved entirely adequate. Wherever possible, all direct fire support ships were given air spotting to supplement the observation of the shore hire control party.

"There is no plane and its aviator which is more important in doing damage to the enemy than the cruiser and battleship spotting plane. This is because the majority of all fire support is indirect fire." So wrote Rear-Admiral A.E. Smith, who succeeded Rear-Admiral Deyo on the 5th May as Commander, Gunfire and Covering Force.[87] The two aircraft carried by his own flagship, the *Salt Lake City*, spent 300 hours in the air between 25th March and 5th May, an average of 6-8 hours daily, including 11 days whilst the ship was replenishing, and consequently no flights were made. The ship originally carried two pilots, but on the 22nd April, a third was added.

Deep support was furnished to Division, Corps, and Army zones of action. A cruiser or battleship was usually assigned to a division for use against targets specified by the divisional artillery commander. When available, one or two battleships or cruisers were assigned to corps, and were given a list of selected deep targets for destruction. Night harassing fire was also designated by corps commanders. Deep support outside the corps zone of action was furnished by C.T.F. 51 or C.T.G. 51.19 against targets asked for by Tenth Army artillery. Little support was delivered in the army zone of action on north Okinawa, but an intensive programme was maintained in the southern sector.

Whilst analysis of indirect fire inshore bombardment indicates that the reported results of damage were usually too high, Japanese prisoners of war stated that naval gunfire was particularly feared.[88]

In the Ryukus operation the Japanese made greater use of artillery against ships than had previously been experienced, though the sum totally was negligible. Much of the enemy artillery fire was at night from scattered, well-defiladed positions. On the 5th April the battleship

87 The U.S. Mark 13 radar, capable of spotting at 34,000 yarda, does not appear to have been installed in the ships of the Gunfire and Covering Force during the Ryukus operation. (*ComBatDir 3 C.T.F.* 32) *Action Report* 28th May-10th June, 1945, p.17 and First Endorsement).

88 Op. Cit., pp.26-7.

Nevada received five hits from coastal guns of 6-inch and 8-inch calibre, and had to return to the rear area. On the 27th the battleships *New York* and *New Mexico*, whilst in the transport anchorage, reported near misses from shore batteries and were ordered to move; the firing was apparently blind, since it decreased in accuracy.

The reports of the ships in the Gunfire and Covering Force furnished impressive picture of continuous rendering of support fire. Twenty of the ships assigned to Task Force 54 spent more than 60 per cent, of their time on firing assignments. Some cruisers maintained constant fire in support for as long as 100 consecutive hours. In 46 days the cruiser *Wichita* had only three "idle" days. The battleship *Texas*, flagship of Rear Admiral P.K. Fischler, Fire Support Unit One (54.1.1) remained at battle stations with only occasional exceptions, day and night, for a period of seven weeks.[89] The light cruiser *St. Louis*, in Fire Support Unit 3, operated continuously for 61 days, during which it was impossible to carry out adequate maintenance.

Smoke cover was used with much success for the protection of ships in the anchorage from air attack after promiscuous automatic weapon firing by ships under smoke screen was stopped. Ammunition was saved and the Japanese were denied information of ships' positions. Smoke posed a difficulty, however, for the fire support ships making their approach to day firing stations at dawn when the large number of transports and sweep units in, or returning to, the area after night retirement, in addition to the many ships of Task Force 54 operating in such restricted waters, caused serious congestion.

When a smoke screen was laid down over the transport area, early morning approach to the fire support stations was virtually impossible until the smoke lifted. The necessity for keeping ships together for mutual support against air attacks sometimes delayed the arrival of retiring Fire Support Ships on day station until after sunrise, or until the day C.A.P. was on station, by which time the protective screen had dissipated.

Ammunition expenditures were high, resulting in a great increase in wear of medium calibre guns, in some cases exceeding their estimated life. Between the 20th March and the 25th May the cruiser *Salt Lake City* fired 23,541 rounds of 5-inch and heavier ammunition, and the *St. Louis* 25,523 rounds – an average of over 400 daily.

---

89 *USS Texas Action Report Okinawa*, 21st *March*-14 *May* 1945, p.23.

Expenditure of the ships of the Expeditionary Force on fire support missions from the 25th March to the 21st June was 584,180 rounds, distributed as follows:

16-inch H.C. – 3,810	5-inch/38 A.A.C. – 327,725
14-inch H.C. – 16,700	5-inch/38 Star – 43,150
12-inch H.C. – 2,700[90]	5-inch/25 Star – 29,170
8-inch H.C. – 31,550	5-inch/25 A.A.C. – 64,425
6-inch H.C. – 45,450	5-inch/51 H.C. – 19,500

The ships of the Gunfire and Covering Force, which at the outset included ten battleships, ten heavy cruisers, two light cruisers, and 27 destroyers, were reduced by the 16th May to four battleships, five heavy cruisers, two light cruisers, and 13 destroyers. From 15th May fire support requirements averaged eight heavy ships and six destroyers until 8th June, and thereafter seven heavy ships and four destroyers by day, and nine destroyers by night, no heavy ships being used at night from 8th-9th June onwards.

61. Attack on the Shuri Line, 11th May

Much of the bombardment by fire support ships was of a very exacting nature. After the small American advance during the latter part of April, the Japanese stood in their heavier defences, centred in the steep rugged hills immediately north of Shuri. Slopes were almost vertical, and defence positions were concealed in interlocking systems of caves and burial vaults.

Key features of the ground were usually honeycombed with these caves, which were integrated into the entire defence of the area. An elaborate system of connecting tunnels, storage rooms and sleeping quarters was found in many of them. Numerous exits were provided for escape. Some cave systems occupied two or more levels, others were merely natural crevices in the sides of steep coral escarpments.

The primary weapon in a cave was usually an infantry weapon, ranging from a light machine gun to a 77-mm. gun. In many of these formidable cave defences, the Japanese were impregnable to all but flame throwers and direct hits by heavy shells. There were few open enemy positions, though open emplacements were provided for

90 To 17th May. This figure is taken from *ConPhibForPac Action Report, 17th Feb-17th May 1945*, p.378. *Operations in the Pacific Ocean Areas* for May 1945, p.20, from which the other figures are taken does not give any figure for the 12-inch.

weapons to cover cave mouths, primarily for use when supporting cave-emplaced weapons were neutralized. In many cases these covering weapons were at such a distance and so well concealed as to be very difficult to find for neutralization. Practically all naval gunfire, whether deep or supporting, was necessarily directed at pin-point targets which had to be destroyed.

On the 11th May, III Amphibious Corps launched a co-ordinated attack against these positions on the entire front, whilst five battleships, four heavy and two light cruisers, and 13 destroyers furnished support. The heavier naval units were assigned directly to the assault units for close support. In some cases, the battleships directed their main battery fire 600-800 yards ahead of the American front lines to take out heavy enemy defences. Shore fire control party spotting was employed wherever feasible, so that heavy calibre fire could be used as closely as possible in advance of friendly troops.

Main battery fire from ships was also used to reinforce the fire of the 36 Field Artillery battalions employed by the Army firing on the 7,000-yard front; and all calibres of naval guns fired separate missions on various objectives. It was not long before the day and night pounding by naval gunfire and other arms began to take effect. There was a reduction in Japanese artillery fire and in the strength of resistance encountered, as the enemy prepared to disengage.

Before commencing to thin out their positions, the Japanese on the 24th May attempted to counter-attack with a heavy night air attack on the objective area. The attack commenced at dusk and continued until 0450 on the 25th, to be followed by daylight attacks from 0730 to 1130 that day. Heavy and persistent attacks were made on units both ashore and afloat. For the first time, the Japanese used airborne troops when five enemy twin-engine aircraft attempted to land at 2225 on the 24th in Yoktan airfield. Four were shot down by A.A., but one landed wheels-up, discharging about 10 enemy soldiers who attacked the transport line with demolition charges, destroying seven aircraft and damaging 25. Before being exterminated, the enemy succeeded in putting the airfield out of action until early next morning.

On the 24th improved visibility after two days of bad weather enabled artillery and fire support ships to operate with destructive effect; but on the 25th the weather again deteriorated, and only a single air support mission could be carried out. Enemy artillery fire during the night was exceptionally heavy, and during the early morning and forenoon of the 25th Japanese troops, under cover of air attacks, attempted counter-attacks and infiltrations, which were repulsed.

Next day, the enemy, under the threat of double envelopment, seized the opportunity of bad weather which slowed the Tenth Army drive, to begin to thin out the Shuri line along most of its length. During the withdrawal, the ships took a heavy toll of the retreating enemy and his equipment with harassing and interdiction fire that covered almost every possible mobilization point or road network.

62. Changes of Command, 17th and 28th May

On the 17th May, Vice-Admiral H.W. Hill, Commander Fifth Amphibious Force with flag in U.S.S. *Ancon*, relieved Vice-Admiral R.K. Turner as Commander Task Force 51. Coincident with this change the command of all forces on shore in the Okinawa area passed to the Commanding General, Tenth Army, Lieut.-General S.B. Buckner, Jr. who assumed responsibility as the Commander Fifth Fleet for the defence and development of captured positions. C.T.F. 51 was responsible to the Commanding General Tenth Army for control of the air defence of Okinawa and of naval forces present.

On the 28th May, Admiral W.F. Halsey, Jr., Commander Third Fleet, took over from Admiral Spruance operational control of all naval forces then attached to the Fifth Fleet, with certain minor exceptions, and all formations changed their numerical designations accordingly, substituting the number "3" for "5", e.g. T.G. 52.1 became T.G. 32.1. Task Force 54 became Task Force 34 (Gunfire and Covering Force). The latter was considerably reduced in strength on this day for the battleship *New Mexico* left for Guam (to disembark Admiral Spruance and his staff) and Leyte; and the heavy cruisers *Mobile* and *St. Louis* were detached to Leyte, without relief.

At the same time, the Commanding General Tenth Army became directly responsible to the Commander-in-Chief Pacific Ocean Areas (Admiral C.W. Nimitz) for the defence and development of captured positions in the Ryukus.

63. Minor Landing Operations

The heavy damage sustained by destroyer type vessels on picket duty north and west of Okinawa resulted in a decision by Vice-Admiral Turner and Lieut.-General Buckner, to capture suitable outlying islands of the Okinawa Gunto on which to establish long-range radar and fighter direction facilities.

It was decided that Tori Shima, to the west of Okinawa; Agum Shima, to the north-west; Iheya Shima, to the north; and Kume Shima, to the west, should be captured in the order named. In the event, the operations were all completely bloodless, and had they been undertaken earlier, the damage received by the radar picket and fighter director ships would have been reduced.[91] However:

> A number of factors hindered the rapid establishment of early aircraft warning sites at Okinawa. Advance planning was not adequate; equipment was scattered and not combat loaded; overwater transportation from island to island could not be readily synchronized with radar equipment unloading and availability on the beach; siting and construction personnel were not readily available. There was a scarcity of high powered, reliable communication material.[92]

Tori Shima was occupied on the 12th May; only two Japanese were seen, both of whom leaped into the sea as the landing force[93] approached their hiding place.

Task Group 31.25 was organized under Rear-Admiral L.F. Reifsneider, with a landing force of Marines, for the occupation of Iheya Shima, which was carried out on the 3rd June, and of Aguni Shima, which was delayed by bad weather and was not accomplished until the 9th June.

The Intelligence Branch of the U.S. General Staff estimated the garrison of Kume Shima at 1,500 men. It was anticipated that a relatively large force would be required to capture the island, and it was doubtful whether troops could be spared for the operation. Consequently, although its geographical position 50 miles to the west of Okinawa made it very desirable for air defence purposes, it was recommended to the Commander Joint Expeditionary Force that its capture should be deferred until the occupation of Okinawa was completed.

On the 13th June, however, a Reconnaissance Battalion, which landed in rubber boats, failed to find any enemy troops or defences. Interrogation of civilians indicated that the island had about 50 enemy naval personnel operating a radio station but was otherwise

---

91 "Earlier installations of radar and G.C.I. facilities on outlying islands near Okinawa would have been advisable." [Com. Fifth Fleet]. *Action Report Okinawa through 27th May*, p.VI-I-8.

92 *C.T.F. 51, Report on Okinawa Gunto Operation*, p.V-D-7.

93 T.G. 51.24, consisting of one reinforced company from the 27th Army Division, with three destroyers and landing ship and landing craft.

virtually undefended. It was not until the 20th June, however, that the occupation took place, and on the 20th the island was declared secure. By this time, the Ryukus campaign was already at an end.

64. The End of Organized Resistance, 21st June

The heavy and unceasing rains, under cover of which the Japanese on the 26th May began to withdraw their troops from the Shuri line to attempt a last stand on the southern tip of Okinawa, affected the Americans in two ways. Not only was their attack slowed by mud and swampy roads, which made tank support impossible, while low ceilings limited air support, but the adverse weather conditions were also complicating supply problems as well as hampering all movement. Unloading was severely curtailed; and critical shortage of artillery ammunition caused orders to be given on the 20th May reducing the maximum daily expenditure allowance to 0-8 unit of fire for 155 mm. guns and 0-2 for howitzers.

Even at this late stage in the operation, and, indeed, until the conclusion of the campaign, a considerable portion of the shipping at Okinawa was still being discharged at the open Hagushi beaches, where the amount of shipping that could be unloaded was limited by exposure to weather, heavy swells and surf as well as the general conditions of roads and dumps. On account of the heavy rains and extremely poor roads, it was difficult to get the necessary supplies to other parts of the island, for the development of bases.

Enemy air raids and alerts also hampered activities; and at the beginning of June the unloading rates fell well behind the tonnage scheduled, and a crisis was precipitated. Improvement of Nakagusuku Wan was rushed. Survey, demolition and dredging of Naha began towards the end of the month, and navigational aids were installed. Yet although at the end of the Ryukus operation the capacity of Okinawa Gunto was approximately 80 Liberty Ships, or 750,000 tons of cargo per month, the limitations enumerated above, reduced the rate of discharge to some 500,000 tons a month.

On the 3rd May the 1st Marines and 77th Infantry Division units completed the reduction of the Wana Ridge, in the centre of the enemy's position, and by the 1st June resistance in the Shuri stronghold was completely overcome.

Events now moved rapidly. By the 18th June, the enemy had been compressed into a very small area on the southern extreme of Okinawa, with very little defensible terrain left to him. Masses of civilians, as well as a great number of fighting and labour troops, were in this area. On that date, a regimental combat team from the Marine Division drove to the south coast of the island, splitting the area held by the enemy into two parts.

Resistance thereafter was purely local in nature. Unprecedented numbers of enemy civilians, labourers and troops were persuaded to surrender, an occurrence brought about partly through the efforts of psychological warfare teams: others committed suicide or made "banzai" charges against the Americans. Organized resistance ceased and Okinawa was declared secure at 1305 on the 21st June. Lieut-General Buckner was killed in action on the 18th, three days before the victory was complete.[94] The Naval Gunfire Support Units were withdrawn two days later.

The enemy casualties in the Okinawa campaign were 131,303 killed[95], 7,401 prisoners of war (military), 3,339 prisoners of war (labourers) and 15 prisoners of war (combat civilians). The American action casualties were as follows:[96]

SERVICE	KILLED	WOUNDED	MISSING	TOTALS
Navy	4,907	4,824	included in killed	9,731
Marines	2,744	13,523	90	16,357
Army	4,288	17,558	91	21,937
TOTALS	11,939	35,905	181	48,028

In the course of the operations, from 1st April to 21st June U.S. carrier and land-based aircraft flew 16,458 sorties on 1,378 missions. They dropped 5,788.3 tons of bombs and 1,496 incendiary tanks, and fired 46,357 rocket projectiles.

From the outset of the operation, the enemy showed a keen appreciation of terrain and the need for conserving his force. He had available a greater diversity of fire power and supporting arm than in any previous operation against the Americans; and he made more effective use of his fire power than ever before, in spite of longer ranges than the Japanese were accustomed to using, co-ordinating it to hold ground, in lieu of mere physical occupation.

94 He was succeeded by Major-General R.S. Gieger, promoted to Lieut.-General on 19th June. On 23rd June General J.W. Stilwell assumed command of Task Force 99 and of the Tenth Army.

95 Counted 107,539, estimated (additional) 23,746.

96 Figures for Army and Marines are for the period 26th March to 30th June. The Navy figures cover the period 1st April to 21st June.

Concentrated and controlled artillery fire was employed from a fire direction centre: the latter was not used to mass the fires of his batteries, rather he co-ordinated the fire of individual guns from widely separated points in engaging a specific target. His fanatical defence was elastic and active. He organized strong points based on intricate cave systems, covering key features and avenues of approach. His strong points were organized in depth, being sited to deliver mutually supporting flanking fire. Both forward and reverse slopes were organized for defence, the stronger defences being on the reverse slopes.

During artillery preparations he would retire to his inter-connected cave positions on the reverse slopes of hills, and re-occupy his original positions when preparation ceased. His anti-tank tactics and appliances were effective and his anti-tank teams were highly trained. Communication difficulties accounted in part for the difficulty experienced by the Japanese in executing manoeuvres of any magnitude.

Chapter IX

BATTLE OF THE EAST CHINA SEA, 7th APRIL

Task Force 51, the Joint Expeditionary Force, troops and ships, had now brought the Okinawa operation to a successful conclusion.

65. Enemy Sortie Reported

But if the Joint Expeditionary Force had won the campaign, the carriers had played a large part in saving it. Tied to a defensive role, in abrogation of the function for which their great speed had been designed, and unable to develop their striking power to the full extent, the fast carriers had stood for ten weeks close by Okinawa, holding above the troops and shipping a shield against the Japanese air attacks which constituted one of the gravest menaces met by the Americans throughout the entire course of the Pacific.

"The achievement of Task Force 58 (and Task Group 52.1 composed of C.V.Es.) in staying within easy aircraft range, under almost constant Japanese aerial reconnaissance, for a period of more than 70 days while furnishing direct air support to the landings on Okinawa, target C.A.P., own C.A.P., aerial interdiction of Japanese suiciders en route to Okinawa, plus several strikes on Kyushu itself, all without losing a single ship sunk, is one which needs no comment."[97]

It is true that no ships were sunk; but in the Fast Carrier Force eight carriers, four battleships, four cruisers, and 16 destroyers suffered damage in greater or less degree; and amongst the escort carriers nine were damaged.[98] Four British carriers, the total number in the force, were hit, two of them twice each.

97 Com. Fifth Fleet, *Action Report, Ryukus Operation*, VI-B-2.

98 Including Service Squadron 6 who supplied the carrier forces and other ships at sea.

But if, in the parlance of the day, the carriers had had to stand and take it, they certainly gave back better than they got; and when on the 28th May, Vice-Admiral Mitscher handed over the command of the Fast Carriers Force to Vice-Admiral McCain, much of the Japanese Air Force lay in ruins about his feet.

The landing was not a week old, however, before the fast carriers were given a mission in keeping with their proper function of reaching out across the ocean to make heavy co-ordinated air strikes. The great Japanese air attacks of the 6th April had just ceased when news was received of a sortie from Japan by units of the enemy fleet.

The Japanese plan for the defence of the Nansei Shoto, termed the "Ten" operation plan, directed naval forces to utilize favourable opportunities to penetrate to Okinawa anchorages and make suicide attacks on the United States ships. In accordance with this, Admiral Toyoda, Commander-in-Chief, Combined Fleet, issued orders on 5th April, to Vice Admiral Ito, Commander-in-Chief, 2nd Fleet, for the First Division Attack Force (2nd Fleet) to sail from the Inland Sea on 6th April and raid the United States Forces at Okinawa at dawn on 8th April. The operation was designated the "Ten-Ichi" (Ten 1) operation. The chances of success were not considered good, but the raid was in keeping with the traditions of the Japanese Navy.

Owing to the shortage of oil fuel it was possible to despatch only a small force, and it is said that difficulty was found in obtaining even the small quantity of 2,500 tons of oil required.

The force under Vice-Admiral Ito was composed of the following fast ships:

Battleship *Yamato* (flagship) (78,000 tons, 9 x 18.1-inch guns).
Light cruiser *Yahagi* (flotilla leader).
Destroyer Division 41 – *Fuyutsuhi, Suzutsuki.*
Destroyer Division 17 – *Isokaze, Hamakase, Yukikaze.*
Destroyer Division 21 – *Asashimo, Hatsushimo, Kasumi.*

It sailed from Tokuyama in Honshu, in the north-west part of the Inland Sea, at 1520 on 26th April, accompanied by the destroyers *Hamatsuki, Kaya,* and *Maki* as anti-submarine patrol; these parted company with the force at 1620.

At 2010 on the 6th, the U.S. submarine *Threadfin* reported a force emerging at high speed from the Bungo Suido, between Kyushu and Shikoku. A second submarine, the *Hackleback,* gained contact soon afterwards, and though the ranges were too great for an attack, the *Threadfin* held on until 2345, by which time the force was fairly well established as two large ships with six or more destroyers, in position 31° 38′ N., 131° 52 E′., off the east coast of Kyushu, steering 213°, at 22 knots.

At the time, three groups of Task Force 58 were operating in their usual combat area, east of Okinawa. The fourth Task Group 58.2, had sailed from Ulithi on the 5th April for a rendezvous with Task Group 50.8, the fuelling group, at 23° 00′ N., 131° 00′ E. It fuelled rapidly in approximately 24° 00′ N., 133° 00′ E., about 350 miles south-east of Okinawa, commencing early on the 7th, and at 1115 steered to join the remainder of the Task Force at high speed.

On Admiral Spruance's instructions, Vice-Admiral Mitscher maintained the fighter protection of Okinawa for the time being, allowing the Japanese force to come to him rather than attacking it at extreme range.

Thus matters rested during the night. All aircraft detailed for strikes were held on the carrier's decks until the results of the searches to be made at daylight next day to a distance of 325 miles from the task force became known.

66. Preparation by Gunfire and Covering Force

Admiral Spruance had warned the Gunfire and Covering force to be ready to destroy the enemy, should they approach Okinawa, which it was calculated they could reach at any time after midnight on the 7th-8th. Rear-Admiral Deyo accordingly organized a force from the strongest ships available, in order to cover the invasion shipping from the north-west. Six battleships composed of the Battle Line, three light cruisers and 11 destroyers formed the Right Flank Forces, and four heavy cruisers and ten destroyers the Left Flank Forces.

At 1530 on the 7th, after a conference of Flag and Commanding Officers, the ships proceeded to a rendezvous north-west of Okinawa. Between 1607 and 1845 a single enemy aircraft penetrated the anti-aircraft fire of the Right Flank cruisers and dropped a bomb which put one of the battleship *Maryland*'s turrets out of action.

67. Approach of the Enemy

Vice Admiral Ito was warned against the possibility of attack in the Bungo Suido. None came on the 6th, however, though he sighted B.29s, while crossing the Inland Sea and intercepted a radio report from one of the American submarines as he emerged from the Bungo Suido.

When well clear of the channel, he turned to a south-westerly course long the south-east coast of Kyushu, until south of the island, when he headed west into the East China Sea. He was sighted on this course south-west of Kyushu, at 0815 on the 7th, by reconnaissance aircraft from the fast carrier *Essex*, flagship of Rear-Admiral F.C. Sherman, C.T.G. 68.8 who reported his force as one battleship, one or two light cruisers and seven to eight destroyers in 30° 44′ N., 129° 10′ E., proceeding at 12 knots.[99] This position was too far south. A contact report from *Essex*'s aircraft by relay at 0823 gave the position of the enemy as 31° 22′ N., 120° 15′ E;[100] this was a little too far north, the actual position at 0600 having been 31° 00′ N., 129° 51′ E.

The weather at the contact was reported to be poor, with ceiling at 3,000 feet, visibility 5 to 8 miles, and occasional rainsqualls. At 0830 a reported change of course to 240° by the enemy indicated that the force was probably making for Okinawa, rather than towards Sasebo for a change of fleet base as the earlier course might have implied. In any event, Rear-Admiral Sherman at 0905 launched a Special Tracking Team of 16 fighters, and two Communication Links, each of four aircraft, to shadow and report the movements of the enemy.

The Tracking Team picked up the force at 1115 and maintained contact, drawing considerable heavy gunfire, but without suffering any damage. No air opposition was encountered, and, in fact, throughout the day from the first sighting of the enemy onwards, very few hostile aircraft were seen, for the only air cover provided for the Japanese force was three to five land-based fighters from Kyushu, which were withdrawn at 1000 on the 7th, though it is stated that land-based aircraft would attack any task force sighted en route. Previous to the arrival of the Tracking Team, Navy reconnaissance aircraft (flying boats) of Task Group 50.5 from Kerama Retto made contact at 1030, and held it until dawn on the 8th.

When the reports of the 0815 sighting came in, showing the enemy on a south-westerly course and indicating that the Japanese might not, after all, be making for Okinawa, Admiral Spruance had ordered Vice-Admiral Mitscher to attack during the afternoon of the 7th. Accordingly, the launching commenced at approximately 27° 10′ N., 129° 45′ E. of a 380-plane strike of all types – fighters, fighter bombers, torpedo bombers and bombers. The wind in the operating area was force 4 to 11 knots; initially from 25°, it veered slowly during the day to 140°. The enemy at the time of launching bore approximately 345°, distance 250 miles from Task Groups 58.1 and 58.3, and 273 miles from Task Group 58.4.

---

99 *Action Report, 14th March-1st June, 1945, Okinawa*, p.22.

100 *Intrepid, Action Report*, p.10.

Task Groups 58.1 and 58.3 launched their aircraft at the same time and were ordered by CTG 58 to make co-ordinated attacks, to be followed by Task Group 58.4, which launched at 1045. The fourth Task Group, 58.2, continued refuelling and took no part in the strike.

68. The Battle; Sinking of the *Yamato*

The first aircraft from Task Groups 58.1 and 58.3 reached the scene of action in approximately 30° 54′ N., 128° 05′ E. at about 1230.[101] The Japanese ships were in circular formation (No. 3 Alert Cruising Disposition) with the *Yamato* at the centre of the destroyer screen, radius about 1,200 yards.

The first air group to arrive was from the *Bennington,* Task Group 58.1. They were directed by the Target Co-ordinator to make the first attack, followed by the remaining air groups of the task group. The *Hancock* was late, however, and never succeeded in locating the target in the prevailing bad weather.

Although the ceiling at the scene of action had lifted and there were spaces of clear sky, throughout the first phase of the battle at least, heavy recurrent rain squalls greatly increased the difficulties of the Target Co-ordinator in directing the attacks and assessing immediate damage. An effort was made to concentrate on the *Yamato,* but attacks were also made on the screening ships, which put up intense anti-aircraft fire.

The Japanese A.A. fire was of all calibres and all types – barrage, predicted concentration, and continuously pointed. Coloured bursts were used: red, yellow, green, and purple, with an abundance of white phosphorous. The *Yamato* used her main battery for anti-aircraft fire, and large back bursts from her 18.1-inch guns followed the American aircraft on retirement to a distance of 12 or 15 miles.[102]

On sighting the American attack formation at 1232, at a distance of 50km (30 nautical miles), Vice-Admiral Ito increased speed to 24 knots and ceased zigzagging. He opened fire two minutes later. Ships manoeuvred independently, increasing to maximum battle speed at 1241, at which time the *Yamato* received her first two bomb hits. Four minutes later she was hit by a torpedo on the port side forward, but this was all the damage she received in the attacks by the first two task groups. The destroyer *Asashimo,* which had fallen astern with engine

---

101 *The Campaigns of the Pacific War,* Plan 332. *C.T.G. 58.1 Action Report* p.25, gives the 1230 position as 31° 18′ N., 127° 35′ E, but this would seem to be too far north.

102 *USS Essex Action Report 14th March to 1st June, 1945, Okinawa,* p.57.

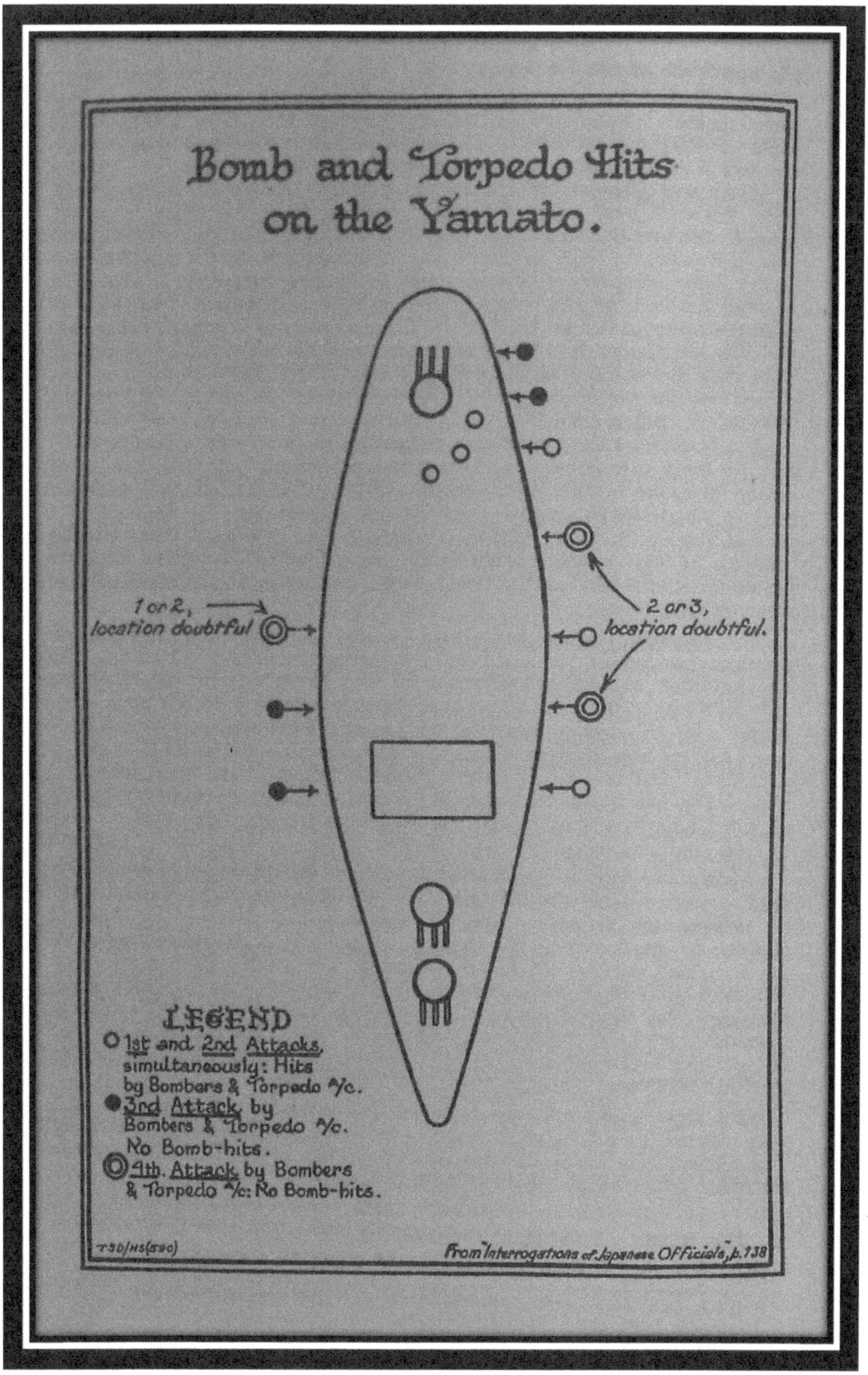
Bomb and Torpedo Hits on the Yamato.
1 or 2, location doubtful
2 or 3, location doubtful.
LEGEND
1st and 2nd Attacks, simultaneously: Hits by Bombers & Torpedo A/c.
3rd Attack, by Bombers & Torpedo A/c. No Bomb-hits.
4th. Attack by Bombers & Torpedo A/c: No Bomb-hits.
TSD/HS(590)
From "Interrogations of Japanese Officials", p.138

trouble, reported being attacked at 1210, and was sunk, her final report being received at 1221. The destroyer *Hamakaze* sank in three minutes at 1248, after being hit by a bomb and a torpedo which broke her back. The light cruiser *Yahagi* was hit at 1246 by bomb and torpedo which stopped her; two bombs had hit the *Kasumi* and a near miss bomb had immobilized her; the *Suzutsuki* was on fire from a bomb hit; and the *Fuyutsuki* had been hit by two rocket bombs which did not explode and by a torpedo which passed through her bottom.

Aircraft from Task Group 58.4 now arrived over the battered enemy and began their attack at 1333. The *Yahagi* was quickly hit and sank at 1406, having sustained 12 bomb hits and seven torpedo hits. The speed of the *Isokaze* was reduced by a near miss aft. By this time the Japanese ships were scattered, and only two or three destroyers remained with the *Yamato*.

The great battleship was hit amidships on the port side in rapid succession by five further torpedoes which reduced her speed to 20 knots, and she took so heavy a list that it was difficult to fire any of the guns still remaining in action. The finishing blow is claimed to have been delivered by six torpedo bombers from the *Yorktown*.

The leader of this attack group (Commander Torpedo Squadron Nine) ordered the torpedo setting to be changed from 10 to 20 feet, and then brought his aircraft in on the high side of the listing ship and attacked with torpedoes. Four, whether fired by this attack group or another, hit the ship between 1407 and 1417.

The leader of the attack group, Commander Torpedo Squadron Nine, attributed the immunity of his force from A.A. fire to the cluttering of the Japanese radars with manoeuvring aircraft and falling window[103] that prevented the enemy from detecting his six unescorted torpedo bombers. In any event, the Japanese ships had been largely incapacitated by this time. For 10 to 15 minutes the *Yamato* continued under way, then capsized and sank at 1417 in 30° 22′ N., 128° 04′ E. She had sustained 10 torpedo hits, seven of them on the port side, and five bomb hits. With her were lost Vice-Admiral Ito, her Captain, and 2,496 officers and men.

The destroyer *Kasumi,* which had been damaged in the first attack, sank at 1657; and the *Isokaze* had to be scuttled at 2240 after her crew were taken off. Thus of the entire force which made this forlorn sortie, only four destroyers, the *Fuyutsuki, Yukikaze, Suzutsuki* and *Hatsushimo*

---

[103] "Window" is a radar countermeasure in which aircraft release a cloud of small, thin pieces of aluminium, metallized glass fibre or plastic, which either appears as a cluster of primary targets on radar screens or swamps the screen with multiple contacts.

escaped and returned to Sasebo for repairs, the latter being very badly damaged. "If half the fighters had been equipped with rockets it is believed that none of the destroyers which screened the *Yamato* would have escaped," wrote Rear Admiral Sherman.

The American losses were very light.[104]

69. The *Hancock* Damaged

At 1340 Vice-Admiral Mitscher gave orders than no more strikes were to be launched against the enemy force, and the fast carriers reverted to the duty of neutralizing the airfields of Amami O Shima.

In the meantime, whilst the striking aircraft were still away from their carriers, about noon heavy Japanese air attacks developed against the ships of Task Force 58. A total of 18 of the attackers were destroyed over or near the force, 15 by combat air patrol and three by ships' gunfire. At 1211, however, one suicide aircraft penetrated the defence and dropped a bomb from 50 feet on to the flight deck of the *Hancock*, and then crashed into a group of aircraft parked on the after end of the flight deck. A large hole was torn in the flight deck, the forward lift was buckled upwards 18 inches, and the hangar deck was dished. Casualties numbered twenty-eight men killed and 32 wounded.

The resulting fires were quickly got under control, and the carrier's strike aircraft were taken aboard at 1615 by manual operation of the barriers. The ship remained with Task Group 58.3 until next replenishment day, when she left for Ulithi for repairs.

---

104 The only figures forthcoming are those of Task Group 58.3 which lost three aircraft in combat (one pilot rescued) and six operationally.

Chapter X

OPERATIONS OF THE AMERICAN CARRIERS

Since the primary task of the American fast carriers of Task Force 58 was to assist the amphibious forces in the occupation of Okinawa, a high proportion of their air activity, particularly during the early part of the operation, before the shore-based air forces were established in Okinawa Gunto, was devoted to operations in direct support of the troops on southern Okinawa.

70. Work of the Fast Carriers in Support of the Troops

From 1st April, when Task Force 58 began launching almost continuous strikes in direct support of the Okinawa assault, the record of the groups shows for the most part of a cycle of two to four days' operating, followed by a day of fuelling.

They were used to centralize enemy coast and anti-aircraft guns which could fire on transport and boat groups; to destroy buildings and obstructions near the landing beaches which might furnish cover for enemy troops; to destroy or neutralize beach defences, field artillery, or mortars which could fire on boats or troops after landing; to prevent the movement of enemy reserves; to furnish combat air patrols and anti-submarine patrols at the objective; to provide air reconnaissance, air spotting for fire support ships and artillery; smokers, photographic aircraft, and to furnish close air support.[105]

105 "The support missions on the whole were satisfactory. Good bombing and strafing being carried out very close to our own front lines, but concern was felt over the misuse of bombs, in that, for instance, 8-12 seconds delay fuses were standing order for all missions for over a week, without attention being given as to what type of target the aircraft were to attack." *Report by BPFLO on First Carrier Task Force Operations*, p.4.

One of the best examples of close support of the troops occurred on 20th May. For more than a week, the ground forces had been held up north-east of Shuri by a small ridge, surmounting a natural amphitheatre sloping to the southward. More than 300 men had been killed in attempting to take this position. The troops finally decided that close-support bombing was the only remaining alternative, and they agreed to accept the risk of bombs on their own lines.

A support mission from Task Group 58.3 landed at Katena Airfield. It was carefully briefed with a photograph of the position, and a Marine officer was detailed to accompany the strike leader to pin-point the precise position. Then, with the American basic forces on top of the ridge only 50 yards away, the twelve Avengers came in in pairs at 200 to 400 feet, each dropping 2 x 500 lb. bombs with 4 to 5-second delay fuses on each of two runs, blasting the enemy dug-outs and gun positions at the base of the ridge.

As the last pair of Avengers made their drop, the artillery reopened its barrage and the troops swarmed over the ridge, and the position was captured with the loss of only two men. The position was proved, two days later, to have been the key to the whole salient, which had been deadlocked for nearly three weeks and then fell apart through the capture and exploitation of this position.

No less important were the fighter sweeps and patrols flown almost daily over the island chain and the airfields of Kikai and Kuno Shima in the Amami Gunto, and Minami Oagari Shima[106] in the Borodino Islands to the south-eastward of the Ryukus. These together with three series of interdiction strikes against the Kyushu airfields, were designed to prevent the enemy's constant and aggressive airborne attacks against the ships and forces in the Okinawa area.

These strikes failed to neutralize the airfields in the Nansei Shoto for more than short periods, though they did destroy most of the facilities and supply dumps around the fields, and wrecked many aircraft. As a consequence, the Japanese were severely hampered in their efforts to stage aircraft through these fields against the ground forces on Okinawa. The Kyushu airfields were, of course, far too numerous to be put out of action completely.

Task Force 58 was not brought up to its full strength of four groups until Task Group 58.2 joined on 8th April, and was soon reduced to three groups once more, so rapid was the attrition amongst the carriers. The number of carriers available in the force varied during the course

[106] Usually referred to in the American reports by its former name Minami Daito Jima.

of the Ryukus operation. Between the 2nd March and 27th April there was an average of seven carriers and six light carriers; from that time until 12th May there were five carriers and four light carriers; between 12th and 18th May four of each type.

71. The *Enterprise* and *Essex* Damaged, 11th April

After the air attack of the 7th April, the Japanese lost little time in mounting a second heavy attack on the fast carriers. On the morning of the 11th, indications pointed to a strong enemy effort. The regular daily support mission over Okinawa was therefore abandoned, and heavy combat air patrols were kept over the islands of Okinawa, Amami, Kikai, and Tokuno, and over the three Task Groups, 58.2, 58.3 and 58.4,[107] which were operating to the eastward of Okinawa in the approximate area 27° N. 130° E.

The *Enterprise*, one of the carriers of Task Group 58.2, had been damaged in the strikes on Kyushu on 18th March and had been undergoing repairs continuously since then; and some 80 per cent of the crew had joined the ship only 7 days previously.

The weather, which was favourable to the enemy in the forenoon with low cloud, broke and lifted by the time the expected attack began at 1330. Cruising disposition was assumed, and the force began evasive manoeuvres at 25 knots. The raid commenced with a few Japanese aircraft coming in singly and making ingenious use of window

Gradually, the number of aircraft was increased, the pilots co-ordinating their dives effectively with the 5/10th cloud cover whose base was at 4,000 feet, and with the sun, and attempting to time their dives with the maximum distraction of the American gunners in finishing off the aircraft immediately ahead. All of them pressed home their attacks with self-destruction on the target as their apparent purpose. Against their elusive preliminary manoeuvers, their straight high-speed dives, and their persistence defence was extremely difficult.

At 1410 the *Enterprise* was hit a glancing blow by a suicide aircraft, which approached in a shallow glide from right astern, where few guns would bear. Its bomb exploded under the carrier on the port quarter, lifting her three to four feet, damaging the ship severely. A second suicide aircraft crashed close aboard the starboard bow at 1501, causing further damage.

A few minutes later, two enemy aircraft approached Task Group 58.8, which was still in cruising formation, from astern. One of them,

[107] Task Group 58.1 was refuelling.

USS *Colorado* (BB-45) firing her after 16/45 guns during the pre-invasion bombardment of Okinawa, 29 March 1945. Photographed from USS *Minneapolis* (CA-36). (USNHHC)

USS *Tennessee* (BB-43) training her guns on Okinawa during the initial landings, 1 April 1945. (USNHHC)

The scene off the invasion beaches during the bombardment of Okinawa, circa 1 April 1945. In foreground are *LCS-16, LCS-15* and *LCS-14*. USS *West Virginia* (BB-48) is beyond them, at left. Firing in right distance is USS *Idaho* (BB-42). (USNHHC)

A wave of LVTs moves past the bombardment line, bound for the beaches of Okinawa on 1 April 1945. An *Idaho*-class battleship is firing in the background. (USNHHC)

The crew of a 40mm quad gun on USS *West Virginia* (BB-48) watch events unfolding as their ship supports the invasion of Okinawa, 1 April 1945. (USNHHC)

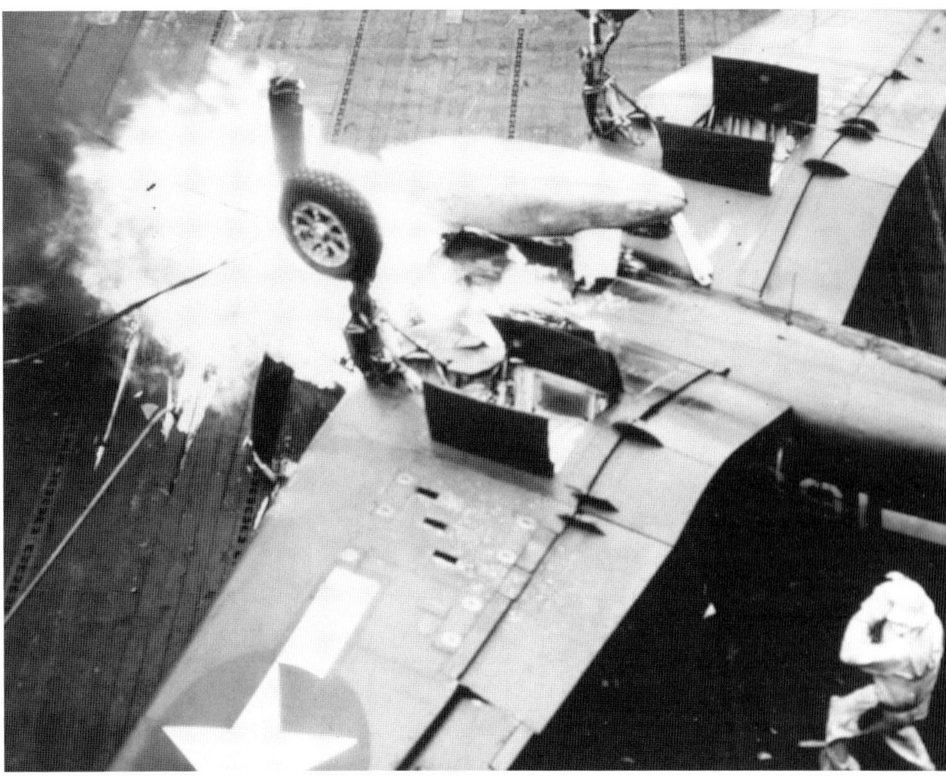

Fire erupts from an F4U Corsair after it crashed into the barrier on USS *Essex*, 8 April 1945. Fuel from the damaged belly tank ignited when it hit the aircraft's hot engine. The fire was quickly extinguished by the flight deck firefighters. (NARA)

Damage to the bridge of USS *Bowers* (DE-637) following a Kamikaze hit off Okinawa on 17 April 1945. (USNHHC)

Firefighters busy on board HMS *Formidable* after a Japanese suicide plane had crashed on the flight deck whilst she was operating off the Sakishima Islands in support of the Okinawa landings in May 1945. The rear part of the aircraft carrier's island is badly scorched, whilst the flight deck is covered in foam and water. (Historic Military Press)

USS *Bunker Hill* (CV-17) burning after being hit by a Kamikaze off Okinawa on 11 May 1945. This photographed was taken from USS *Bataan* (CVL-29). (USNHHC)

USS *Idaho* pictured firing on Japanese positions on Okinawa during the American invasion in 1945. Among the other bombarding ships is USS *Salt Lake City*, in the right distance. (USNHHC)

USS *Louisville* (CA-28) off the southern coast of Okinawa, 30 May 1945. She was hit by a kamikaze a few days later. *LCI-1090* is alongside. (NARA)

The author stood between the 16-inch guns of USS *Iowa* at the battleship's berth at San Pedro, Los Angeles. *Iowa* arrived off Okinawa on 15 April to relieve her sister ship USS *New Jersey*, and from 24 April, supported carrier operations. (Hannah Fadairo)

passing unhurt through the barrage, dived on the *Essex* and dropped a bomb close to her port side, causing minor damage. No ships in the task force received direct hits, but the destroyer *Kidd* was severely damaged by a near miss, and the battleship *Missouri* and three other destroyers received slight damage.

During the day, fighters from Task Force 58 shot down 17 of the attackers, and ships' gunfire accounted for 12 more, but it was evident from the day's action that the problem of the suicide aircraft had not been solved. That night, however, when the enemy renewed the attack, they were less successful; they inflicted no damage on the task force, but they lost 11 aircraft to night fighters and seven by ships' gunfire, in badly executed attacks mainly by single or small groups of aircraft that presented little danger to a well-handled force.

At midnight the Japanese shifted the main weight of their air strikes to the ships anchored at Okinawa, which they attacked heavily or intermittently for nearly 24 hours, and except for a short attack on Task Group 58.1 the Task Force was left alone. Strong combat air patrols drawn from Task Force 58, the Support Carriers, and the Marine Air Group ashore, had again been placed over Okinawa and the islands to the north. Of the total of at least 208 Japanese aircraft destroyed that day fighters from Task Force 58 accounted for 151.

72. Attacks on Kyushu, 15th-16th April; *Intrepid* Hit

In an attempt to reduce the weight of the Japanese air attacks against the forces engaged in the Ryukus operation Admiral Nimitz, at the request of the Commander Fifth Fleet, now arranged with General Amold for the diversion of part of the effort of XXI Bomber Command's long-range heavy bombers to Kyushu.

On the 15th April, the aircraft of Task Group 99.2 commenced direct air support of the troops from bases in Okinawa Gunto. This rendered it possible to spare the last carriers for a strike elsewhere; and as there were indications of a further heavy Japanese air attack being organized for the 16th, Task Force 58, with only short notice, sent a long range fighter sweep of 125 aircraft against airfields in S. Kyushu.[108] About noon on the 15th, Task Groups 58.1, 58.2 and 58.3 were ordered to eliminate all support missions at Okinawa

108 B.P.F.L.O. in his *Report on First Carrier Task Force Operations, 9th April la May, 1945* p.3, states that Vice Admiral Mitscher was not in favour of strikes on Kyushu by T.F. 58. In his opinion higher losses in pilots, aircraft and petrol were caused to the Japanese by shooting them down when they came into Okinawa, than by attacks on well dispersed aircraft on heavily defended airfields; and in view of the work that lay before Task Force 58 he did not wish to waste the Naval Air Force unnecessarily.

and prepare a fighter sweep on Kyushu in the afternoon. The attack apparently came as a complete surprize to the Japanese, for many aircraft were caught and destroyed on the fields. Twenty-nine were also destroyed in the air.

During the night a group of 20 Japanese bombers carrying a number of Baka bombs and escorted by 20 fighters, was met over Tokuno. All the bombers were destroyed, and the fighters shot down or dispersed before they could get through to the Force.

Next day, April 16th, whilst Task Group 58.2 fuelled, their place was taken by Task Group 58.4. During the morning, in an effort to break up a heavy Japanese air attack which was clearly impending, sweeps were again launched against airfields in Kyushu. More than 50 aircraft were destroyed on the ground. This, however, did not prevent the Japanese from launching heavy air attacks, both against Okinawa and against Task Force 58. The attacks continued throughout the day and all air support for the ground forces was cancelled so that every effort could be concentrated on fighter defence.

During the afternoon, Task Group 58.4, which so far had not been engaged, was attacked by several aircraft. At 1336 one of them crashed on the flight deck of the *Intrepid* and almost simultaneously a second narrowly missed the ship. The engine and part of the first suicider pierced the flight deck and went through to the hanger deck, carrying a heavy bomb with them. The resulting explosion dished the armoured hangar deck about 4 inches, raised the flight deck 12 inches, started large fires among the parked aircraft, and damaged No. 3 lift beyond repair. Although at 1544 the *Intrepid* reported that she could take 20 aircraft at 1615 and the remainder an hour later, the damage was such that it was considered necessary to send her back to Ulithi next day, and she had eventually to proceed to a Navy Yard for repairs.

Task Force 58 reported they shot down 155 aircraft that day, losing only nine themselves.

73. Fast Carrier Force Reorganized, 17th April

Task Group 58.2 was dissolved next day, 17th April, and the fast carriers were re-organized in three groups. Only two carriers remained in Task Group 58.2; one, the *Randolph*, joined Task Group 58.3 to replace the damaged *Enterprise* which was sent back to Ulithi for repairs and did not re-join until 6th May; the other, the light carrier *Independence*, took the place of the *Intrepid* in 58.4. The new carrier *Shangri-la* joined Task Group 58.4 on 24th April and next day, whilst the remainder of the group was refuelling, she launched a strike against Okino Oagari Shima.

The extra support ships made available through the dissolving of Task Group 58.2 were much appreciated on 17th April, for the fast carriers bore the brunt of the enemy attack that day. The *Bataan* was near missed but suffered no damage; and 55 enemy aircraft were reported shot down, including six by gunfire.

On the 27th April, Task Group 58.1 was ordered back to Ulithi for ten days replenishment and overhaul, the intention being that each group should have 10 days' rest in rotation.

Since leaving Ulithi on 14th March the ships of this task group had been called upon to defend themselves with gunfire against enemy aircraft on 105 occasions. Fifty-one of the attackers were reported shot down by ship gun-fire and one destroyed itself by crashing into the destroyer *Sigsbee*. On the 14th April, when the *Sigsbee* was hit, the three destroyers of the Radar Picket Line, *Sigsbee, Dashiell* and *McKee* shot down ten out of 15 attacking aircraft in half an hour. Against the concentrated gunfire of the task group whilst disposed for air defence no Japanese suicide aircraft was ever able to effect his mission and not one got away. Anti-aircraft ammunition expenditure by Task Group 58.1 during the period was as follows:

6-inch	5-inch/38	40mm	20mm
59 rds.	13,658 rds.	52,536 rds.	90,266 rds.

The amount of ammunition required to destroy each aircraft was thus: 1.25 rounds of 6-inch; 268 rounds of 5-inch/38; 1030 rounds of 40mm and 1777 rounds of 20mm.

74. The *Bunker Hill* Damaged, 11th May

In spite of the heavy night air attacks on the Expeditionary Force shipping on the 27th and 28th April the Japanese were able to mount a heavy attack on Task Force 58 on the 20th. No serious damage was suffered, however, until late in the afternoon, when the destroyer *Haggard,* stationed in the picket group, was hit by one suicide aircraft and narrowly missed by a second. The destroyer *Hazelwood,* sent to stand by the *Haggard,* was also hit. Both ships were seriously damaged, and the *Haggard* had to be taken in tow. Fires on board the *Hazelwood* burned for more than eight hours. Both destroyers were sent back to Ulithi next day, for repairs.

After nearly a week of calm, the night 10th-11th May witnessed the unusual occurrence of simultaneous enemy air attacks on the Expeditionary Force at Okinawa and the Covering Force to the eastward of the island. After Task Force 58 had been almost constantly shadowed during the night, a major air battle developed overhead in the morning. At 1009 a screening destroyer, the *Ault*, reported enemy aircraft overhead, and within a minute two suiciders crashed into the Task Force flagship, the carrier *Bunker Hill* in Task Group 58.3, almost simultaneously, coming out of the low clouds near the ship at great speed. A third was shot down by ships' gunfire.

The task group at the time was in cruising disposition 5V but was not at action stations.[109] No ship in the group detected the enemy by radar, the last report of any enemy aircraft having been at 0955, when Task Group 58.4 reported their Combat Air Patrol shooting down one aircraft bearing 090° 70 miles from Task Group 58.3. It is believed that two aircraft which attacked the *Bunker Hill* came in very low and on sighting the group climbed rapidly into the clouds over the force and closed quickly, being undetected amongst friendly aircraft circling overhead, because of the limitations of the American identification equipment.[110]

The first suicider crashed on the flight deck just abaft No.3 lift, released its 500-lb. bomb whilst still airborne, then penetrated the flight deck and the island at their intersection. The bomb passed through the flight deck, exploded on the galley deck, bulging these and the hangar deck and starting large fires which soon became continuous from No.2 lift to the fantail. The light cruiser *Wilkes-Barre* and three destroyers assisted in putting out the fires, and Vice-Admiral Mitscher later transferred to the *Enterprise*. Casualties in the *Bunker Hill* were very heavy, no less than 52 missing and 352 killed, mostly by asphyxiation from the heavy volumes of smoke which penetrated everywhere owing to her ventilation fans having been running when she was hit. The ship had to be sent to the rear area for repair.

75. Attacks on Kyushu, 13th-14th May

By now, the shore-based fighters in Okinawa Gunto were strong enough to release the fast carriers for a few days,[111] and at 12.15 on 12th May Task Force 58 received orders to discontinue support of

---

109 Actions stations was sounded off as the first suicider hit.

110 *C.T.G. 58.3 Action Report*, pp.60-61.

111 Report by B.P.F.LO. (covering letter dated 18th May, 1945), states that C.T.F. 58 felt that the use of the Fast Carrier Force at Okinawa was now over and that it was merely providing a stationary target for the training of the Japanese Air Force. C.T.F. 58's proposal that Task Force 58 should return to advance base for a fortnight before resuming attacks on Japan or Formosa was not, however, concurred in by Commander Fifth Fleet who considered that air defence at Okinawa was not yet entirely satisfactory.

the troops and patrols over the northern islands of the Nansei chain, and to set course for a launching area in approximately 30° 30′ N., 132° 30′ E,[112] south-east of Kyushu. Task 58.4 had left for replenishment at Ulithi on the previous day; and Task Group 58.1 which had now re-joined the Force after replenishment proceeded in company with Task Group 58.3. At noon on the 12th the carrier *Monterey* transferred from Task Group 58.1 to 58.3, bringing the number of carriers in this group to five.

Since re-joining the group on 6th May after repair of damage suffered on 11th April, the *Enterprise*, in Task Group 58.3, had carried out valuable night nuisance raids on the airfields of the Nansei Shoto[113] and southern Kyushu. Her greatest effectiveness was demonstrated, however, on the nights preceding these third strikes on Kyushu.

Since she was the only night carrier with the task force, her scope of operations covered the entire island of Kyushu, and during the nights 12th-13th and 13th-14th May her nuisance raiders attacked virtually every airfield of importance thereon. Before the day launches on 13th May her night aircraft attacked with incendiary clusters, rockets and machine guns airfields at Kanoya and Kanoya East, being fortunate in striking the latter when exhaust flames showed aircraft being readied for take-off and strike, either against the approaching carriers or the shipping at Okinawa.

The long list of raided airfields included Kushira, Shibushi, Kokobu, Kagoshima, Chiran, and Inujo in the extreme south; Miyazaki, Nittagahara, and Tomitaka along the east coast; and Kermamoto, Omura and Sasebo in the middle west. Numerous fires and explosions were reported; and 12 enemy aircraft were destroyed in the air by night fighters, three of them over the task force.

The Americans followed up their night nuisance raids by a dawn fighter Combat Air Patrol over the same area, to pin down the enemy on his home fields until relieved by the strikes from the day carriers.

Sunrise was at 0525. The first strikes were launched at 0145-0500 from a position about 30° 00′ N., 132° 30′ E., Kanoya bearing about 310° distance 125 miles, in good weather, skies partly cloudy, sea calm. In all, 700 sorties were launched against assigned target areas during the day. There was a noticeable absence of enemy airborne opposition, and AA fire was meagre to moderate, inflicting no appreciable damage on

112 Position as shown in *U.S.S. Enterprise, Action Report, 3-16, May, 1945*, Okinawa, Track Chart, p.16.

113 C.T.G. 58.3, Action Report, p. 24, says "on the airfields of the Ryukus", but the night heckler work of the *Enterprise* was not confined to the Ryuku Is. alone.

the attackers. Not a single attack was made on the task force, although the C.A.P. shot down one or two enemy aircraft, and the northern pickets took under fire a raid which closed to nine miles.

During the night 13th-14th May, night fighters from the *Enterprise* again covered all the principal airfields on Kyushu and some on Shikoku. In spite of this deterrent, however, the enemy was able to launch an early and sustained air attack against the ships of the task force on the morning of the 14th.

Enemy aircraft were on the screen with little interruption during most of the night, and soon after 0600 on the 14th raids commenced and continued unremittingly for over four hours. A group of 25 or 26 enemy aircraft apparently passed the force well to the west at low altitude, and then approached from the south-west, thereby avoiding the radar picket group to the north-west of the task force.

At 0658 four of these aircraft penetrated the C.A.P. screen and got over Task Group 58.3 which had formed cruising disposition 5V about half an hour previously. Three were shot down by AA fire, but the fourth dived out of cloud cover on the *Enterprise,* crashing just abaft the forward aircraft elevator. The 500-lb. delay action bomb which it carried penetrated the flight deck, passed through the decking of the elevator pit and exploded in the rag storeroom on a 4 to 6 feet thick layer of rag bales, demolishing the lift and bulging the flight deck upwards to a maximum of 3 feet.

The ship had been at action stations for over three hours when struck, and as with her two previous hits, she was ready to cope with the resulting fires and damage: and in 30 minutes the fires were extinguished. Casualties included 13 killed and 68 injured. For the second time within a week Vice-Admiral Mitscher had to shift his flag, this time to the *Randolph,* whilst the *Enterprise* was sent to rear areas for repairs. Combat Air Patrol shot down 19 of the enemy, and ships' gunfire six.

The three sweeps scheduled for the day were launched and completed successfully. Their experiences were substantially the same as those of the previous day: they met virtually no air opposition and found very few aircraft on the fields attacked. At sunset Task Force 58 retired to Okinawa.

Two days of strikes resulted in the destruction of 72 enemy aircraft in the air; whilst 78, and probably a further 167, were destroyed on the ground. Damage was caused to 17 Japanese airfields., many of which had been damaged already by long range bomber raids. The American losses for the two days were 14 aircraft. A pilot and a gunner from an American aircraft shot down by A.A., were rescued by seaplanes from the Inland Sea, within close range of the enemy's shore batteries, whilst U.S. fighters damaged and drove off two enemy vessels that tried to seize the airmen.

The *Randolph* during the two days' operations launched 388, the *Bennington* 307, and the *Hornet* 437 aircraft.

76. The Final Operations of the Fast Carriers

On the 24th May, Task Groups 38.1 and 38.8, whilst engaged in patrols over Amami Gunto, launched a clean-up sweep of 18 fighters against airfields in Southern Kyushu, from the usual operating position east of Okinawa, with Kanoya Airield bearing 015° distance 290 miles. At this airfield, 70 aircraft in revetments, with Baka bombs under their wings, were machine gunned; but little activity was found on the other fields, the result, it was considered, of the effectiveness of the previous strikes against the area.

The Americans lost three aircraft by A.A. fire off Kanoya, and destroyed 84 of the enemy in the air and on the ground. Task Group 58.4 re-joined from Ulithi on the 27th May, and next day Task Group 38.3, as Task Group 58,3 became on the 28th when Vice-Admiral J.S. McCain (USS *Shangri-la*) succeeded Vice-Admiral Mitscher in command of the Fast Carrier Force, left for Ulithi for rotation replenishment.

Further long-range fighter sweeps were launched on the 2nd and 3rd June by Task Force 38 from a distance of some 350 miles, but on both days bad weather made the operations difficult. Time for briefing for the first day's strikes was short. The lack of alternative approach track from the launching position off Okinawa enabled the enemy to receive ample warning. The Americans' losses were heavy, 16 aircraft and 12 men, for these fighter sweeps encountered some Japanese pilots and aircraft of very different calibre from the inferior Kamikaze pilots, often flying training aircraft since the numbers of Japanese bombers and fighters had dwindled to insufficiency.

In a total of 178 sorties only eight Japanese aircraft were destroyed in the air and 22 on the ground. Wide dispersal of targets also contributed to these relatively heavy losses, which in proportion to those of the enemy were the highest for many months. One American pilot was rescued inside Kagoshima Bay without any interference by the Japanese.

Next morning, all aircraft on support missions were recalled by C.T.F. 38 and the Fast Carrier Force steered eastward to avoid a typhoon approaching from the south-west. Task Groups 38.1 and 38.4 met at 2006 and proceeded in company with the Logistic Support Group (30.8), under Vice-Admiral McCain's orders. At 0505 on the 5th Task Group 38.1 was separated whilst manoeuvring in an unsuccessful attempt to avoid the storm centre which was much nearer to this group than to 38.4. An hour and a half later Task Group 38.1 passed through the centre of the typhoon, with serious results.[114]

The heaviest damage inflicted by the high winds and seas was the loss of 100 feet of the bow of the heavy cruiser *Pittsburgh*. The missing bow was subsequently sighted about six miles from Task Group 38.1 and was taken in tow by the tug *Munsee*. Two more cruisers of the same class, the *Baltimore* and the *Duluth* also suffered serious structural damage, whilst the forward 25 feet of the flight decks of the carriers *Hornet* and *Bennington* collapsed. Other ships which suffered damage that day were three battle ships, two light carriers, four escort carriers, one heavy cruiser, four light cruisers, 12 destroyers, two destroyer escorts, two oilers and one ammunition ship. Task Force 38 lost 29 aircraft. The *Pittsburgh*, light cruiser *Duluth*, the destroyer *Blue*, and the *Munsee*, with the *Pittsburgh*'s bow in tow, were sent to Guam for repairs.

On the morning of the 6th June, Task Force 38 was reformed in the fuelling area, and supporting operations for Okinawa were resumed.

Although the typhoon passed clear of Okinawa, the Typhoon Plan which had been prepared in view of the high probability of tropical storms during the summer, was put into action at the anchorages.[115] The most dangerous weather encountered at Okinawa Gunto itself, however, in the course of the operations was that caused by cold fronts moving in from the north-west as on the 4th-5th April when so much damage was caused to landing craft. A more violent front on the 10th of that month caused less damage because all concerned took the necessary precautions at the first warning.

For the 8th June a final fighter strike on Kyushu was planned, and during the early evening of the 7th Task Groups 38.1 and 38.4 steered towards the launching area in about 27° 00′ N., 133° 30′ E., 280 miles from Kyushu. In accordance with the American method of immediate ruthless analysis, which may have accounted for much of their success, the operation was specifically planned to avoid the mistakes made in the previous attack.

The attack was concentrated on the air installations at Kanoya, the strike group of 200 fighters being in four parts to each of which was assigned a limited specific area for bombing. They found the enemy alert, the aircraft in the revetments, and no aircraft activity on the

---

114 The matter is commentated on fully in *T.G. 38.1 Action Report, 28th May-13th June, 1945*.

115 The Typhoon Plan is given in *ComPhibForPac, Action Report 17th February-17th May 1945, 17th February-17th, May, Okinawa*, Appendix III.

ground at Kanoya or the neighbouring fields. The 200 aircraft attacked within less than five minutes, completely saturating the defences. One of the very few Japanese aircraft encountered was shot down and 28 were destroyed on the ground. Americans lost four aircraft, but all the pilots were rescued.

On the same day Cruiser Division 16, consisting of the large cruisers *Guam* and *Alaska*, light cruisers *Flint* and *San Diego*, and the 107th Destroyer Division (*Remey, Wadleigh, Norman Scott, Mertz* and *Monssen*) was detached from Task Group 30.4 and proceeded towards Okino Oagari Shima to carry out a surface bombardment on the 9th.

The bombardment was carried out as planned, covered by air patrols from the task group. During the afternoon, Task Group 38.1 launched a strike of 74 aircraft against the island for the purpose of testing the effectiveness of napalm against suitable targets. The pilots reported that, as far as could be observed. napalm was 75 to 90 per cent effective. The targets had already been heavily worked over, and it was therefore impossible to estimate the damage caused by either the air strikes or the surface bombardment.

That day the battleships *Massachusetts, Indiana* and *Alabama* and destroyers *De Haven, Mansfield, L.K. Swenson, Collett,* and *Maddox* were detached temporarily from Task Group 38.1 and were formed into Task Group 30.2 for the purpose of bombarding Minami Oagari Shima on the 10th. The target was well worked over under C.A.P. from Task Group 38.4, and useful training was provided for the ships involved. As on the preceding day, aircraft from Task Group 38.1, together with 38.4, launched strikes simultaneously with the ships' bombardment in order to obtain an additional test of the efficacy of napalm. Similar results were reported.

This was the third occasion on which the Borodino Islands had been attacked. On the 20th March, Minami had been bombarded by the large cruisers *Guam* and *Alaska*. On April 21st, Task Group 58.1, en route to a fuelling rendezvous, steamed by Minami Oagari Shima and Kita Oagari Shima[116] whilst the cruiser *San Juan* and 15 destroyers[117] conducted short bombardments of both islands, working over the phosphate plant on Kita and starting many large fires near the radio station on Minami.

On 10th June, Task Force 38 left the strike area and proceeded towards Leyte for rest, replenishment, maintenance work and voyage repairs.

116 Called by its old name, Kita Daita Jima in the only report on this bombardment which has been seen, *C.T.G. 58.1 Action Report, 14th March-30th April*, Encl. F. p.2.

117 Group 1, *John Rodgers, Harrison, McKee* and *Schroeder* of DesRon 25, *Wedderburn, Stockham* and *Collett* of DesRon 61; Group 2, *De Haven, Mansfield, L. K. Swenson, Maddox, S.N. Moore, Taussig, Blue* and *Brush* of DesRon 61.

Their part in the Ryukus operation was concluded, for they were still at Leyte on 21st June when resistance on Okinawa was declared at an end.

77. Work of the Escort Carriers

Whilst the Fast Carriers had been engaged in these operations the Escort Carriers of the Support Carrier Group (Task Group 52.1) had been engaged on parallel tasks under the orders of Rear-Admiral Durgin. During the operations preparatory to the main landing on Okinawa, the Support Carrier Group - "was the backbone of the attacks against the defence installations, and provided the close support for the assault of the Western Islands attack the Support and the UDT operations. It was apparent that this Force realized what was required of it far better than did the Fast Carrier Force, and its pilots were far more assiduous in engaging concealed defences. It was this Force also that was called upon to do all the various odd jobs."[118]

The escort carriers continued their close support of the troops subsequent to the landing, and also alternated with Task Force 57, the striking force of the British Pacific Fleet, in rendering continuous the work of neutralizing the airfields of the Sakishima Gento on the days when the British carriers withdrew to refuel. Amongst their varied duties was that of providing air cover for Service Squadron 6 (Task Group 50.8) and fleet units in the fuelling and supply area south-east of Minami Oagari Shima, when the escort carriers of that group were not available.

The escort carriers suffered less severely from enemy action than the fast carriers, for none were sunk, and their numbers suffered little diminution from the 14 which comprised Task Group 52.1 at the outset of the operation. During April their numbers varied for the most part between 17 and 18, though they dropped to 12 at the end of the month. Including the two escort carriers of the Anti-Submarine Warfare Group (Task Group 50.7) and the six escort carriers of the Logistic Support Group (Task Group 50.8), a total of nine suffered damage in greater or less degree, mainly from the weather, and only three from enemy action all from suicide attack.

Statistics of this force are meagre but up to the 27th May, when Admiral Spruance relinquished charge of the 5th Fleet, they destroyed 200 enemy aircraft and sank four ships and a number of small craft.

So completely was the Escort Carrier Force the Cinderella of the Fleet, that operation orders from "higher authority" directed that the escort carrier groups should keep clear of all others in the operating area; consequently, the carrier group commander was often faced with the possibility of having to land-on a large group of his aircraft at dark

118 *British Combined Operation Observers' Report*, p.21.

with his wind line fouled by an approaching group which could have avoided him by a small change of course. "With planes low on gas and darkness approaching it is not a pleasant picture to dwell on," wrote Rear-Admiral Henderson, Commander Carrier Division 25.[119]

The same commander also made representations regarding the overcrowding aboard the escort carriers, mainly caused by detailing specialists to the ships. "The problem of transferring these specialists from one group to another when fuelling operations necessitate departure from the target area is one that often contains more headaches than the Japanese attack."[120]

The *Saginaw Bay* had 148 officers on board with 120 bunks normally available and this during extended operations.

78. Summary[121]

Between the 23rd March when Task Force 58 commenced its strikes on Okinawa, and 13th June when it anchored in San Pedro harbor, Leyte, the aircraft of the Fast Carriers flew 29,949 sorties. They expended 7,680.1 tons of bombs, 34,003 rockets, 624 napalm tanks, 178 torpedoes, and 31 Tiny Tims[122]. One of the task groups, 58.3, operated at sea for 79 consecutive days, on 52 of which offensive missions were flown; one of the carriers of the group, the *Essex*, Rear-Admiral F.C. Sherman's flagship, was present throughout the entire operation. In another task group, 58.1, some pilots averaged more than 100 hours of combat flying per month.

During these 81 days of operation 1,908 Japanese aircraft were reported destroyed, 1,352 in the air. "It is probably conservative to say that at least 50 per cent of those destroyed were either bomb-carrying or suicide attack planes. Had they succeeded in getting through to Okinawa, the Fleet and landing Forces would undoubtedly have had a far rougher time than they did," wrote Rear-Admiral Sherman.[123] In addition, 188 ships and 283 small craft were sunk and 437 ships and 769 small craft were damaged.[124] The fast carriers lost in all 441 aircraft, 195 in combat and 246 operationally.

Personnel losses amongst air crews were 188. At least 60 per cent of the pilots shot down were picked up, a remarkable record when the location of the operations is taken into consideration.

119 *C.T.U. 52.1.2, Brief of Action Report, Okinawa, 21st March – 29th April, 1945,* p.2.
120 ibid.
121 Operating Statistics for T.G. 58.3/38.3 are given in Appendix I. No complete statistics for other task groups are available.
122 Air-to-ground rockets.
123 *C.T.G. 58.3 Action Report, 14th March-1st June, 1945,* p.38.
124 Between 1st April and 1st July.

Suicide air attacks were the most serious problem for the Fast Carrier Force. Eighteen ships were damaged in this way, though the manner in which the Americans[125] gradually got the upper hand of the Japanese Air Force is demonstrated by the fact that only two of these eighteen were damaged after the end of April.

Instances of damage by other forms of enemy attack were few. An enemy aircraft torpedo pierced and passed completely through the hull, of the destroyer *Murray* 18 inches above the waterline, but did not explode. Four other destroyers were slightly damaged in various ways by enemy attack, and the battleship *North Carolina* was hit by an enemy shell which damaged one of her directors.

There were a number of instances of operational damage, in addition to those caused by the typhoon of 4th-5th June. The battleship *New Jersey* and destroyer *Franks* were in collision, and three ships were damaged by A.A. fire from vessels of their own force. The battleship *South Dakota* received some damage from an ammunition explosion whilst in the fuelling area.

Numbers of Japanese mines were encountered in the operating area east of Okinawa. Task Group Task Group 58.1 destroyed 56 up to the end of April, and 58.3 68 during 79 days of operating. In spite of mines being an ever-present menace no ship ever struck one.

Conditions of readiness prescribed in U.S. Fleet Orders were subjected to a severe test during extended operations and proved inadequate to meet the situation where ships were liable to surprise air attacks. The various task groups and ships met the matter in their own ways. Personnel fatigue was aggravated by personnel shortages. A shortage of seamen is a serious matter in any ship, but especially so in a carrier engaged in 24-hour flight operations.

During April the *Hornet*, which had suffered no action casualties, was short of 175 seamen. This reduced the efficiency of her flight and hangar deck personnel, and the alertness of her guns' crews during long periods at action stations. On arrival at Ulithi on 3rd April for replenishment almost all the heavy ships in Task Group 58.1, to which the *Hornet* belonged, were seriously under-manned. Requirements of non-rated men were 500 seamen, 250 firemen, and 50 steward's mates: this, moreover, before transferring large drafts on orders and with the prospect of resuming active operations in ten days' time.

125 Including the strategic air forces.

Chapter XI

LOGISTICS[126]

The great number of ships and landing craft employed, coupled with the long distances involved, created a problem of supply, maintenance, and repair of greater magnitude than any heretofore encountered by the Americans in the Pacific.

79. Administration

The Joint Expeditionary Force (Task Force 51) was composed of over 1,200 ships and landing craft of all types, and the Fast Carrier Force (Task Force 58) numbered at the outset a further 88 ships. The assault phase of the operation required the embarkation of 182,821 persons and 746,850 tons of cargo into 433 assault transports and landing ships by eight embarkation authorities at 11 different ports extending 6,000 miles from Seattle to Leyte.[127] Between 1st April and 21st June, 1,921,955 tons of supplies and equipment were discharged at Okinawa.

Initially all ships loaded ammunition, fuel and lubricants to authorized capacity; fresh provisions to maximum capacity, and clothing, dry provisions, general stores, ship's stores, and medical stores for 120 days[128] (thus eliminating the need for victualling store ships during the assault phase). Forces embarking in the South Pacific completed at Ulithi with fuel and provisions. Vessels sailing from Leyte proceeded direct to Okinawa. There were no supply installations at Leyte and issues were made direct from the supply ships to the forces

126 This chapter deals only with the U.S. Forces' logistics. The operations of the Fleet Train B.P.F. are dealt with in Chapter XIII.

127 The loading ports were: San Francisco, Roi, Seattle, Oahu, Saipan, Tinian, Guam, Guadalcanal, Espiritu Santo, Russell, Leyte.

128 Dry provisions for 60 days for embarked troops.

sailing from there, despite distances of 40 to 50 miles between rehearsal beaches and logistic areas.

The administration of fleet manning and supply for the Ryukus operation was as follows:

(a) Commander Service Squadron 10 (CTG 50.9) was charged with responsibility for replenishing the fleet at forward area bases, and routeing and sailing supply ships required by the forces operating in the combat area.

(b) Commander Service Squadron 6 (C.T.G. 50.8) commanded the fleet supply ships in the combat area, co-ordinated fuelling schedules for the Fast Carrier Task Force and the Amphibious Forces, and exercised direct command of replenishment activities at sea.

(c) Responsibility for replenishing ships in their area was assigned to Forward Area commanders.

(d) Replacement aircraft, air crews and pilots, and aircraft spares were supplied through Commander Air Pacific representatives at the forward area bases by Commander Logistics Support Group (C.T.G 50.8) in the combat area.

(e) After the occupation of Kerama Retto, an amphibious group commander was established there to administer supply at the objective.

The extent of the supplies furnished by Service Squadron 6 during the period 14th March to 11th June was as follows:

Fuel oil (M Bbls)	10,133
Diesel (M Bbls)	323[129]
Aviation Spirit (M Gal)	25,573
Ammunition (tons)	16,373
Aircraft	998
Aircrews	220
Refrigerated provisions (tons)	2,219
Dry provisions (tons)	4,005
Ships' store stocks (tons)	575
Mail (bags)	15,398
Passengers	2,282

129 This figure is not understood, since another table in *Operations in the Pacific Ocean Areas during May, 1945*, from which these figures are taken, shows 455 M Bbl issued at the Ryukus between 1st April and 30th May alone, whilst Com. Fifth Fleet reported that the requirement on D+15 day alone was nearly 150,000 barrels.

80. Kerama Retto

The sheltered anchorages at Kerama Retto rendered this group of islands a valuable supply base. This base was originally set up as a temporary expedient in anticipation of further movement to eastern Okinawa at an early date. To handle the heavy battle damage, however, several large repair ships were stationed in this area, and the protection afforded by its land-locked anchorages was utilized to full advantage. A large number of oilers, ammunition, provision and water ships were also stationed here for the supply of ships of the Expeditionary Force.

Ammunitioning, storing and provisioning of ships of the Joint Expeditionary Force was largely carried out at Kerama Retto, the necessary shipping being sailed by Commander Service Squadron 10, principally from Ulithi though, on 7th May, the movement of this principal base of operations of Task Group 50.9 to Leyte in the Philippine Islands, 300 miles closer to the objective area, was begun.

Until 17th May forward supplies were the joint responsibility of the Senior Officer Present Afloat at Kerama Retto and the Commander Joint Expeditionary Force who arranged supply schedules at Hagushi, Ie Shima, and Nakagusuku Wan, and called forward and sailed supply shipping. On 17th May a representative of Commander Service Squadron 10 assumed responsibility for supplies in the entire Okinawa area.

81. Servicing of the Fast Carrier Force

The Covering Force was serviced at sea south-eastward of Minami Oagari Shima by the Logistic Support Group (T.G. 50.8). This task group operated ferry carriers, fleet oilers, fleet tugs, ammunition ships, general supply ships, and at a somewhat late date in the operations a hospital ship, at sea in areas close to Okinawa.

The group supplied all necessary stores and services from fuel to cinematograph films. In addition to fuelling ships of the Covering Force, tankers were used to supply lubricating oil and also aircraft drop tanks for the carriers, provisions for the destroyers, and to receive empty ammunition details for all ships. Fresh and frozen provisions were not available for more than a very few days after the operation commenced, but dry provisions were issued at every replenishment period. Delivery of ammunition to the Fast Carrier Force at sea was an innovation that proved outstandingly successful.[130] "It is considered that complete servicing of Task Groups at sea is not only feasible but also marks a definite forward step in Fleet operations" wrote C.T.G. 58.1.[131]

---

130 Com. Fifth Fleet, *Action Report, Ryukus Operation through 27th May, 1945*, p.VI-F-2.

131 *C.T.G. 58.1, Action Retort, 14th March - 30th April, 1945*, p.55.

In the fast carrier force there were two apparently chronic shortages. The first, certain aircraft spares which it was the province of an officer with the formidable short title ComAirPacSubComFwdArea to supply, was alleviated to a great extent by the escort carriers and tankers. The supply of replacement aircraft, aircraft crews, and pilots to Task Force 58 by the transport escort carriers was adequate only because a large number of aircraft carriers received battle damage. Numbers of their aircraft which were in the air at the time consequently landed on other carriers and were retained to make up deficiencies.

The other shortage, namely personnel, has already been referred to. Petty Officers and men were available on board the tankers of the Logistic Support Group, and were drawn by ships of the Task Group during each replenishment period. Drafts also left the task groups at each replenishment period, but replacements were never sufficient to make good the drafts withdrawn and keep the ships at full battle strength. In particular, there were never enough seamen.

82. Fuelling Task Force 51

The ships of the Joint Expeditionary Force replenished either at Kerama Retto or at anchorages in or close to Okinawa Shima, the sole exception being the Support Carrier Group (52.1) which fuelled every nine days in their operating area from tankers of the Logistic Support Group. Screening and fire support ships could fuel at Kerama Retto or near the landing beaches at Okinawa, from oilers or liberty tankers refilled from fleet oilers, which were sailed to the objective from the pool of fleet oilers operating with the Logistic Support Group. The screening vessels could also fuel under way between Okinawa and Kerama Retto, direct from the fleet oilers on their way to replenish the station tankers and other ships at Kerama Retto.

The estimates for the supply of heavy oil to the ships of the Joint Expeditionary Force were based on the assumption that those transports and landing ships which had been at the objective since L-Day (1st April) would require refuelling about L+16 Day (17th April). It was found, however, that ships of the transport squadron which arrived at Kerama Retto on L-6 Day (26th March) required replenishment about L+2 Day (3rd April), on account of the heavy demands made upon them to refuel screening vessels, high speed destroyer transports, and fire support destroyers, both en route to and at the objective, prior to the arrival of the first fleet oiler. On this account consumption of heavy oil at the objective reached 8,500 tons a day by L+2 Day (3rd April), but dropped to half this figure by L+16 Day (17th April).

With regard to diesel oil also "the peculiarities of operation of L.S.Ts., L.S.Ms., and similar diesel-burning craft are such that in any large amphibious operation the delivery of a large amount of diesel oil about D+15 is necessary. In an amphibious operation the size of the Okinawa operation, this requirement approaches 150,000 barrels (21,430 tons)."[132]

83. Damage Repair

Three supply ships were sunk and 18 damaged, and ten landing ships and rafts were sunk and 50 damaged by enemy action during the Ryukus operation. The ideal number of cargo ships in the Okinawa area would have been the number that could be continuously unloaded. As, however, prior to the removal of Service Squadron 10's base from Ulithi to Leyte, six days elapsed between the sailing of garrison troops and supply ships and their arrival, and owing to the high rate of consumption of all supplies, especially ammunition, ashore it was necessary to send forward more ships than could be discharged immediately upon arrival, or worked continuously.

Seven ships and 43 landing ships and craft suffered accidental damage. Much of this was damage from weather to landing craft and ships, practically all caused during the storm on the 4th and 5th April. "Considering the large number of landing craft and other small craft employed in this operation, the operational casualties were surprisingly low in number."[133] Reference has already been made to the methods for dealing with salvage operations off the reef which were so effective that there were none of the scenes of shipping devastation on the beaches which marked the Iwo Jima operation.

From L+2 Day (3rd April) onwards the repair facilities included in the original Task Force were overtaxed, and it immediately became evident that a large amount of assistance in dealing with battle damage would be required. At the outset of the operation the Service and Salvage Group (Task Group 51.6) included three landing craft repair ships and one battle damage repair ship. To these were subsequently added four mobile floating dry docks, four repair ships, two destroyer depot ships, and a radar maintenance ship. They accomplished a great amount of work, but a large backlog of damaged ships accumulated prior to the organization of the unit and a considerable time elapsed before it could be overtaken. In the repair of ships at the objective,

---

132 Com. Fifth Fleet, *Action Report, Ryukus Operation through 27th May. 1945*, p. VI-F-3. A ton of oil fuel equals seven barrels.

133 *ComPhibForPac, Action Report 17th Feb – 17th May, 1945, Okinawa*, p.538.

highest priority was given to the least damaged to ensure their earliest possible return to duty.

At the forward area bases also repair facilities were overloaded by the large amount of battle damage sustained. The salvage and towing work by Task Group 51.6 exceeded that undertaken in any other Pacific operation. The Task Group included three salvage vessels, five fleet tugs, and two rescue tugs. These proved quite inadequate, and at times during heavy enemy air activity twice the number could have been utilized to the fullest extent.

84. Port Development at Okinawa

The physical characteristics of Okinawa Gunto lent themselves to the development of fairly good harbours. The general development plan called for two harbours and certain additional waterfront facilities to be developed in order to provide a large, advanced fleet base and quays for unloading cargo vessels. The responsibility of Service Squadron 12, which had been temporarily appointed to develop the harbours, extended over the water areas up to the pierhead and bulkhead or beach line and involved survey, clearance, dredging, blockship placement, and salvage.

The existing harbours in Okinawa Gunto were blocked with Japanese vessels sunk or shattered by American air attacks. In Naha harbour, 146 wrecks were examined; 33 were disposed of by beaching and burning; seven were raised, towed out to sea, and sunk; and two were partially disposed of on the spot. The north slip, including the marine railway in the north-west comer, was entirely cleared. In Buckner Bay, the name given by the Americans to Nakagusuku Wan after 5th July, some 69,000 cubic yards had to be removed by dredging; but at Baten Ko, in the south part of Yonabaru Wan (south-west corner of Nakagusuku Wan), where the preliminary dredging surveys were not completed before the operation ended, it was anticipated that even more extensive dredging would be necessary.

The task of transforming open anchorages into secure harbours was complicated by heavy ground swells which made work impossible on many days. Many working hours were also lost through enemy air raids, alerts, and the threat of impending typhoons which failed to materialize.

Harbour development was far from complete when resistance ceased on Okinawa, and it was not until July that the critical arrears in unloading of shipping, so pronounced in June, began to decrease. In the first ten days of July 30,000 tons of cargo were unloaded.

Chapter XII

OPERATIONS OF THE BRITISH PACIFIC FLEET

During the first two months of the Ryukus operation the British Pacific Fleet had covered the left flank of the Americans.

85. Role of Task Force 57

Admiral Sir Bruce Fraser, Commander-in-Chief of the British Pacific Fleet, felt that not only on strategic grounds but also from a national point of view and for reasons of prestige the British Fleet operating in the Central Pacific should co-operate with the U.S. Fleet in its most advanced operations against Japan; and he secured acceptance of this view by Fleet Admiral Nimitz, Commander-in-Chief Pacific Fleet and Pacific Ocean Areas.

In the course of over three years of war in the Pacific the Americans had become masters of the large-scale strategic deployment of big naval forces at long distances from their home bases, and the tactical operation of these forces at previously unheard of distances from their most advanced bases. The U.S. Fleet had been gradually built up to suit the new type of naval warfare in the Pacific, the most modern yet evolved. It called for the employment of fast carriers, armed with numbers of aircraft serviced by ample maintenance personnel and operated by air crews who, when worn out by intense striking activity, over periods varying from four to six month, were taken out of the ship and replaced completely by a fresh group.

Quite apart from a natural doubt in the minds of the Americans as to the ability of the British Pacific Fleet to operate in the Pacific manner, they considered that our fleet might create a further drain on their logistic resources.

From the British point of view several factors must constantly be remembered when studying the operations of the British Pacific Fleet as part of the United States Pacific Fleet. Though considerable planning of the Australian base had taken place, the final decision that this base should be set up and the Fleet should take part in Pacific operations, was taken so late that much of the plan could not come to fruition before it became necessary to send the Fleet into action.

As a consequence, the Fleet sailed from Australia with little opportunity of working together and with an assignment to a type of warfare which under the conditions of the German war it had not been able to practice before. It is almost true to say, moreover, that it had at that time to rely on the resources which each ship carried on board, and even at the time of sailing initial supplies of stores, air stores, aircraft and men were arriving from the United Kingdom.

The whole venture was therefore necessarily a scramble. Essential support was always a little late and there was the continued aggravation of unavoidable teething troubles. The account which follows is therefore so often one of difficulties overcome by sheer improvisation. Nevertheless, though the fault for deficiencies lay solely with the necessities of war, justification was complete in that the British Fleet played its part in the Pacific war.

The British Pacific Fleet was a balanced fleet consisting of the battleships *King George V* (flagship of Vice-Admiral Sir H. Bernard Rawlings, C.T.F. 57) and *Howe*; the four fleet aircraft carriers *Indomitable* (flagship of Rear-Admiral Sir Philip L. Vian, A.C. 1 and Second-in-Command T.F. 57). *Victorious, Illustrious,* and *Indefatigable*; a cruiser squadron and destroyer screen. When air operations were being carried out tactical command of the Fleet was delegated to the Rear-Admiral Commanding First Aircraft Carrier Squadron.

Thus, it approximated to an American task group. Ship for ship the carriers contained little more than half as many aircraft as the U.S. (fleet) carriers. Nor was there, at the date of the conference between Mr Churchill and President Roosevelt in September 1944, when the role of the British Pacific Fleet was decided on, much visual evidence of the existence of the Fleet Train which, by rendering the striking forces independent of shore bases, formed an indispensable part of the fleet.

Although assignment of the British Pacific Fleet to Operation "Iceberg" was eventually arranged in detail, the necessity for confirmation by the Commander-in-Chief, U.S. Fleet, Fleet-Admiral E.J. King, rendered it two days late in commencing operations. On 14th March, 1945, most of Task Force 113 (as the striking force, which later became Task Force 57, was then known) consisting of the 1st Battle

Squadron, 1st Aircraft Carrier Squadron, 4th Cruiser Squadron, 25th, 4th and 27th Destroyer Flotillas, was at sea exercising from Manus in the Admiralty Islands. Task Force 112 (ships of the Fleet Train and Escort Vessels) was in harbour at Manus. On the forenoon of 15th March, whilst exercising at sea, Vice-Admiral Sir Bernard Rawlings, commanding Task Force 113, received instructions from the British Commander-in-Chief, whose headquarters were at Sydney, N.S.W. to report his force and Task Force 112 to the Commander-in-Chief, Pacific, for operations connected with "Iceberg".

The employment of his force was to be such that it could be disengaged and re-allocated to the South-West Pacific Area at seven days' notice from the Commander-in-Chief, U.S. Fleet. In point of fact the Commander-in-Chief, U.S. Fleet, ordered re-allocation of part of the Fleet shortly after it had become engaged in the Ryukus operation, and it was only combined representation by both the U.S. Area Commanders that prevented the fleet from being thus withdrawn in the middle of an operation. Admiral Nimitz allocated the British Force to Admiral Spruance's Fifth Fleet, in which the striking force (Task Force 113) received the designation Task Force 57;[134] and on 18th March it moved up to Ulithi, sending on ahead a tanker group to a position where it could refuel at the last prudent moment.

The Order of Battle-Aircraft-at the commencement of the operation was as follows:[135]

Indomitable	29 Hellcat,[136] 15 Avenger[137]
Victorious	7 Corsair,[138] 14 Avenger, 2 Walrus[139]
Indefatigable	10 Seafire,[140] 20 Avenger, 9 Firefly[141]
Illustrious	36 Corsair, 16 Avenger
Total aircraft	218

134 This designation was assumed at 0715 (T) on 23rd March.

135 These figures are those given in the report by the Flag Officer Commanding First Aircraft Carrier Squadron which forms Enclosure 1 to the report of Vice-Admiral, Second-in-Command, B.P.F. (*Operation "Iceberg"*). Slightly different figures are given in the section "The British Pacific Fleet in Operation 'Iceberg'" (*Operational Research Reports by Fleet Operational Officer B.P.F.*)

136 Fighter bomber.

137 Torpedo bomber employed throughout the operation almost exclusively as bombers.

138 Fighter.

139 Amphibian Reconnaissance Bomber (Air Sea Rescue).

140 Fighter.

141 Fighter.

The aircraft which constituted the main offensive weapon of the Fleet left much to be desired. The multiplicity of types – the *Chaser* on one occasion took out no less than seven different types for transfer to Task Force 57 in the service area – was a grave hindrance in carrier borne warfare. The characteristics of the Seafire made it very nearly incapable of reaching the enemy, and, in fact, during the first part of the operation their effort was entirely defensive. Finally, the American aircraft (Avengers, Corsairs and Hellcats) which constituted almost the entire complement, had been so altered to British requirements as to render impossible any pooling of resources with the U.S. Navy even in this American product.

The armoured decks of the British carriers much interested the Americans. They proved their worth, not against bombs, but against suicide aircraft with their comparatively small penetrating power, which in this particular operation carried out so high a proportion of the Japanese air attacks.

United States signal publications and doctrine were used throughout the operation. The task assigned to the British Fleet was to neutralize the airfields in the Sakishima Gunto as continuously, and for as long as possible, in order to cover the left flank of the invasion against Japanese air reinforcements from the south-west.

The Fleet was not able to play its full part, having insufficient forces to form a second Task Group, since the effort of one, alternately striking and refuelling, was necessarily discontinuous, and uneconomical of force. American task groups had to continue the work when Task Force 57 was fuelling. The six primary airfield targets in the group, three of which were situated on each of the two islands Ishigaki and Miyako, were as follows: On Iskigaki – Ishigaki, Miyara, Hegina; On Miyako – Hirara, Nobara, Sukama.

Photographs showed that two, Ishigaki and Hirara, were heavily defended against air attack, the former having 26 heavy A.A. and 66 light A.A. guns and the latter 12 heavy A.A. and 54 light A.A. guns. At the remaining four airfields there were concentrations of light A.A. guns only. A substantial proportion of the air effort was devoted to neutralizing the anti-aircraft gun positions, in order to reduce losses from flak and diminish the adverse effect on bombing accuracy.

Few of the airfields appeared to be in active use; and after initial heavy bombing and machine gunning the work of Task Force 57 consisted principally of maintaining a combat air patrol over the islands, searching for heavily camouflaged aircraft, and delivering bombing attacks against the airfields and installations.

The Japanese aircraft were for the most part widely dispersed and camouflaged with care and intelligence; and discernment was called for in order to avoid attacking camouflaged dummies or non-operational machines. The flying-off positions varied between 80 and 100 miles from the target area.

86. First Part of Operation "Iceberg"; First Strikes, 26th - 27th March

The date of sailing of Task Force 57 from Ulithi to commence operations, like that of sailing from Manus, was dictated by the arrival of the tankers in the fuelling area. The Force sailed at 0630 on 23rd March and met the tanker group and escort at 0600 on the 25th in position Ant (18° 30′ N. 120° 08′ E.). Owing to various unexpected difficulties, refuelling took nearly six hours longer than anticipated, and a high speed run at 23½ knots had to be made through the night, in order to avoid being late on their first appointment.

The destroyers sailed 30 per cent short of full stowage, with consequent effect on operations two days later. Two, the *Quality* and *Whelp*, had to be left with the fuelling group on account of defects; they were exchanged for the *Whirlwind* from the screen of the ferry escort carrier (Task Unit 112.2.1) and the *Kempenfelt* from the screen of the escort carrier for C.A.P. duties (Task Unit 112.2.5.) respectively.[142] A third, the *Wager* remained behind to continue fuelling when the Task Force proceeded at 1530; and re-joined next morning.

The general task of Admiral Rawling's force during this phase of "Iceberg" was to crater the runways of all Miyako and Ishigaki airfields and to maintain a combat air patrol over them by day, to prevent repair work, destroy any airborne enemy, and machine-gun grounded aircraft.

At sunrise, 0635 on 26th March, strong fighter sweeps were flown off 100 miles 180° from Miyako Jima to attack the airfields at Ishigaki and Miyako. They reported little activity. These sweeps were followed by two escorted bomber strikes and one fighter bomber strike on airfields and associated buildings. At dusk, after the last aircraft had flown on, the fleet withdrew to the south-eastward.

The night was fine and the fleet was shadowed by an enemy aircraft in the bright moonlight. Soon after 0300 on the 27th the *Indomitable* flew off a Hellcat, which drove off the enemy and then remained up until dawn. This incident at the very outset of the operation may have

---

142 *Quality* and *Whelp* re-joined T.F. 57 on 29th March and *Kempenfelt* and *Whirlwind* re-joined the Tanker Groups.

given the Japanese the mistaken impression that the Task Force was equipped with night fighters.

During the day (27th March) two bomber strikes from the previous day's fly off position were directed against radio stations, barracks and airfields not already covered, and coasters were also attacked off the islands. After a final small fighter-bomber strike, the task force began withdrawal for the night at dusk. It was intended that Task Force 57 should continue to operate off Sakishima Gunto next day, the programme including a bombardment of Ishigaki. However, Guam reported a typhoon to the southward, whose position and estimated track appeared to threaten the fuelling area.

There was risk of bad weather completely dislocating fuelling for some time, which would have precluded the return of Task Force 57 to the operating area in time to continue the strikes from L-1 until L+1 Day (31st March to 2nd April). Vice-Admiral Rawlings believed that the Commander 5th Fleet attached great importance to the maintenance by Task Force 57 of the neutralization of the Sakishima airfields during this special period; consequently, he cancelled the air and bombardment programme for the next day, and the Fleet withdrew to the fuelling area after the second day's strikes had been landed on. The necessity to withdraw was increased by the shortage of fuel in certain ships at the commencement of the operation.

Fuelling began at 0730 on the 28th in area Midge, a rectangle extending 50 miles to the south and 100 miles to the west of 19° 55′ N., 129° 40′ E. On this, as on the previous occasion, the force was divided into two groups, the "non-fuelling force" taking full A/S precautions at some distance from the fuelling force. As this method was found to be uneconomical in the use of escort vessels and fuel, and was also tiring for Flag and Commanding Officers, the United States Naval method of fuelling at sea was adopted for the last three periods and was found satisfactory. It required the main body of the fleet, consisting of capital ships, carriers, and cruisers to take station astern of the line of oilers.

All available escort vessels of the combat and fuelling force formed a circular screen within which the necessary movements to and from the oilers, flying operations by the carriers and escort carriers and movements connected with transfer of stores and so forth took place. Except for individual movements within the screen, the speed of the whole force was governed by the speed of the oilers.

The fleet always disengaged from the tanker group at night. Fuelling proceeded with constant interruptions and delays caused by defective state and shortcomings of the tankers' fuelling gear, until 1430 on 30th March, when Task Force returned to the operating area.

87. Second Series of Strikes, March 31st-April 2nd; The First Air Attack

C.A.Ps. and A.S.Ps. were part of the normal daily flying programme, though the latter were dispensed with after April 7th. Before the first fighter sweep was sent off, the cruiser *Argonaut* and destroyer *Wager* were detached in a position 300° 30 miles from the Fleet centre to act as radar pickets to prevent enemy aircraft from returning with British strikes.

At 0630 on 31st March a fighter sweep was sent in from a flying-off position 23° 10′ N., 125° 23′ E., and thereafter fighter patrols were maintained over Ishigaki and Miyako. Two bomber strikes were sent against Ishigaki airfield, installations and barracks, and at dusk the Fleet disengaged to the south-westward.

The *Argonaut* and *Wager* opened out to their picket positions next morning, 1st April, before the fighter sweep was sent in at 0640 from a flying-off position 23° 26′ N., 125° 25′ E. Ten minutes later enemy aircraft were detected by radar 75 miles to the westward, height 8,000 feet, closing at 210 knots. The fighter sweep was recalled to intercept, and additional fighters were flown off. The raid split up more than 40 miles from the Fleet, and four of the enemy were shot down, but some of the attackers penetrated to the ships.

At 0727 an enemy aircraft dived into the base of the *Indefatigable*'s island, killing and wounding a number of officers and men. The flight deck was put temporarily out of action, but within a very short time aircraft were again being operated from the ship, although on a reduced scale for the rest of the day. At about 0755 the *Ulster* was near missed by a bomb, her engine-room and the after boiler-room were flooded, and when the raid was over the *Gambia* took her in tow for Leyte.

At 1215 a bombing strike was sent against airfields and runways at Ishigaki. Reports received at 1430 from combat patrols over the islands showed that more aircraft had been sighted there and at Hirara. A fighter sweep was sent to reinforce the fighter patrols and about 14 enemy aircraft were destroyed on the ground.

Two enemy aircraft penetrated to the fleet soon after 1730, pursued by friendly fighters right on to the ships' guns. One dived on to the *Victorious*, which avoided it by using its helm, so that the enemy's wing only grazed the flight deck's edge; the aircraft spun harmlessly into the sea where its bomb exploded clear of the ship and blew the manuscript instructions to the pilot, giving priority of targets for suicide aircraft, on board the *Victorious*.

It was evident that the Japanese had commenced using the Sakishima airfields, and it was therefore decided to cancel the bombardment planned for 2nd April in favour of air operations, a more profitable means of destroying aircraft staging through or operating from an airfield. Patrols were flown off by moonlight early that morning and sent over the airfields as it was thought likely that the enemy might be leaving at first light; but no activity was reported from Ishigaki, and the two aircraft destined for Miyako were unable to proceed on account of radio failures.

At 1045 the Fleet withdrew to refuel in position Mosquito One, 19° 37 'N., 124° 42' E., but it was not until 0730 on the 4th that the weather moderated sufficiently to enable fuelling to commence. At 1930 on the 5th, when the Fleet disengaged from the Tanker Group and set course for the operational area again in order to relieve the American fast carrier group which had assumed the duty of neutralizing Sakishima Gunto in their absence, the two battleships were nearly 50 per cent short of their full stowage and aircraft carriers had been able to embark only enough Avgas for the forthcoming two days' operation.

88. Third Series of Strikes, 6th-7th April

C.A.Ps. flown off at 0635 on 6th April from position 23° 16' N., 125° 36' E. to cover Ishigaki and Miyako, reported the craters at the latter airfield filled in. The day's air operations included bombing raids on Hirara runway and town, and Nobara, Sukama and Miyara airstrips; and fighter attacks on radio and radar stations and junks.

A small Japanese air raid at about 1700 was preceded by enemy jamming of British fighter direction frequencies which disorganized the fighter defence to some extent. Two of the enemy reached the destroyer screen and one penetrated to the *Illustrious,* which took violent avoiding action and received only slight damage when a suicider's wing tip hit her island and the aircraft spun into the sea. Gunfire of the fleet unfortunately shot down one of our own Seafires.

Meanwhile, heavy attacks had been taking place on the Americans at Okinawa. It was thought that some enemy aircraft had probably passed north of the Sakishima Gunto to join in these attacks, but no use was made of the Sakishima airfields.

Already during the forenoon of the 6th American intelligence pointed to strong enemy reaction against the invaders of Okinawa, and Vice-Admiral Rawlings again cancelled the bombardment of Ishigaki, planned for the afternoon of the 7th, in favour of air operations only, a decision also influenced by cloud over the island. The plan was to maintain a constant C.A.P. over the enemy airfields during daylight, bombing and strafing any targets offered. The bomb craters on Ishigaki had been filled in, and Hirara and Nobara airfields appeared serviceable. Consequently, three bomber strikes were sent in during the day, and successfully re-cratered the airfields. By the end of the day all runways in the islands were unserviceable.

During the 8th and 9th April, Task Force 57 fuelled in an American area known as Cootie One, in 21° 12′ N., 128° 44′ E., which was closer to the British operating area than Midge or Mosquito. H.M.C.S. *Uganda* and the destroyers *Urchin* and *Ursa* joined as reinforcements and the *Whelp* was despatched to Leyte with defects.

89. Strikes on Formosa, April 12th-13th; Poor Co-Operation from South-West Pacific

By this time British pilots and aircraft alike were beginning to show signs of strain. The extended operational periods, too, brought considerable strain on the maintenance and handling personnel, which in numbers could not compare with the great American crews.

The programme envisaged Task Force 57 carrying out final strikes on Sakishima on 10th and 11th April, before returning to Leyte for a short spell of replenishment and rehabilitation. These plans, however, had to be altered in order to deal with troublesome air attacks from Formosa, the enemy's strongest and best developed permanent base south of Japan itself. Although the number of enemy aircraft based there was comparatively small, they were more skilfully handled than those from Kyushu, and had been responsible for much of the damage to ships at Okinawa.[143]

On the forenoon of the 9th April, therefore, Admiral Spruance obtained from the Commander-in-Chief Pacific, approval for the British Fleet to raid Shinchiku and Matsuyama airfields, in the northern part of Formosa on 11th-12th April, whilst the South-West Pacific air forces struck the southern airfields simultaneously, the neutralization of Sakishima being maintained by Task Group 52 which had assumed the duty on 8th April whilst Task Force 57 fuelled. On account, however, of intermittently adverse weather and other reasons, the requests by Admiral Nimitz and the Commander 5th Fleet for heavy strikes on Formosa by South-West Pacific Aircraft evoked, during the month of April, only 1,636 out of a total of 25,239 sorties by the land-based air forces in the South-West Pacific Areas.

The Formosa operation involved the maximum strength of the Task Force and 50 miles flying over enemy country. The operation was named "Iceberg Oolong". The final plan was to strike Matsuyama

143 "They have scored perhaps five times more hits than their Kyushu compatriots." (*Operation "Iceberg" B.P.F.L.O., Com. Fifth Fleet's Second Report*, para 31.

airfield from a dawn flying-off position 23° 58.5′ N., 122° 46 ′E., retiring to the south-east after the strike returned. A similar strike was planned for the morning of the 12th on Shinchiku, after which the Fleet would return to the oiling area. Both strikes were to be with the maximum available aircraft, and as the Fleet would be operating some 50 miles from Formosa, a C.A.P. of 20 was put in place of the normal 16. The Japanese attacks usually came in at heights between 25,000 ft. and sea level, and as the available instruments were not sufficiently accurate to determine height the combat air patrol was staggered at four different heights 20,000, 10,000, 6,000 and 3,000 ft.

To obviate the Task Force remaining close to Formosa after strikes the Americans provided aircraft for air-sea rescue, the fighter escort being British. American submarines had also carried out rescue work for the British Fleet since March 27th, when the Kingfisher [floatplane] was detailed.

As the weather on April 11th proved unsuitable, with cloud base about 1,000 ft. and intermittent rain and drizzle, the operation was postponed 24 hours. It improved considerably during the night, and at 0715 on the 12th the main strikes for Shinchiku and Matsuyama respectively, each consisting of 24 bombers and 20 fighters, were flown off from position 23° 58.5′ N., 122° 46′ E., and proceeded in company around the coast, cloud preventing either strike from crossing the mountains. At Shinchiku the bombers encountered flak but, no airborne opposition.

On account of cloud over Matsuyama the other strike attacked their alternative target, Kiirun harbour, where hits were made on the chemical plant, dock area and shipping. In the evening, the enemy made a sortie from Ishigaki. It was intercepted by fighters and failed to reach the fleet, eight of the enemy being shot down.

Signals showed Vice-Admiral Rawlings that the Japanese were making very heavy air attacks on the American forces in the Okinawa area and that Formosa-based aircraft were taking part.

He therefore decided that Task Force 57 must remain for a further period, for even if it could do little more than occasionally strike at the Sakishima Gunto it would at least provide an alternative target for the enemy. The morning of the 13th opened with an ineffective attack by four enemy aircraft, one of which dive bombed but missed the *Indomitable*. Matsuyama airfield was successfully bombed, though few aircraft were seen on the field. Another force of Avengers bombed Shinchiku airfield, and the fighter C.A.P. for the Air-Sea Rescue service destroyed a suspected radar station on Yanakuni Shima in the Sakishima Gunto.

90. Fifth Series of Strikes, April 16th-17th

The next two days were spent by Task Force 57 in fuelling and replenishing in position Cootie One (21° 12′ N. 128° 44′ E.). *Formidable* joined on the 14th to relieve the *Illustrious* whose structural defects, the legacy of past underwater damage, were beginning to increase, moreover, her Corsair squadrons were overdue for relief and her pilots were showing signs of operational fatigue. She left for Leyte on April 14th, escorted by the *Urania* and *Quality*. The change left the number of complement Corsairs unaltered, but increased the Avenger bombers by three. Owing to shortage of fighter aircraft no picket cruiser was stationed on the 16th.

The first strike took off at 0630 in position 23° 28 'N., 125° 18′ E. to attack the Ishigaki airfields, and another was flown off at 1230. All runways at Ishigaki were left unserviceable. At Miyako the craters were found to have been filled in and every endeavour made to keep the airfields serviceable. Two attacks put all the airfields on the island out of action. Some unlocated fast-moving bogeys during the day were believed possibly to have been piloted flying bombs launched so far away that they failed to reach the fleet.

In view of the apparent success of the day's operations the number of bombers in the main strikes on 17th April was reduced. Ishigaki was not attacked as no attempt had been made to repair its airfields. Considerable effort had been made to fill in the runway craters at Miyako, and three strikes were sent there, the first two of which left all the airfields unserviceable and the third attacked municipal buildings and barracks.

91. Final Strikes of First Part of "Iceberg", 20th April

Straining his resources to the limit, Vice-Admiral Rawlings had offered to Admiral Spruance to make final strikes on 20th April, an offer which Admiral Nimitz warmly appreciated. The fleet fuelled on the 18th in Mosquito area, but a second day in the replenishing area was necessary in order to rest aircrews and carry out maintenance work on aircraft. Captain D. 7 in the *Napier*, with the *Norman* and *Nepal*, joined Task Force 57 on the 18th.

The plan for the day followed generally the pattern of previous strikes. Four bomber strikes were sent in from a position about 23° 33′ N., 125 ° 02′ E. They found that on both Ishigaki and Miyako Islands most of the craters on the runways had been filled in. By the end of the day all runways were unserviceable, with the exception of those at Hirara on Miyako, which were only partially cratered. Two strikes were also made on coastal shipping and ground installations by rocket firing Fireflies. At 1910 the Fleet set course for Leyte, where it anchored in San Pedro Roads on April 23rd, 32 days out from Ulithi. No British fleet in history had kept the sea for so long under conditions of continuous offensive operations. This ended the first part of the operation by the British Pacific Fleet in the Ryukus.

92. Comment on the First Part of the Operation

From the beginning it was apparent that however thoroughly the airfields were neutralized by day, the enemy was determined and able to effect repair by night. The lack of night intruders was keenly felt as it was evident that intermittent night attacks on the airfields would have slowed down the enemy repair parties. There was also a need for night fighters to counter dusk and night shadowing of the Fleet. Night missions during this period were flown by the *Indomitable*'s Hellcats, which were dependent on moonlight.

The enemy flak positions on Miyako remained unsubdued to the last and continued to inflict casualties on the British aircraft. The high explosive bombs with which the fleet was provided proved unsuitable for their reduction.

The unsuitability of the *Indefatigable*'s Seafires, which constituted more than a quarter of the total number of fighters in the Task Force, became more apparent every day. Only five replacements were received by the *Indefatigable* for 25 Seafires lost or damaged beyond repair; and several more aircraft remained unserviceable for a time owing to lack of spares. The accident rate was such that, although no losses were suffered in action, the numbers available for flying in the later stages of the operation were less than one-third of the standard load; and for one reason or another, about one-third of these failed to leave the deck.

On the other hand, in the second part of the operation there was a remarkable increase in Seafire effort, the proportion of sorties per complement aircraft per strike day being actually higher than any other aircraft. The rate of landing accidents decreased from 7.0 per 100 in Part I of the operation to 1.9 in Part 2.[144]

The scale of effort by the Hellcats, 1.22 sorties per complement aircraft per strike day throughout the period, and the scale for the Corsairs, only slightly lower, were comparable with standard American carrier flying effort. The Avengers, with the exception of the *Formidable*'s, were relatively under- employed, not on account of unserviceability, as with the Seafires, but because of a lack of suitable targets for them to attack.

---

[144] The matter is analysed by F.O.N.A.P. in his report dated 28th June 1945. Para 8; (*The British Pacific Fleet in Operation "Iceberg" May 1st-30th*).

93. Short Replenishment at Leyte, 23rd April-1st May

Task Force 57 had just made British naval history by operating off the enemy's coast in face of continual attack for a period of 32 days. American task groups, with their mastery of the technique of replenishing at sea, did the same thing for twice as long. But with its few slow small tankers and inadequate Fleet Train the British Pacific Fleet had now exhausted its effort for the time being, and a period for replenishment and reliefs was essential before it could again take its part in the operation.

It was unfortunate that when the operation began no less than three Fighter Wings[145] in the Fleet Carrier Squadron were near, at, or beyond the end of an operational tour of accepted limits. All the original members of those wings were operationally fatigued and had now to be relieved, and consequently the second part of the operation began without any of the most experienced pilots.

During the operations, moreover, an added strain had been imposed on pilots flying American-type fighters owing to the necessity for their undertaking duty which should have been done by the British Seafires that proved so unsuitable, since there was, of course, a minimum below which it was not possible to reduce the number of fighter sorties necessary to a 13-hour striking day. In the final strikes on April 20th, for instance, the planned sorties were:- Seafires (one ship), 16 sorties of 2 hours; Corsairs, per ship, 40 sorties of 3½ hours each. The Seafires could do no more.

Leyte, though superior in climatic conditions to Manus, was far from an ideal spot for the rehabilitation of aircrews:

> It is feared that the period at Leyte will not produce all the restoration of stamina and morale that might be expected by the flying world of 6-7 days' stand-off, since the ship will be miles from the shore with virtually no boats and living conditions on board, as in all British Fleet Carriers, are pretty grim for the young aircrews still unaccustomed, and imperfectly conditioned, to ship life ... a change of air in a camp or station anywhere on shore would be a valuable restorative.[146]

The replenishment of the Fleet commenced on the afternoon of arrival at Leyte, and continued throughout the week, aided by favourable weather. There was little time for rest or relaxation. Owing to the lack of local facilities and the work in hand, few harbour exercises were carried out. Precautions were taken against possible attack by midget

145 Nos. 15, 47 and 5.

146 C.O.H.M.S. *Victorious, Report,* (Operation "Iceberg", Enclosure No.8).

submarines, explosive motorboats, and suicide swimmers, but no attack developed and no air raids were experienced.

The future employment of Task Force 57 was under consideration, and there was a question of its withdrawal from Operation "Iceberg" and engagement off Borneo, where a landing by the Australians at Tarakan was planned for 1st May. On 28th April, however, the Commander-in-Chief Pacific Fleet, ordered Task Force 57 to continue with the Ryukus operation, its role as before being the neutralization of airfields in the Sakishima Gunto. Operations were planned by Vice-Admiral Rawlings for a cycle of two days of strikes followed by two for replenishment, commencing on 4th and 5th May.

By the evening of 30th April the replenishment of the Fleet was complete. A Tanker Group, to top up the Fleet on their passage north to the operating area, sailed from Leyte at 0700 that day.

94. Second Part of "Iceberg"; Opening Air Strikes, 4th May

When Task Force 57 sailed from Leyte at 0630 on 1st May there were a few changes in the organization. The *Formidable* had replaced the *Illustrious*. The *Argonaut* had left the 4th Cruiser Squadron to refit; but the *Euryalus*, which had carried the flag of Rear-Admiral J.H. Edelsten (R.A. (D)), temporarily, had joined the cruisers, which had been reinforced by H.M.C.S. *Uganda*. The composition of the 25th, 4th and 27th Destroyers Flotillas had changed. The *Ursa* and *Urchin* were now with the 25th DF whilst the *Ulster* remained at Leyte for temporary bomb damage repairs to fit her to proceed to another port for major repairs. The *Quilliam* had taken over the 4th DF, and the *Kempenfelt*, *Whirlwind* and *Wessex* had returned from Task Force 112 to replace the *Wager* and *Whelp* which were to refit at Sydney.

On 3rd May the cruisers and destroyers refuelled from the Logistic Support Group in position Mosquito One, 19° 37′ N., 124° 42′ E., and at 1530 the Fleet left for the operating area.

The plan for the opening of operations was as follows:

(a) To render airfields of the Sakishima Gunto unserviceable by bombing runways and air installations.
(b) To conduct an offensive against flak positions and to assist in cratering runways by ship bombardment.
(c) To maintain an offensive C.A.P. over the islands.

The particular plan for the first day was for the bombardment of Miyako airfields and flak positions at about noon, from medium range.

The Carrier Force would remain some 30 miles to the southward, so that their radar would not be fouled by land.

A combat air patrol was flown off at 0540 on 4th May in position 23° 44′ N., 125° 11′ E. Ten minutes later enemy air activity was detected near Sakishima, the general trend of traffic being easterly. One small group approached the fleet, but only one Zeke was shot down. Another enemy aircraft approached at 0827, but was never detected visually. Bomber strikes were flown off at 0605 for Miyako and at 0815 for Ishigaki. At the former, repair work on the airfields had apparently been proceeding by night, whilst Task Force 52 had been carrying out day strikes in the absence of the British carriers.

All A.A. batteries opened fire on our aircraft. Runways at Hirara were well bombed and a direct hit was seen on an A.A. position. On Ishigaki one runway of Miyara airfield found serviceable was left well cratered. Life saving aircraft were provided by C.T.F. 51 (Joint Expeditionary Force) from 0800 to 1700 and were stationed between the target and the carrier force.

95. Bombardment of Miyako, 4th May

Vice-Admiral Rawlings decided to carry out the bombardment although the Fleet had been sighted, for this had happened several times before without being followed by any attack on the ships. Bombardment was considered necessary to reduce A.A. fire ashore, although it was not easy for ships to knock out enemy flak positions, without previous practice and liberal expansion of ammunition. But the Vice-Admiral considered that the effect on morale would be most beneficial, as many men of the ships' companies were young and untried, and there was a tendency for the personnel of ships other than the carriers to become stale. Conditions near the target had been reported excellent.

At 1000 the bombarding force parted from the carriers in position 23° 54′ N., 125° 10′ E., and closed Miyako at 24 knots. The carriers provided an additional C.A.P. for this force as well as aircraft for spotting. The bombarding force passed through position 24° 33.5′ N., 125° 10′ E., at 1155, on the bombarding course 070° at 15 knots. The *King George V* and *Howe* were in open order line ahead, screened by the 25th Destroyer Flotilla and by the *Euryalus* and *Black Prince* who occupied the two port, i.e. inshore, positions on the screen. The *Swiftsure, Gambia,* and *Uganda* in open order line ahead were stationed 270° 3 miles, i.e., fine off the port quarter of the Fleet Flagship.

Fire was opened at 1205. The *Euryalus* and *Black Prince* carried out a simultaneous "air burst" shoot, the former using V.T. fuses, on the A.A. defence area of Nobara airfield. *King George V* and *Howe* bombarded Hirara airfield and the A.A. defence area to the north of the airfield, respectively. On completion of the "air burst" shoot the *Swiftsure* and the *Gambia* bombarded Nobara airfield and the *Uganda* Sukuma airstrip.

Gambia bombarded Nobara airfield and the Uganda Sukuma airstrip. Ammunition expenditure and mean ranges were as follows: 14-inch H.E. 195 rounds 25,000 yards; 6-inch H.E. 598 rounds 18,000 yards; and 5.25-inch H.E. 378 rounds 17,000 yards.

In general, control procedure and spotting were good, but in some cases were marred by bad communications. There was no opposition from the shore. Photographs showed the runways at Nobara and Sukama heavily hit and that all rounds from the *Howe* fell in the target area, but no photographs were obtained to show results by the *King George V*.

Meanwhile, during the absence of the heavy ships the carriers had been under air attack. Accordingly. Vice-Admiral Rawlings expedited the latter part of the bombardment, finally ending it a little earlier than planned: his force turned to the southward at 1247 and closed the carriers at 25 knots.

96. Air Attack on the Carriers, 4th May and Strikes, 5th May

Meanwhile, at about 1100, an hour after the departure of the Bombarding Force, three small groups of enemy aircraft, shortly followed by a fourth, were detected by the carrier force to the westward. Apparently, 16 to 20 enemy aircraft were employed with some acting as decoys. Fighters engaged one group working round to the southward, but one Kamikaze group penetrated to the carriers and was first detected when an aircraft was seen diving on the Force.

This group escaped earlier detection either because, in the absence of the bombarding force too many of the reduced number of radar sets were fully engaged in tracking the diversionary aircraft, and too few acting as warning sets, or because the enemy made a very low approach followed by a very high climb at about 15 miles range.

There were no enemy on the screen within 20 miles when at 1131 a Zeke was seen diving from a great height on to the *Formidable* and was taken under fire. Rear-Admiral Vian thereupon manoeuvred his force at high speed by successive emergency turns. The suicide aircraft was reported hit by the *Formidable*'s close-range weapons, nevertheless it crashed into the ship's flight deck near the island structure, and started a large fire in the deck park of aircraft. It appeared to release its bomb just before hitting the deck.

Casualties were 8 killed and 47 wounded, and 11 aircraft were damaged beyond repair. The flight deck was holed and badly dented over an area of 16 square feet and 2 feet deep in the centre, and other damage was caused, including slight loss of steam from an armoured deck splinter which passed through the centre boiler room and pierced the inner bottom. Nevertheless, by 1254, an hour and 23 minutes later, the ship was capable of making 24 knots, and by 1700 she was again flying on aircraft.

Three minutes after the attack a Zeke was taken under fire, and after disappearing temporarily in cloud, dived at an angle of 60° on the *Indomitable*, which was turning under full helm. Although heavily engaged by close-range weapons and set on fire it flattened out at the last moment, landed on the flight deck, bounced over the side, and its bomb appeared to explode under water, doing no damage except to the ship's radar.

At 1142 another Zeke dived steeply on the *Indomitable*, hit hard and often by her close-range weapons and those of the *Quality*, the aircraft burst into flames and crashed harmlessly into the sea 10 yards off the *Indomitable*'s starboard bow. The *Indomitable* and *Indefatigable* each shot down another attacker soon after midday.

By 1420 the Bombarding Force was close to the carriers, and the Fleet reformed in Cruising Disposition 5B at 1450. During the afternoon several enemy aircraft were shot down, but it was not until 1720, whilst the Fleet was withdrawing to the south-eastward for the night, that the development of another attack became evident. This was broken up very satisfactorily by our fighters. Fourteen enemy aircraft were destroyed in the air, 11 by fighters and three by gunfire, including those which struck the *Indomitable* and *Formidable*.

At 0120 on 5th May repairs to the *Formidable*'s centre boiler room were complete and the ship was once more capable of full speed. Miyako and Ishigaki were well bombed during the day and all left unserviceable. No flak was encountered over Miyako, a welcome, even if temporary, change for the airmen, due, undoubtedly, to the previous day's bombardment. A reconnaissance aircraft detected about 0730 was finally shot down from 30,000 feet at 0920 after a 300-mile chase by Corsairs of the *Formidable* operating from the *Victorious*.

97. Second Series of Strikes, 8th-9th May, *Victorious* and *Formidable* Hit

Whilst Task Force 57 fuelled on 6th and 7th May, U.S. Task Group 52.1 covered Sakishima. The *Formidable*'s repairs were completed by the 7th and at 1400 the fleet sailed for the operations area.

Four bomber strikes were flown off on 9th May, two to each island, the first being launched at 0830 in position 23° 40′ N., 125° 34′ E. All runways were re-cratered.

At 1145 the fleet was sighted by an enemy aircraft which escaped. Five hours later, 4 enemy aircraft approached the fleet, aided by decoys which drew off the British fighters, and at 1651 a suicider made a 10° angle dive on the *Victorious*. Although hard hit by close-range weapons, it crashed on to the flight deck near the forward lift, and its bomb detonated. The resulting fire was quickly brought under control, but the explosion had holed the flight deck and damaged one lift motor.

Another suicider made a shallow power glide on the *Victorious* from astern at 1656. Though hard hit by gunfire, as well as on fire, it struck the flight deck a glancing blow, and burning furiously passed over the side, damaging four Corsairs beyond repair but doing little other harm.

A third suicider made a pass at the *Victorious* a minute later, but shifted target to the *Howe* further ahead, and approached her from the starboard quarter in a long shallow dive. This time the attacker was hit at a longer range and continued to be hit until it crashed in flames 100 yards from the *Howe* after passing over her quarter-deck.

At 1705 a fourth aircraft approached the *Formidabl*e and *Indomitable* in turn. Both ships engaged it without apparent result, it then turned and dived into the after deck park of the *Formidable*. A large explosion and fire followed, but fortunately little structural damage was caused, though no less than 18 aircraft were put out of action.

By 1755 the *Formidable* was once more fit to land-on aircraft, though she had only four bombers and 11 fighters serviceable. The *Victorious* could operate a few aircraft at a time, but the damage to her lift seriously reduced her speed of handling, and in addition she had only 28 fighters available. At 1950 therefore, Vice-Admiral Rawlings withdrew towards area Cootie, and Task Group 52.1, which covered Sakishima on days when Task Force 57 was absent, had once more to alter its programme.

98. Third Series of Strikes, 12th-13th May; Change of Launching Position

When Task Force 57 resumed action on 12th May, the launching position was moved further eastward, on the assumption that the enemy might be fixing the position of the force in daylight by shore radar on the C.A.P. The change proved effective, and after it was made no further attacks of a serious nature were made on the task force.

The low approach adopted by the enemy suiciders in lieu of their previous practice of a high approach greatly reduced the warning period and rendered fighter interception much more difficult. To overcome this, measures were taken, including the stationing of two radar pickets, each consisting of a 6-inch cruiser and a destroyer, 12 miles north-west and south-westward of the fleet, in order to increase the range of detection.

Two fighters were allocated to each picket, and additional fighters would be sent to the threatened sector at first contact with the enemy. The 5.25-inch cruisers were brought in from the screen and stationed with the main body of the fleet to increase A.A. protection for the carriers in the operation area. A destroyer was stationed astern of each carrier to afford more gun protection in what appeared to be the enemy's favourite position for attacking carriers.

Finally, a new cruising disposition 5F designed to increase mutual gun support was now given a trial, the carriers being brought in to the 2,000-yard circle, the battleships and cruisers stationed 2,000 yards

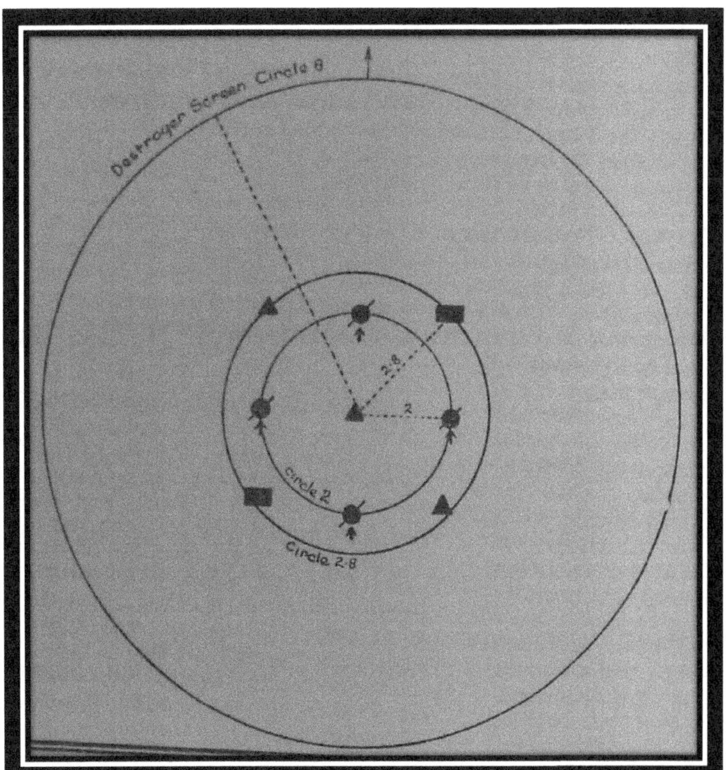

Cruising Disposition 5F

from adjacent carriers, and the destroyers on circle 8. No opportunity occurred to test the efficacy of this formation since no further enemy air attacks were experienced during the remainder of the operation period.

Four bomber strikes were flown off during the 12th May, the first at 0540, 12 minutes before sunrise, in 23° 40′ N., 126° 51′ E. One attacked Ishigaki and three Miyako; a second strike planned for Ishigaki was cancelled owing to bad weather. However, the runways of Miyara and Ishigaki, on Ishigaki Island, which were found to have been rendered serviceable, were again put out of action and A.A. and dispersal areas were strafed. Miyako, one runway at Hirara and both at Nobara, found to be serviceable, were put out of action by the first strike. Subsequent strikes attacked A.A. positions and installations, a direct hit being made on a 4-inch A.A. battery. The radar pickets re-joined at 1915. At 1930 the dusk C.A.P. was landed on and the Fleet withdrew to the southward for the night.

On 13th May three bomber strikes were again flown to Miyako and one to Ishigaki. At the former, all runways were left unserviceable: a new revetted dispersal area was discovered at Hirara. At Ishigaki, installations were hit and a radio station was left in flames.

Task Force 57 fuelled in area Cootie and transferred stores and aircraft on 14th and 15th May. The Fleet was due to replenish in the rear bases early in June in readiness to resume operations in July and in order that the slow tankers and repair ships of the Fleet Train, based at Leyte, might reach their new stations in time to meet the Fleet it was decided to conclude the current operations on 25th May.

99. Task Force 57 Operates Under Handicaps, 16th to 21st May

On 16th May three bomb strikes on Miyako, and two on Ishigaki from the new launching position, rendered all runways unserviceable.

Very light winds handicapped operations next day. Defects to the *Indomitable* made high speeds most undesirable, and damage to the *Victorious* caused by deck crashes necessitated 20 of her aircraft being accommodated in other carriers. Three strikes were made, two on Miyako and one on Ishigaki, and all airfields except possibly Miyara, were left unserviceable. Ohama and Hirara towns were also bombed.

Whilst fuelling and exchanging aircraft and stores in Area Cootie on 18th May the *Formidable* suffered a serious fire when a Corsair in the hangar accidentally fired her guns into an Avenger, which exploded. About 30 aircraft were destroyed or damaged.

By evening, however, the ship was capable of operating once more, with emergency lighting in her hangar, and it was decided she should continue in operation, her damaged aircraft being replaced as far as possible. The work of replacement next day was seriously upset by the weather.

Soon after reaching the flying-off position on the 20th May, Task Force 57 ran into dense fog. At 0524 the destroyer *Quilliam*, endeavouring to form astern of the *Indomitable*, collided with her. Little damage was done to the carrier, but the *Quilliam*'s bow was wrecked and she was taken in tow for the fuelling area by the *Norman*, with the *Black Prince* as escort.

A slight improvement in the weather at 0745 enabled one strike to be flown off. This strike had great difficulty in finding Miyako island, where Hirana town was bombed and ground installations were attacked with rockets. The next two strikes were cancelled on account of the weather. In view, however, of a signal from C.T.F. 51 at 0725Z on the 19th May, stressing the importance of evening strikes on Sakishima in order to reduce the weight of dusk and moonlight attacks on Okinawa, an attempt was made to carry out strike D. This was flown off at 1530 for Ishigaki, but the weather was so bad that it had to be recalled to the fleet.

C.T.G. 99.2 had indicated on the 19th his intention of striking Miyako with shore-based aircraft from Okinawa at 1700 on the 20th. Consequently Rear-Admiral Vian withdrew his C.A.Ps. from that island by 1600, but C.T.G. 99.2 cancelled his strike, presumably on account of the weather.

Five bomber strikes were sent off next day (21st May) to Miyako at 0655, 1210 and 1610; and to Ishigaki at 0835 and 1440. The runways at Nobara and Hirara were well plastered with bombs, both runways at Ishigaki airfield were left unserviceable and Miyara airfield was hit, though low cloud varying between 7/10ths and 9/10ths made bombing difficult at both islands.

100. The Final Strikes, 24th 25th May

On the 22nd the *Formidable* was detached from the Fleet in the fuelling area, and proceeded to Sydney via Manus, to expedite repairs in order to ensure that four carriers would be available for subsequent operations.

Task Force 57 sailed for the operations area next evening with only three carriers in company. It had been hoped to bombard Miyako on the 24th, but with the reduced number of aircraft Vice-Admiral Rawlings judged it wiser to forego this in favour of an entirely air effort. Four strikes were planned for each day, 24th and 25th May, the first to be flown off two hours later than usual in order to provide the late afternoon strikes desired by C.T.F. 51. Bad weather, however, reduced the strikes to three.

Strikes on Miyako were flown off at 1045 and 1515. Cloud over the target was 10/10ths at 6,000 to 9,000. Nobara runways were left unserviceable, Hirara runways were hit, and other damage was caused, The Ishigaki strike took off at 1245 and all runways at Ishigaki airfield were left unserviceable.

The unfavourable dawn weather cleared earlier than usual next day, 25th May, and the first strike to Miyako was flown off at 0600 in 23° 40′ N., 126° 32′ E., further strikes being sent at 1115 and 1400. The Nobara runways were left unserviceable and 14 hits were made on Hirara runways, but low cloud prevented the results of the last strike from being seen. At Ishigaki, eight hits were made on each of the main runways of Ishigaki and Miyara airfields. A new airstrip was seen under construction near Hegina airfield. The returning strike from Ishigaki made contact with the U.S. lifesaving submarine, *Bluefish,* which reported that on the previous night, observing lights on Ishigaki airfield, she carried out a bombardment.

At 2200 Vice-Admiral Rawlings set course for Guam in the *King George V* with the *Troubridge, Tenacious* and *Termagant* in company. The remainder of the Fleet, under the command of Rear-Admiral Vian, set course for Area Cootie to refuel en route for Manus, where they were to disperse to their rear bases for major storing.

This concluded the part played by the British forces in the Ryukus operation, for during their major storing period organized enemy resistance at Okinawa was declared at an end, and the next assignment of the British Pacific Fleet was against the Japanese homeland.

101. Comment on Operation "Iceberg"

The fact that Vice-Admiral Rawlings had no opportunity of personal conference with Admiral Spruance before Operation "Iceberg" did not prevent satisfactory co-operation. Two days after the conclusion of participation in the Ryukus operation by the British Pacific Fleet, Admiral Spruance relinquished the command of the United States Fifth Fleet he made a signal expressing his thanks to Task Force 57 for their work[147]and in his report he stated:

147 "To C.T.F. 57. Info. C. in C.B.P.F. CincPacAdv, Fifth Fleet from Com. Fifth Fleet. On completion of your two months' operations as a Task Force of the Fifth Fleet in support of the capture of Okinawa, I wish to express to you and to the officers and men under your command, my appreciation of the fine work you have done and the splendid spirit of co-operation with which you have done it. To the American portion of the Fifth Fleet, Task Force 57 has typified the great traditions of the Royal Navy. Signed Spruance. D.T.G. 270948Z May."

> The operations of the British Carrier Force (TF 57) were carried out with commendable initiative and reflected credit on the British person concerned and their leadership. Between 20th March and 25th May, T.F. 57 carried out twenty-two days of strikes against Sakishima Gunto and two days against Formosa airfields. Complete neutralization of Sakishima Gunto airfields by this means was not to be expected, but the efforts of the British Carrier Force in that direction unquestionably greatly reduced the magnitude of enemy attacks upon our forces in the Okinawa area by aircraft from or staging through Sakishima Gunto, thereby reducing our losses or damage and contributing materially to our success. T.F. 57 was handicapped by their lack of night fighters, the relatively small number of planes on board their carriers as compared to U.S. large carriers, and by the shorter endurance of their ships and certain of their planes (Spitfire [sic] and Firefly). They gained experience in sustained operations and American carrier task force methods and tactics and are considered ready to undertake operations with our Fast Carrier Force.[148]

Over the whole period Task Force 57 was at sea for 62 days, broken by eight days' re-storing at Leyte. During this time the carriers flew 4,001 sorties,[149] dropped 127 tons of bombs and fired 950 rocket projectiles, destroyed 100 enemy aircraft and damaged 70 more. Shipping, W/T stations, etc., were also attacked, six small ships being sunk and 180 or more probably sunk or damaged.[150] British aircraft losses totalled 160, including 20 shot down in combat and 72 destroyed operationally.[151]

Various other targets such as suicide attacks accounted for 32, and 30 were lost in the *Formidable*'s hangar fire. Deck landing crashes were responsible for the loss of 61 aircraft, a higher total than that caused by the efforts of the enemy. Flying casualties numbered 41 killed and missing, non-flying casualties 44 killed and 83 wounded.

The decisive factor governing the ability of the Task Force to continue operations was the armour of the carriers. Four fleet carriers were hit by suiciders, one, the *Formidable*, twice; but all four remained operational, three at full strength. During the same period, four American fast carriers were similarly hit, one of them twice; all

148 *Action Report, Rynkus Operation through 27th May, 1945*, VI-A-2.

149 Exclusive of sorties flown on non-strike days. The figures give 4,893 sorties on strike days out of a total of 5,335 sorties on strike and non-strike days together, though another table gives 4,152 and 5,335 respectively. It is not clear whether any of these figures includes sorties abortive due to early landings.

150 Operation "Iceberg", Second Phase, covering letter by Vice Admiral. 2nd i.c. B.P.F.

151 It has not been possible, however, to check any duplication of claims.

four had to be withdrawn from operations. The cost of the armoured deck, however, in terms of aircraft carried and speed of operation was enormous, and it did not prevent heavy destruction of aircraft which, from the immediate operational point of view, was one of the most serious results of suicide attacks.

In his report, the Commander Fifth Fleet remarked on the short endurance of the British ships. In the Pacific, however, distances were all so vast that practically no operations could be contemplated without Fleet attendant tankers, and Admiral Fraser reported that the low endurance of any particular unit, although it was as Admiral Spruance stated, a handicap, was not a limiting factor as had generally been the case in other areas in which ships were normally refuelled in harbour. The comparable figures for the American and British air efforts respectively throughout the Ryukus operation are not immediately available.[152]

Moreover, the conditions under which the two forces operated differed greatly. Nevertheless, some explanation must be attempted of the vast disparity in the totals of Japanese aircraft destroyed, namely 100 by the British Pacific Fleet though the U.S. Commander-in-Chief allows no more than 75 as against 1908 claimed by Task Force 58. Even if allowance is made for the fact that the participation of the American Carriers extended over 81 days against 34 by the British, and that the American Fast Carrier Force carried more than four times as many aircraft, namely 919 as against 218 in Task Force 57, it is clear that the number of enemy aircraft destroyed by the British Pacific Fleet was comparatively small.

The particular part played by Task Force 57, however, was one which offered little opportunity of inflicting high losses on the enemy. On the other hand, it must be borne in mind that much of the American effort was expended in direct support of the land forces and gave no return in enemy aircraft destroyed. The majority of the Japanese aircraft destroyed by the Americans were brought down in the air – two and a half times as many as were destroyed on the ground. In the British Pacific Fleet the numbers destroyed in each manner were equal.

The few air attacks on Task Force 57 never offered a group of enemy aircraft at which to fire. No massed attacks were made on the British

152 The British figures have been analysed in *Operational Research Reports by Fleet Operational Research Officer, B.P.F.* (First part of the operation) and *The British Pacific Fleet in Operation "Iceberg" – May 1st to 30th, 1945* (Second part of the operation). Comparable American figures are not forthcoming.

comparable, for example, with those on Task Force 58, the landing forces, and the shipping at Okinawa which the Task Force was defending on 6th April. On that occasion two task groups claimed to have brought down 248 of the enemy. Again, on the 12th April, fighters of Task Force 58 alone claimed 151, and on the 16th 155 were claimed to have been brought down in the air.[153]

The extent to which these massed attacks contributed to swell the figures of Japanese losses is clear from a comparison between the figures of the first part of the operation, when these attacks were of frequent occurrence, and the second part, when far fewer Japanese aircraft offered themselves to the Americans as targets. In the first period the ratio of enemy aircraft destroyed in the air to those destroyed on the ground was 3½ to 1; in the second part of the operation it was little more than 1¼ to 1.

Whilst there is no suggestion that British fighter pilots were less efficient than the American it is questionable whether the same can be said for the anti-aircraft armaments of the British ships. The armament of the latter had been designed primarily from an anti-ship point of view and it was said of our ships by the Americans, that generally speaking they were "not able to look after themselves". Suicide air attacks introduced new complications into the A.A. systems, particularly as this type of attack proved to be invulnerable to anything smaller than 40-mm. guns whereas the British Fleet was largely equipped with the 20-mm. gun which had proved effective against torpedo bombers. Only 2 per cent of the British sorties were offensive, compared with the American figure of 65 per cent.

The British figure was reduced by the high percentage of defensive sorties which had to be made by the fighters – 69 per cent and 76.3 per cent respectively in the two periods of Operation "Iceberg". It is, of course, a fact that fighter defensive effort is an "overhead cost" which does not appreciably change as the forces to be defended are decreased or increased; consequently, the greater the number of aircraft operating in any given force, the larger the proportion free to undertake offensive action.

It was a handicap that no cluster or fragmentation and incendiary bombs were available to the British for their attacks on airfields and dispersed aircraft.

---

153 C.T.G. 58.3 in his *Action Report*, pp.37-8, refers to the manner in which the score of enemy aircraft destroyed was run up on the days when large-scale attacks occurred.

Rather higher losses of aircraft were caused to the British force by suicide crashes than by Japanese anti-aircraft fire. In the American Fast Carrier Force gunfire accounted for the majority of the losses, due in part to the weather and low ceilings preventing high speeds over the target. Thirty-six aircraft fell or landed in the sea. Of the 64 airmen involved 41, ie. 64 per cent, were saved. Destroyers picked up 28, lifeguard submarines eight and Walrus and Mariner aircraft five.

Chapter XIII

THE FLEET TRAIN, BRITISH PACIFIC FLEET

One of the conditions on which Admiral Nimitz accepted the co-operation of the British Pacific Fleet in the operations against Okinawa, was that the Fleet should be self-supporting.

102. A Break with Tradition

The American logistic plan had been carefully worked out, and their bases had been assigned and their supplies estimated on the scale considered necessary to keep their fleet in operation at the intense rate envisaged, and no more. With the best will in the world, there was little to spare for an Ally, though, in fact, the U.S. Navy did help the British Pacific Fleet out of many a tight corner. The only recognized supply agreement with the Americans concerned oil fuel, and petroleum products, and W/T and radar stores. Such dockings as were necessary were also carried out by the U.S. Navy, since the British floating docks were on passage at the time of the operation.

The ability of the British to operate in the Pacific had, consequently, to depend upon an organization entirely new to the Royal Navy – the Fleet Train. Ever since the advent of steam, a British fleet had been accustomed to return to a shore base for replenishment of stores and ammunition: the Fleet Train had now been designed to enable it to keep the sea for periods comparable to those of sailing ship days, under conditions of ceaseless expenditure of fuel, ammunition, and supplies of every description.

With the shortage of shipping available to the British, both in quantity and appropriate kind, and the poor state of repair of several of the fleet auxiliaries and merchantmen selected, it was impossible to reach the standard of the ideal Fleet Train, but a series of ingenious improvisations and a high degree of co-operation with the fleet enabled the fleet train adequately to fulfil its function.

The unexpectedly rapid advance of the Americans into the Philippines had placed the advanced anchorage of the British Pacific Fleet at Leyte, rather more than twice as far ahead of its shore bases as had originally been contemplated. The British striking force had to operate approximately 3,500 miles ahead of its nearest Empire base. This naturally increased the number of ships required to keep the fleet supplied at the advanced anchorage. Australia in turn was 12,500 miles from the Fleet's home bases and was not extensively equipped with naval base facilities.

In planning the organization, the comparatively new American policy of replenishment at sea had not been provided for. Yet the British striking force, operating nearly 800 miles from its advanced anchorage, had to adopt this policy or content itself with no more than spasmodic raids.

103. Organization of the Fleet Train

The Fleet Train was under the command of Rear-Admiral D.B. Fisher, C.B., C.B.E., R.N., whose duties were defined as follows:

(a) Operations. The Rear-Admiral Fleet Train is responsible for the operation of the Fleet Train as a whole. He will transfer to the Operational Task Force Commanders the detailed operational control of the Fleet Train groups while employed on servicing their Task Forces at sea.

(b) Administration. The Rear-Admiral Fleet Train is responsible to the Commander-in-Chief for the administration of the ships of the Fleet Train.

(c) Logistics. The Rear-Admiral Fleet Train is responsible to the Vice-Admiral, Second-in-Command, British Pacific Fleet, for: (i) keeping the Fleet directly supplied. This includes the detailed logistic planning for each specific operation and the transport of supplies from the supply bases to the Fleet, in ships of the Fleet Train; (ii) the maintenance and repair of H.M. ships, auxiliaries, and aircraft (in accordance with the policy promulgated by the Flag Officer, Naval Air Stations (Australia)) of the Fleet within the capacity of the Fleet Train; (iii) arrangements for the evacuation of sick and wounded by sea; (iv) mails, distributing authorities, chart offices afloat; (v) amenities for the fleet; (vi) salvage and tugs.

Organization of the Fleet Train began on 1st January, 1945. At this date the organization of the British Pacific Fleet and the place of the Fleet Train in it were not known. It was thought that the fleet would commence operating in July, 1945.

There was no precedent on which to base the size and composition of its staff, and the staff actually provided proved to be about half that which was found to be necessary: a state of affairs due in part to the restricted accommodation on board the vessel selected as flagship, H.M.S. *Montclare*. Incidentally, none of the typists could type. Moreover, it was not visualized that the administration of bases and anchorages would devolve on the Rear-Admiral Fleet Train – an extensive and exacting duty which had been envisaged in R.A. (Q), who, however, never materialized in the forward area. Further, H.M.S. *Lothian*, employed as a temporary flagship, whilst the *Montclare* was delayed in England, had to function not only as the communication centre of the Fleet Train, but also as a Base W/T ship taking the place of a shore W/T transmitting station.

The short time available before the Fleet commenced operating apparently impeded thorough study of U.S. experience of logistic work, and it was perhaps inevitable under the circumstances that when the Fleet Train came functioning it did so under conditions of praiseworthy extemporization rather than planned efficiency.

As the result of practical experience, the Chief Staff Officer undertook general supervision and was responsible for operations and supply. The Maintenance Captain was responsible for repairs, personnel, and harbour administration. Responsibility for the development of bases was eventually transferred to the Vice-Admiral (Administration), Pacific Fleet.

104. The Ships

The Fleet Train was composed of various different classes of ships, of which the replenishment carriers and Store Issuing Ships (constituting the Logistic Support Groups) were capable of carrying out their functions whilst under way at sea. It included oilers; escort carriers for ferrying aircraft to the advanced base and for replenishing the Fleet Carriers at sea; armament store issuing ships capable of transferring bombs and all types of ammunition at sea; hospital ships; victualling store issuing ships; heavy machinery, aircraft, and radio repair ships; a collier, a tug, a water boat, and so forth: the whole, when moving from one base to carriers and screened by escort vessels.

The fact that the group was established from vessels not originally intended for the purpose, threw a great strain on the newly formed

Fleet Train. The flagship, the *Lothian*, had been fitted out as a Headquarters ship for combined operations in northern latitudes. In the tropical heat of the Pacific, under "conditions which can only be described as appalling, 110 officers and 650 men lived and worked in a space suitable for two-thirds of their number."[154]

The limitations in endurance imposed by the construction of the merchant ships which constituted the majority of the Fleet Train, their inadequate complements, the poor state of repair which delayed several in joining – one, the *Kelantan*, never joined at all – and necessitated an abnormal amount of maintenance; and the heterogeneity of ships within types and classes both as to speeds and loads rendered planning and operation difficult.

The lighters and vessels intended to provide floating storage at Leyte and Manus did not come forward during the operation. The U.S. authorities could allot no shore space, however, and lack of adequate transit space for stores arriving in the forward area from Australia by sea and air, and the absence of other facilities normally established ashore, were further adverse factors.

By the end of the operation the Fleet Train, which at the outset comprised 65 ships, had increased in number to 109 vessels.

105. The Crews

The majority of the ships in the Fleet Train were manned by merchant seamen. The shortage of trained naval personnel in the British Commonwealth rendered it impossible to replace their crews by naval officers and ratings. Many of the ships were entirely foreign manned: Dutch, French, Belgian, Norwegian, Danish, Lascar, and Chinese seamen were all represented in this heterogeneous assembly of foreign merchantmen, H.M. ships, and red and blue ensign ships. From time-to-time difficulties arose over the behaviour of the crews of merchant vessels, though the *Denbighshire*, a merchantman just withdrawn from commercial service, appears to have been unique in that during the working of cargo the ship's officers and crew "confined their assistance to standing about and criticizing".[155]

In order to provide men for working cargoes in the issuing ships and for other purposes such as working parties ashore in the Fleet Mail Office and on the airstrip, a permanent working party, termed for reasons of *esprit de corps* "Fleet Train Porters" was raised, numbering 15 Petty Officers and Leading Hands, and 150 others.

---

154 *Fleet Train History*, Vol. II, p.10.

155 *R of P Fleet Train*, Appendix G, Report of Fleet Train N.A.A.F.I. Officer.

The administration of this force in which not only the crews, but also the ships and their functions, were so diverse, was a most difficult problem for the Commodore, Second-in-Command, Fleet Train (COFT).

106. Logistic Support Groups

The role of the Fleet Train was to "provide logistic support for Task Force 57". This consisted in ferrying supplies from Leyte to the fuelling area, to which the striking force returned approximately every third or fourth day.

To achieve it three or four task units were formed to ply between Leyte and the fuelling area, a distance of 700 miles each way. In the early days, a typical task unit would consist of three tankers, one escort carrier, and two or three escort vessels. The escort carriers and escort vessels were under the operational control of the Rear-Admiral Fleet Train, though not administered by him. At Leyte, the tankers loaded cargoes of fuel oil and aviation spirit from U.S. bulk supplies, and the escort carriers took as many serviceable aircraft as possible to fly across to the fleet carriers.

In the comparative absence of any submarine threat, the escort vessels closed Task Force 57 and transferred the mails, passengers, and stores, which were transported by them in preference to other ships for this very reason that they could transfer without transshipment. This practice had, however, two serious disadvantages: it weakened the A/S screen, and necessitated continually moving around in what should have been, in effect, their "harbourl" period, i.e. fuelling time.

On arrival in the fuelling area, the ships reported to and were turned around by the Commander Logistic Support Group,[156] casualties, mails and personnel being transferred from the Task Force to an oiler or escort vessel returning to the forward base. C.A.P. and A.S.P. were furnished by an escort carrier and screen. They operated under the orders of the Commander, Logistic Support Group, and remained in the fuelling area throughout. In the event of an enemy attack, which, however, never occurred, the Senior Officer present was to take charge. During fleet fuelling the Senior Officer took charge of the combined force.

---

156 During the first part of "Iceberg" these duties were carried out by Capt. C.P. Frend, R.N. (Capt., Escort Forces B.P.F.) and during the second part of the operation by Acting Capt. P.T. Love R.N.

107. Air Logistics Groups

The responsibility for aircraft maintenance in the forward area and delivery of replacements to Task Force 57, were among the responsibilities of the Rear-Admiral, Fleet Train.

Replenishment carriers for transferring aircraft to the fuelling area and flying them across to the Fleet Carriers, had not been allowed for in planning the composition of the Fleet Train, and it became necessary to reduce certain fighting escort carriers to a transport role. The escort carriers also performed a variety of tasks in connection with the transfer at sea of stores and casualties, as there was no other means of performing them.

For all these duties, the Rear-Admiral Fleet Train had six escort carriers of the 30th Escort Carrier Squadron, two aircraft repair ships, and one air stores issuing ship. Rear-Admiral Fisher had no staff to deal with air logistics;[157] and, moreover, whilst the Fleet Train anchorage was largely fixed by question of fuel tankers, the Air Train was tied to its airfields and replenishment ports, which might or might not be at the same place.

The responsibility for the whole of the air logistics was therefore delegated on arrival in the forward area to the aircraft repair ship *Unicorn*. Subsequently, the Air Logistics Groups were separated from the Fleet Train under the title Air Train, which was placed under the command of a Commodore (Comat) who was himself responsible to Rear-Admiral, Fleet Train.

The replenishment escort carrier had to achieve efficient maintenance of all types of operational aircraft and to carry out lying operations to meet the ever rapidly changing circumstances in the fuelling area. At the commencement of the operation the ships were not worked up for the duties they were called upon to perform. Their complements of air maintenance ratings were inadequate and had to be made up by drafting ratings, many of whom had never been to sea. All ships had a most limited range of air stores and had to maintain operational aircraft for far longer periods than had been expected.

108. First Replenishment at Manus, 7th-19th March

The striking force of the British Pacific Fleet or Task Force 113 as it then was, arrived at Manus in the Admiralties on 7th March, to undertake fuelling and provisioning before moving up to the combat area. At Manus the Americans had formed one of their logistic support bases, and the British found awaiting them such vessels of the Fleet Train as

157 He had one Lieut. Commander (E). A Lieut. Commander (A) was subsequently appointed.

the Admiralty had been able to provide and the authorities to load and despatch from Sydney, viz., seven escort carriers, one hospital ship, and 19 auxiliaries in the intervals between the dockers' strikes which made working to a date so difficult when loading ships in Australia.

The necessity for fleet training during this period added to the difficulties of replenishment. The U.S. authorities could give very little assistance to the British Pacific Fleet, ill-provided though the latter was to meet the conditions prevailing in this huge anchorage. The swell made large and strong catamarans a necessity for fuelling heavy ships; the British had none.

The great distances over water called for numerous harbour service craft; but they were in very short supply, for although the requirement for boats had been forecast with a high degree of accuracy the paucity of suitable shipping to move them forward resulted in their not being where they were needed. In both victualling store issuing ships stocks were over-stowed by large quantities of beer, which had to be discharged in heavy rains that reduced to pulp the paper bags in which the beer bottles were packed. Small gales blew.

There were difficulties of communication with the fleet auxiliaries anchored miles away from the fleet. Refrigerated stores were affected by the prevailing heat. Daily water requirements in excess of distilling capacity were about 179,000 U.S. gallons per day, but there was little water at Manus, and in any case the Fleet Train had no proper water boat. Nevertheless, as the result of extemporisation and great exertions the Fleet Train "just got away with it"; and when on 19th March it moved to Leyte though the convoy "may not have looked very warlike, it was an inspiration to see the Fleet Train both in being and under way for the first time."[158]

109. Oiling at Sea

In order to have the Tanker Group in position for the Fleet to top up with fuel at the last prudent moment Task Ünits 112.2.1 and 112.2.5. sailed from Manus on 17th March. The former consisted of the escort carrier *Striker* wearing the broad pendant of Commodore Commanding, 30th Aircraft Carrier Squadron, with 18 replacement aircraft and screen (*Crane, Findhorn* and *Whirlwind*), and three tankers; the latter of the escort carrier *Speaker* with 16 Hellcats to provide C.A.P. for the oiler force, and screen (*Pheasant* and *Kempenfelt*). Rendezvous was made with Task Force 57 at 0600 on the 25th in position "Ant" in 18° 30′ N., 129° 08′ E., 400 miles south-east of Sakishima Gunto, and

158 *R. of P. Fleet Train*, Appendix I, Report of Fleet Train Engineer Officer.

the fuelling of the destroyers, and of the *Black Prince*, *Argonaut* and *Euryalus* commenced.

It had been hoped to complete fuelling by 1100, but a strong north-easterly wind together with hose troubles soon ruled this out. To enable the Task Force to keep this, its first appointment, on time, both battleships and the *Striker* were ordered to fuel destroyers. In spite of this, of leaving one destroyer to follow later and accepting other destroyers up to 30 per cent short, the operation had to be stopped at 1450, and the Task Force proceeded at 23½ knots in order to reach the operating area by dawn next day.

Between 25th March and 23rd April when Task Force 57 arrived at Leyte for a short replenishment period, fuelling at sea took place on six occasions, and opportunity was taken to transfer stores, fresh provisions, mails and spares from the oilers and ships of the Escort Force. On each occasion the time taken to fuel was far greater than had been anticipated from peace-time fuelling at sea.

During the first part of Operation "Iceberg", which from the supply point of view was marred by the failure of the operation of oiling at sea, delays were caused by bad weather and heavy swell. Apart from the all too small number of tankers available (three for the first two fuels and thereafter five, with a sixth on one occasion) inherent causes of slowness in re-fuelling were the insufficient pumping capacity of the tankers and lack of sufficient means of transferring fuel and aviation spirit. For example, some tankers could only pass through one hose astern, others carried no aviation spirit, hoses for aviation spirit were too small, etc.

The method adopted for fuelling big ships astern was much slower than the United States Navy method of fuelling all ships alongside. Both H.M. ships and tankers had had insufficient practice, resulting in bad station keeping and slow handling of gear. Oiling gear, hoses and fittings were in bad condition and there was a lack of spare hoses. The expenditure of hoses was so greatly in excess of anything anticipated, that at one time the Vice-Admiral Second-in-Command, British Pacific Fleet signalled to the C.-in-C. that "shortage of fuel hoses owing to weather damage and lack of initial spares may become the deciding factor in the length of time the British Pacific Fleet can continue operations". As an immediate answer to this situation, sufficient spares were flown from Australia to enable operations to continue till long-range measures were worked out. Supplies were sufficient to provide for the second part of Operation "Iceberg", but with no margin whatever.

Delivery of petroleum products to the Task Force constituted only one part of the fuel problem with which R.A.F.T.(Rear-Admiral Fleet Train) had to contend. Arrangements had been made for the U.S. Navy to furnish these products to the Fleet Train, and Rear-Admiral Fisher's problems included the necessary estimating and accounting procedure to enable the U.S. Navy to ensure the flow of supplies to the loading ports at the time required. In this respect also, the methods agreed upon did not, in practice, work out so well as was expected. In the first place, shortage of R.A.F.T.'s staff necessitated the matter being handled by an officer as a mere collateral duty. Another aspect which added to the problem was imperfect liaison between officers concerned in operational and logistic planning. "The Fleet gave no detailed order of what they required except that they, the Fleet, must be supported for a certain time and in places sometimes uncertain."[159]

No fleet operation was ever curtailed or postponed, however, solely on account of lack of fuel or delay in its delivery. The performance of the Royal Fleet Auxiliary *Wave King* on April 14th furnishes a good example of the effect of efficiency and enthusiasm on the part of the officers and crew of an oiler in countering shortcomings. On this day she delivered 5,050 tons of oil fuel between 0700 and 1900 hours to one carrier, three light cruisers, and four destroyers, both the astern and alongside methods being employed.

110. Summary of Effort During First Part of Operation "Iceberg"

Between 25th March and 23rd April, the following ships were employed in maintaining Task Force 57 in the Combat Area, about 900 miles from the advanced base at Leyte:[160]

24 Escorts	4 Escort Carriers
2 Repair Ships	1 Aircraft Repair Ship
4 Victualling Store Issuing Ships	2 Hospital Ships
10 Tankers	3 Naval Store Issuing Ships
1 Destroyer Depot Ship	1 Distilling Ship,
1 Net Layer	8 Armament Store Issuing Ships
4 Tugs	

159 *R. of T. Fleet Train*, F.T. Engineer Officer's Report. I. 1 (e).

160 This is the list given in *Operational Research Reports*, and it differs somewhat from the list given in Appendix C (9) which was taken from an American source, no complete nominal list having been found in any British report.

The following were supplied to, or landed from, the Fleet: 93,000 tons of fuel oil, 1,300 tons of aviation spirit, 1,064 bags of letter mail, 43 aircraft, as well as many tons of fresh vegetables, stores of all descriptions, and personnel including 20 casualties brought back to base.

111. Short Replenishment at Leyte, 23rd April-1st May

On April 23rd, on the conclusion of the first part of Operation "Iceberg", Task Force 57 arrived at Leyte, in order to replenish with stores, provisions, fuel and ammunition. The approximate date of arrival had been made known some time beforehand. Actually, the anticipated date was postponed about a week, with the result that more tankers were available, and the only adverse effect of the delay was that half the perishables went bad before they could be issued.

The following ships of the Fleet Train took part in the replenishment:

Assault transports:	*Lothian, Empire Spearhead, Glenearn*
Heavy machinery repair ships:	*Artifex, Resource*
Aircraft repair ships:	*Unicorn, Deer Sound*
Oilers:	*Wave King, Wave Monarch, San Ambrosio, San Amado, Arndale, Cederdale, Dingledale, Aase Maersk;*
Water tanker:	*Brown Ranger*
A.S.I.S.:	*Heron, Kheti, Pacheco, Prince de Liege, Gudrun Maersk Hermelin, Thyra S, Robert Maersk*
V.S.I.S.:	*Fort Edmonton, Denbighshire, Fort Alabama, City of Dieppe*
Distiller:	*Stagpool*
Collier:	*Atlas*
Hospital ships:	*Oxfordshire, Maunganui, Tjitjalengka*
N.S.I.S.:	*Bacchus, Fort Colville, Bosphorus*

This replenishment was easier than the former one, at Manus. The berthing plan, which had been arranged by R.A.F.T., gave distances much less than at Manus, and the heat and the lethargic effects of the climate were less severe. Seven days had been allotted for replenishment, but thanks to the perfect weather the work was virtually over in five. The Fleet was extremely lucky, for had there been any swell an extension of the period in harbour might have been necessary, largely owing to the fact that the British had no suitable tenders.

Once again, the shortage of harbour craft was acute. In order to make every boat of the Fleet Train available, all shore leave was stopped and all other extraneous activities were curtailed. Work went on 12 hours a day, assisted by landing craft lent by the Americans.[161] Provisions and naval stores were brought alongside the ships of the Force by landing craft from the store ships; but ammunition ships went alongside battleships and cruisers, and destroyers went alongside the ammunition ships.

The tankers were overworked. Some arrived back in harbour after the Task Force, and others sailed for the next operation before it left, whilst the remainder were kept busy supplying fuel to the Task Force on its arrival and again before its departure. Consequently, they had little rest or opportunity for repairs; one of the unhappy results of working on a bare margin.

In a period of hard work in great heat and an absence of amenities, beer assumed an exaggerated importance. After the Task Force anchored, permission was given for beer to be consumed on board H.M. ships since there were insufficient boats for libertymen to be landed. By now, every landing craft in the boat pool had been allotted for other work, and on a tight schedule none could be diverted. However, though some of the ships applied incessantly for boats to draw their beer the more enterprising found ways and means of doing it for themselves. Having drunk his beer, the British seaman proceeded to exercise his traditional right of grumbling at the price.

112. Second Part of Operation "Iceberg"

Task Force 57 left Leyte on 1st May and the second part of Operation "Iceberg" began. The Tanker Group, to fuel the Fleet on the passage north, sailed from Leyte on the previous day. The escort carriers, *Striker* (AC 30) and *Ruler* sailed at 0700 on 3rd May. The *Ruler* carried 18 Hellcats and four Avengers for C.A.P. duties, and of these no less than six Hellcats and one Avenger were lost whilst landing or taking off, three pilots losing their lives.

The high accident rate was attributed chiefly to the inexperience of some of the Hellcat pilots, six of whom had not previously deck-landed this type of aircraft and had no deck-landing training apart from that provided during their initial training.

As far as the Fleet Train was concerned events followed the previous pattern closely, the activities of the Fleet Train being confined to general support of the Task Force, the major work being, as before, the

161 In terms of lift, 54% of the bottoms were American.

turnaround of tanker groups and despatch of stores to the forward area, storing of escorts, etc. The ships employed were the nine oilers which had been used at Leyte, the ammunition ship *Robert Maersk*, and three escort carriers. Conditions were such that the strike and refuelling programmes could be more rigidly adhered to by the Task Force, which facilitated the operation of tanker groups.

The weather was ideal for fuelling at sea, and it was possible by placing small working parties on board the tankers to complete fuelling the task force in one day. Two days, however, were consistently required in the fuelling area in order to permit the limited maintenance crews of the carriers time to conduct normal upkeep and overhaul work on their aircraft, as well as to keep pilot fatigue down to an acceptable maximum.

During this period, an additional escort carrier for combat air patrols was provided in the Service Area, a hospital ship was also stationed in the neighbourhood of the Service Area, and a rescue tug was sent forward as part of Task Unit 112.2.5. Use was found for the tug when the destroyer *Quilliam* was damaged in collision with the *Indomitable* on 20th May. About 15 escort vessels were employed.

During this part of Operation "Iceberg" the following were supplied to the Fleet: 87,000 tons of oil fuel (estimated), 756 tons aviation spirit, 1,473 bags of letter mail, in addition to aircraft and personnel. No provisions were supplied.

During the entire operation the total sorties of the nine tankers amounted to 18. The average tanker fuel capacity was about 1,000 tons, the average amount of fuel supplied per tanker's sortie was 4,633. In other words, nine tankers were able to maintain the Fleet at sea between 700 and 900 miles from its base for 30 days with a margin of some 40 per cent to spare.

The two repair ships, H.M.S. *Artifex* and H.M.S. *Resource*, with the destroyer depot ship *Tyne*, successfully effected all necessary repairs to the fleet that did not require docking; and they also carried out much light construction work, such as fenders for harbour fuelling of carriers and compatible re-modelling and alteration work. The biggest task was the repair of the *Indefatigable*'s battle damage, which was carried out in six working days, and the ship sailed fully operational. The floating docks were still on passage at the time of the operation, and such dockings as were necessary were carried out by the U.S. Navy. Two light cruisers, seven destroyers and two escort vessels were docked at various times for brief periods; and two more destroyers were docked for longer periods to affect temporary repair of comparatively serious battle and collision damage.

The 30th Aircraft Carrier Squadron brought forward 190 replenishment aircraft, 140 of which were supplied to Task Force 57. The squadron transferred 100 casualties from the fleet to hospital ships in the advanced base.

During the fuelling and replenishment periods the Fleet and the Fleet Train had necessarily to steer steady courses at slow speeds for long periods; yet not a single submarine or air attack was made on any ship by the Japanese during these periods of extreme vulnerability.

On completion of the second part of Operation "Iceberg" the Fleet underwent a major replenishment and rehabilitation from 1st June to 24th June. During this period the greater part of Task Force 37 – as it had become on 28th May – and some of the Fleet Train went to Australian ports to replenish. Those ships of the Fleet for which there was no room at Australian ports had to undergo their replenishment from the Fleet Train at Manus; and requirements for fuel and ammunition had to be met in order to make good that expended in exercises and in a minor operation against Truk.[162]

During this major replenishment period Okinawa Gunto was declared secured, and the next assignment of the British Pacific Fleet was in the raids on the Japanese homeland.

162 Operate "Inmate", bombardment and air strikes at Truk, 13th-15th June.

Chapter XIV

CONCLUSION

The Ryukus operation was at an end. The American Tenth Army, supported by Allied naval and air forces, landed on a fortified, enemy-held island within 350 miles of that enemy's industrial home base and captured or destroyed its garrison to the last man.

113. Summary of the Ryukus Operation

The entire Japanese 32nd Army was blotted out as if it had never had an existence; 131,000 men were killed. The U.S. Army and Marines lost 7,032 officers and men killed, 181 missing, and 31,081 wounded. Amongst the killed was the Army Commander, Lieutenant-General S. B. Buckner, Jr.

The Japanese fought with skill and tenacity in prepared defensive positions amongst difficult terrain which often called for the use of scaling ladders and special equipment. For the first time, the Americans used tactical propaganda on a large scale, and to this may undoubtedly be ascribed the high total of 7,400 prisoners taken. Amongst the Americans, all components of the Tenth Army, troops and Marines, executed their assigned tasks with competence and speed. In 81 days of campaigning the rain, mud and fatigue were overcome by courage.

The U.S. Fifth/Third Fleet including the British Task Force which supported the operation suffered heavy casualties. The operating statistics of the British task force have already been noted (Section 101); those of the American task forces may be summarized as follows: - Of 525 fighting ships which at the outset comprised the fleet, 22 were sunk and 254 damaged. Amongst landing craft and auxiliaries 14 were sunk and 117 damaged. The fleet lost 539 aircraft in support of the Ryukus operation.[163] Personnel losses were 4,907 killed and missing and 4,824

163 Between 1st April and 1st July.

wounded.[164] They destroyed 1,908 enemy aircraft and sank 188 ships and 283 small craft, besides damaging 437 ships and 769 small craft.

In no previous operation had the American naval losses in ships and men been so high, both in sum and in relation to those of the ground forces as in the capture of Okinawa; and this, despite the inactivity of the enemy surface fleet, the almost entire lack of success of his submarines, and the decline which had already begun in 1945 of Japanese air power, their only effective arm of offence, from its former peak.

Against this, however, had to be set three factors: the proximity of the scene of action to the enemy's homeland and main resources in air power; the high proportion of his effort which he devoted to suicide attack; and the length of time that the Allied shipping was exposed to attack whilst supporting and covering the operations ashore.

It is not necessary to emphasize the manner in which proximity facilitated the Japanese pressure: the shorter the distance, the greater the intensity of the attack than can be delivered at the far end. Then, too, the span of the Ryukus operation was much longer than in any previous amphibious operation in the Pacific and during all that time the Allied ships were by the nature of their role deprived of their most positive safety measure against attack from the air at any place – to wit, not being there when the attack comes.

The suicide attack is as old as history. For perhaps the first time in history, however, it became a serious menace at Okinawa through three factors which then came into combination, namely: the importance in modern war of vulnerable structures such as ships, floating docks, and airfield installations; the great destructive power contained in comparatively small charges of modern high explosives; and the ability of air power to convey these charges at great speed over great distances to the selected target.

In particular circumstances, defence by evasion was not feasible, and active defence was handicapped by the incomplete technical development of U.S. warning apparatus at that date. But their attacks cost the Japanese 6,810 aircraft, and a further 1,020 were destroyed on the ground.

The Okinawa campaign created a new problem in morale and well-being of the crews of the ships concerned. For nearly three months officers and men were subjected to almost daily air attacks and night nuisance raids; they were seldom free from the menace of suicide boat and submarine. On the whole, it is clear that the men responded with alertness, skill, and determination. The success of the American

164 For the period 26th March to 30th June.

method of maintaining morale by "bread and circuses" has already been mentioned.

In all seriousness Rear-Admiral Sherman could write: "Other than mail, probably the greatest morale aid was for the men to get apples and oranges."[165] In total war of to-day the high cause alone is not enough; and Bonaparte's dictum that an army marches on its stomach was fully recognized and acted upon by the Americans in the Pacific, with highly satisfactory results.

The capture of Okinawa Gunto provided the U.S. forces with air and naval bases within 330 miles of industrial Kyushu. A major fleet anchorage and 26 potential airfields were now available for the final assault on Japan, an operation which, however, owing to the prior surrender of the enemy, which was never carried out.

---

165 *C.T.G. 58.3, Action Report 14th March-1st June, 1945*, p.63.

Appendix A

AIRCRAFT TYPES

S.E. = Single engine
T.E. = Twin engine
M.E. = Multi engine

F4U	Corsair. Landplane. S.E. Fighter. Navy aircraft.
F6F	Hellcat.[166] Landplane. S.E. Fighter. Navy aircraft.
F7F	Tigercat. Landplane. T.E. Fighter. Navy aircraft.
FM-1	Wildcat.[167] Landplane. S.E. Fighter. Navy aircraft.
LB-30	Liberator. Landplane. M.E. Heavy Bomber. Army aircraft.
OY	Artillery spotting aircraft.
P-38	Lightning. Landplane. T.E. Fighter. Army aircraft.
PB2Y	Coronado. Flying boat. M.E. Patrol Bomber. Navy aircraft.
PB4Y	Liberator. Landplane. M.E. Patrol Bomber. Navy aircraft.
PBM	Mariner. Flying boat. T.E. Patrol Bomber. Navy aircraft.
SB2C	Helldiver. Landplane. S.E. Dive bomber. Navy aircraft.
VB	Bomber (H = Heavy, M = Medium).
VD	Photographic aircraft.
VF	Fighter.
VF(N)	Night fighter.
VF(P)	Fighter equipped for photographic work.
VLR	Very long range.
VOS	Seaplane.
VP	Patrol aircraft (H = Heavy, M =Medium).
VR	Transport aircraft.
VSB	Dive bomber.
VSO	Kingfisher Floatplane. S.E. Observation Navy aircraft.
VT	Torpedo bomber.

166 Originally called Gannet.
167 Originally called a Martlet.

Appendix B

Organization of Pacific Fleet and Pacific Ocean Area Forces (Fleet Admiral C.W. Nimitz, Cincpac-Cincpoa)

(1) NORTH PACIFIC FORCE (Vice-Admiral F. J. Fletcher)
Task. Contain enemy naval and air forces in North Pacific by conducting reconnaissance and harassing enemy positions in Kuriles.

(2) FORWARD AREA CENTRAL PACIFIC (Vice-Admiral J. H. Hoover)
Task. Support operation for capture of Okinawa with air and naval forces and bases under his command. This to include A.S.W. coverage, neutralization of enemy bases, by aircraft, A.S.R. services, air evacuation and transport service and repair facilities.

(3) SOUTH PACIFIC FORCE (Vice-Admiral W. L. Calhoun)
Task. Provide logistic support as directed.

(4) MARSHALLS-GILBERTS FORCE (Rear-Admiral W. K. Harrill)
Task. Hold positions needed for security of lines of communication and for support of air, sea, and amphibious operations against Japan.

(5) AIR FORCE, PACIFIC FLEET (Vice-Admiral G. E. Murray)
Task. Provide logistic support as directed.

(6) SERVICE FORCE, PACIFIC FLEET (Vice-Admiral N. W. Smith)
Task. Provide logistic support as directed.

Note. Forces (5) and (6) had the duty of providing facilities for the Commander Logistic Support Group (C.T.G. 50.8) (see Appendix E).

(7) ARMY FORCES, PACIFIC OCEAN AREAS (Lieut. General R. G. Richardson, Jr.)
Task. Provide logistic support as directed.

(8) WESTERN SEA FRONTIER (Admiral R. E. Ingersoll)
Task. Provide logistic support as directed.

(9) STRATEGIC AIR FORCES, PACIFIC OCEAN AREAS (Major-General W. H. Hale)
Tasks. (a) Neutralize enemy bases in Carolines and Nanpo Shoto.
(b) Destroy enemy aircraft and air installations in Nansei Shoto and Japan as practicable.
(c) Provide fighter cover for XX Air Force strikes on Japan)

(10) RYUKUS FORCE (Lieut.-General S. B. Buckner, Jr.)
Task. When released by C.T.F. 50, defend and develop captured positions in Nansei Shoto.

(11) CENTRAL PACIFIC TASK FORCES (Com. 5th Fleet – Admiral R.A. Spruance)
Tasks. (a) Capture, occupy and develop air and naval bases on Okinawa Retto.
(b) Gain and maintain control of the Nansei Shoto area.
(c) Protect air and sea communications along the Central Pacific axis.

(12) SUBMARINE FORCE (Vice-Admiral C. A. Lockwood, Jr.)
Tasks. (a) Provide accurate intelligence of enemy naval units.
(b) Interdict sea approaches to Okinawa from Japan and Formosa.
(c) Provide lifeguard services as ordered.
(d) Be prepared to concentrate for strategic or tactical support of Central Pacific Task Forces.

Appendix C

Covering Forces and Special Groups of Fifth Fleet (Task Force 50, Admiral R. A. Spruance)

Note: (1) Lists of ships are as at the commencement of the operation. (2) U.S. classification of types has been employed for U.S. ships, and British classification for British ships.
TASK. Cover the operations of the Expeditionary Force and utilize every opportunity to destroy the enemy fleet:

Fleet Flagship Group (Task Group 50, 1) *Indianapolis* (cruiser) (Capt. C. B. Mc Vay)
Relief Fleet Flagship (Task Group 50.2) *Missouri* (Capt. W. M. Callaghan)

1
Fast Carrier Task Force (Task Force 58)

Vice-Admiral M. A. Mitscher, U.S.S. *Bunker Hill*, Flagship

TASKS: 1. Will provide aerial R/C and strikes against the Empire, Formosa, and Nansei Shoto.
2. Prevent interference by enemy air action with capture and occupation of Okinawa.
3. Protect the Joint Expeditionary Force and Okinawa after U.S. occupation from attack by enemy surface forces.

TASK GROUP 58.1 (Rear-Admiral J. J. Clark)
Carriers: *Hornet** (Flagship), *Bennington**; Light carriers: *Belleau Wood***, *San Jacinto***; Battleships: *Massachusetts*, *Indiana*; Light cruisers: *Vincennes*, *Miami*, *Vicksburgh*, *San Juan*; Destroyers: *De Haven*, *Mansfield*,

L.K. Swenson, Collett, Maddox, Blue, Brush, Taussig, S.N. Moore, John Rogers, Harrison, McKee, Murray.

TASK GROUP 58.2 (Rear-Admiral G.F. Bogan)
Carriers: *Randolf** (Flagship), *Enterprise****; Light carrier: *Independence***; Battleships: *Washington, North Carolina;* Heavy cruisers: *Baltimore, Pittsburgh;* Light cruisers, *Oakland, Flint;* Destroyers: *Owen, The Sullivans, Stephen Potter,*[168] *Tingey, Hickox, Hunt, Lewis Hancock, Marshall.*

Note: Dissolved 17th April and ships remaining undamaged were reassigned to other task groups.

TASK GROUP 58.3 (Rear-Admiral F.C. Sherman)
Carriers: *Essex** (Flagship), *Bunker Hill***, *Hancock**;[169] Light carriers: *Cabot***, *Bataan***; Battleships: *New Jersey, South Dakota;* Light cruisers: *Pasadena, Springfield, Astoria, Wilkes-Barre;* Destroyers: *Ault, English, C.S. Sperry, Waldron, Haynsworth, W.L. Lind, I.W. Welks, Hank, Erben, Walker, Hale, Stembel.*

TASK GROUP 58.4 (Rear-Admiral A.W. Radford)
Carriers: *Yorktown** (Flagship), *Intrepid**; Light carrier: *Langley**; Battleships: *Missouri, Wisconsin;* Large cruisers, *Guam, Alaska;* Light cruiser: *San Diego;* Destroyers: *McCord, Trathen, Hazelwood, Heerman, Franks, Hailey, Remey, Norman Scott, Mertz, Monssen, McDermut, McGowen, Mc Nair, Melvin.*

* Aircraft = 36 F6F, 36 SB2C and 19 TBF, or 150 FM, or 120 F6F or F4U, or 52 F7F
** Aircraft = 24 F6F and 9 TBF, or 42 FM, or 33 F6F or F4U.
*** Aircraft = 36 F6F, 36 SB2C and 19 TBF, or 120 FM, or 96 F6F or F4U.

2
Striking Force (Task Force 59)

Vice-Admiral A.W. Lee Jr.

Task. Destroy enemy naval forces when specifically directed (to be formed from units of Task Force 58)

3
Destroyer Scouting Group (Task Force 58.8)

Capt. H. S. Jarrett

168 Her Task Group Commander always called her *Stephan Potter*.

169 *Hancock* and *Bataan* joined on 22nd March; they did not take part in the strikes of 18th-19th March.

Duty. From scouting line ahead of T.F. 58 to destroy enemy pickets and aircraft.

4

British Carrier Force (Task Force 57)

Vice-Admiral Sir H. Bernard Rawlings, K.C.B., O.B.E. (All H.M. ships unless otherwise stated)

TASK. Neutralize airfields in the Sakishima Gunto.

1st Battle Squadron: T.U.1 *King George V*, Capt. T.E. Halsey, D.S.O. (flag of C.T.F. 57)
Howe, Capt. H.U.W. McCall, D.S.O.
1st Aircraft Carrier Squadron: T.U.2 *Indomitable* (29 Hellcat,[170] 15 Avenger[171]) Capt. J.A.S. Eccles (flag of A.C.1 and Second in Command T.F.57). Rear-Admiral Sir Philip L. Vian, K.C.B., K.B.E., D.S.O.
Victorious (37 Corsair,[172] 14 Avenger, 2 Walrus[173]) Capt. M.M. Denny, C.B., C.B.E.
Illustrious (36 Corsair, 16 Avenger) Capt. C.B. Lambe, C.B., C.B.E.
Indefatigable (40 Seafire,[174] 20 Avenger, 9 Firefly) Capt. Q.D. Graham, C.B.E, D.S.O.
4th Cruiser Squadron: *Swiftsure* (9 x 6-in., 10 x 4-in.) Capt. P.V. McLaughlin (Flag of C.S. 4), Rear-Admiral Sir E.J.P. Brind C.B.
H.M.N.Z.S. *Gambia* (12 x 6-in., 8 x 4-in.) Capt. R.A.B. Edwards C.B.E., R.N.
Black Prince (8 x 5.25-in.) Capt. G.V. Gladstone
Argonaut (8 x 5.25-in.) Capt. W.P. McCarthy
25th Destroyer Flotilla T.U.8 *Euryalus*,[175] Capt. R. Oliver-Bellasis (flag of R.A.(D) temporarily, Rear-Admiral T.H. Edelsten, C.B., C.B.E.
Grenville Capt. H.P. Henderson (Capt. D. 25)
Note: *Ursa* was docking *Ulster* Lt.-Com. R.J. Hanson, D.S.C. & Bar
at Manus. *Undine* Com. T.C. Robinson
Urania Lt.-Com. D.H.P. Gardiner, D.S.C.
Undaunted Lt.-Com. C.E.R. Sharp
4th Destroyer Flotilla R.A.N. *Quickmatch* Com. O.H. Becher, D.S.C (Capt. D.4)
R.A.A. *Quiberon* Lt.-Com. G.E.F. Knox

170 Fighter bomber.
171 Torpedo bomber fighter employed throughout the operation almost exclusively as bombers.
172 Fighter.
173 Amphibian reconnaissance bomber.
174 Fighter.
175 Joined the 4th C.S. on 28th March, when R.A. (D) proceeded to Leyte.

Queensborough Com. P.L. Saumarez D.S.C.
Quality Lt.-Com. The Viscount Jocelyn
Whelp Com. G.A.F. Norfolk
Wager Lt.-Com. R.C. Watkin
Note: *Kempenfelt*, Capt. E.G. McGregor, D.S.O. (Capt. D.27) was attached to T.U. 112.2.5, the group remaining in the replenishment area. *Whirlwind*, Com. A.W.F. Hawkins, D.S.O., O.B.E., D.S.C., and *Wessex*, Lt.-Com. R. Horncastle, were attached to T.U. 112.2.1 and T.U 112.2.2 respectively, the Tanker Group proceeding between Leyte and the replenishing area.

5
Search and Reconnaissance Group (Task Group 50.5)
(Cdre. D. Ketcham)

TASK. Aerial R/C and offensive missions against Nansei Shoto, Kyushu, Honshu and in the China Sea area.

50.5.1. Advanced Seaplane Group (Capt. G.A. McLean)
Seaplane tenders (large) *Hamlin, St. George, Chandeleur.*
Seaplane tenders (small) *Yakutat, Onslow, Shelikof, Bering Strait.*
Aircraft: 45 PBM5, 6 PBM-3B.

50.5.2. Saipan Group (Cdr. James)
Seaplane tenders (small) *Castle Rock, Suisun, Casco.* Aircraft: 24 PBM5.

50.5.3. Tinian Search Group (Cdr. Masterton)
Aircraft: 48 PB4Y-1-2, 24 PV-1.

50.5.4. Ulithi Group (Capt. E. Grant)
Seaplane tenders (large) *Cumberland Sound, K. Whiting, Norton Sound.*
Seaplane tenders (small) *Corson, Cook Inlet, Chincoteague, Duxbury Bay, Mackinac.*
Aircraft: 45 PBM5, 6 PBM-3B.

50.5.5. Advanced Land-plane Group (Cdr. Harper)
Aircraft: 24 PB4Y-2.

6
Anti-Submarine Warfare Group (Task Group 50.7)
(Capt. J. C. Cronin)

TASK. A.S.W. operations in the vicinity of logistic support group operations.

50.7.1. A.S.W. Unit Able (Capt. G. C. Montgomery)
Escort carrier *Anzio*
Cortdiv 72 Escort vessels *L.C. Taylor, M. R. Nawman, O. Mitchell, R. F. Keller*.

50.7.2 A.S.W. Unit Baker
Cortdiv 64 Escort vessels *Raymond, R. F. Clark, Silverstein, Lewis.*
50.7.3 A.S.W. Unit Charlie (Capt. J. C. Cronin)
Escort carrier *Tulagi*
Cortdiv 70 Escort vessels *W. Sieverling, U.M. Moore, K.C. Campbell, Goss.*

7
Service Squadron 10 (Task Group 50.9)
(Cdre. W. R. Carter)

TASK. Administer services afloat at anchorages in the Marianas and Western Carolines.

9 destroyer tenders or depot ships, 8 fleet auxiliaries, 5 AG miscellaneous auxiliaries, 1 oiler, 4 gasoline tankers or small tankers, 2 cavalry transports, 2 labour transports or barrack ships, 1 hospital ship, 2 salvage vessels, 2 ocean tugs (auxiliary), 12 ocean tugs (fleet), 3 ocean tugs (old), 7 rescue tugs, 1 high speed minesweeper, 3 repair ships battle damage, 6 floating dry docks, 4 repair ships internal corruption, 1 repair ship heavy hull, 33 unclassified.

8
Logistic Support Group (Task Group 50.8)
(Service Squadron 6)
(Rear-Admiral D.B. Beary)

TASK. Furnish direct logistic support to 5th Fleet units in and near combat zone.

50.8.10 Flagship *Detroit* (Light cruiser) (Capt. D. Curry, Jr.)

50.8.1 First Replenishment Unit (R.A.D.B. Beary)
Oilers *Platte, Marias, Aucilla, Taluga, Chipola, Chikaskid, Cossatot, Ashtabula*
Cargo vessel *Mercury*
Ammunition ships *Shasta, Lasseu*

50.8.22 Screen
Destroyer *Welles*
Escort vessels *Lake, Lyman, Mitchell, Donaldson, Reynolds*

50.8.4 Carrier Transport Unit (Capt. H. F. MacComsey)
Ferry escort carriers *Attu, Admiralty Islands, Bougainville, Windham Bay*

50.8.4 Carrier Screen
Escort vessels *Greiner, Lovering, Sanders, Wyman*

50.8.23 Second Carrier Covering Unit
Escort Carrier *Makassar Strait*
Destroyers *Dale, Farragut*

50.8.12 Screen
Destroyers *Stevenson, Thorn, Hobby, Stockton, Buchanan, Gillespie, Kalk*

50.8.7 Third Shuttle Unit (Cdr. Smyth)
50.8.71 Train
Oilers *Kaskaskia, Guadaloupe, Cimarron, Manatee*
50.8.72 Screen
Escort vessels *Hilbert, McCoy Reynolds, Kyne*

50.8.5 First Shuttle Unit (Cdr. Eagleton), 50.8.51 Train
Oilers *Tomahawk, Sabine, Pamanset, Pecos*

50.8.52 Screen
Escort vessels *Brackett, Waterman, Clones, Crowley*

50.8.13 First Carrier Covering Unit
Escort carrier *Shamrock Bay*
Destroyers *Dewey, Aylwin*

50.8.6. Second Shuttle Unit (Cdr. McKenzie)
50.8.61 Train
Oilers *Cowanesque, Cache, Nantahala, Patuxeut*
50.8.62 Screen
Destroyer escorts *Bangust, Weaver, Lemons, Conklin*

50.8.8 Advance Replenishment Unit (Capt. A.C. Allen)
50.8.81 Train
Oilers *Neshanic, Saugatuck, Housatonic, Schuylkill*
50.8.82 Screen
Escort vessels *Strauss, J. Miller, La Prade, Corbesier*

50.8.9 Reserve Unit (Capt. V. Bailey)
50.8.91 Train
Oilers *Cacapon, Neches, Merrimack, Enoree, Monongahela, Suamica, Niobrara*
50.8.92 Screen
Escort vessels *Raymond, Silverstein, H.F. Clarke, Lewis*

50.8.2 Replenishment Unit (Capt. W.I. Stevens)
50.8.81 Train
Oilers *Escalante, Tappahannock, Lackawanna, Atascosa, Kankakee, Tallullah, Millicoma*
Ammunition ships *Wrangell, Mouna Loa*

50.8.3 Salvage Unit (Lt.-Cdr. Howard)
Ocean tugs (fleet) *Cree, Ute, Molala, Sioux*

9
British Logistics Task Force
(Rear-Admiral D.B. Fisher, C.B., C.B.E.)

TASK. To furnish logistic support to the British Carrier Force

Escort carriers
*Striker**, Capt. W.P. Carne (Cdr, 2nd Class), *Speaker** Capt. U.R.H. James (act.), *Ruler** Capt. H.P. Currey, *Slinger**, Capt. B.L. Moore, *Fencer*** Cdr. A.M. Harris (act.) (emergency), *Chaser** Capt. R.G. Poole.
Destroyers
*Napier****, Capt. N.L. Buchanan, D.S.O. (Capt. D.7), *Nepal****, Lt.-Cdr. C.J. Stephenson, *Nizam****, Cdr. C.H. Brooks, *Norman****, Cdr. J. Plunkett-Cole.
A/A Sloops
Crane, Lt.-Cdr. R.G. Jenkins, D.S.O., *Pheasant*,[176] Cdr. J.B. Palmer (act.), *Woodcock*, Lt. S.J. Parsons, D.F.C., *Whimbrel*, Lt.-Cdr. N.R, Murch
Frigates

176 S.O. Escort Group.

Avon, Lt.-Cdr. P.G.A. King, D.S.O., R.D., R.N.R., *Findhorn*, Lt.-Cdr J.C. Dawson, D.S.C., R.N.R., *Parret*, Lt.-Cdr. T. Hood, R.N.R.

Landing Ship Headquarters (Large)
Lothian (HQ ship), Capt. G.C.F. Branson (act.) (ret.).

Landing Ships, Infantry (Large)
Empire Spearhead (Base Ship), Lt. A.F. Benton, R.N.R., *Glenearn* (Transport) Capt. C.A.G. Hutchinson, D.S.O., (act.) (ret.).

Hospital Ships
Oxfordshire, Tjitjalengka, Maunganui,

Minesweepers
*Pirie****, Temp. Lt. D.S. Tompson, R.A.N.R., *Whyalla*, Cdr. N.R. Read (act.), *Launceston**** Temp. Lt.-Cdr. E.J. Barron, (act.) R.A.N.R., *Burnie****, Lt.-Cdr. E.M. Andrewartha, R.A.N.R., *Ipswich****, Temp. Lt. R. H. Creasey, D.S.C., R.A.N.R., *Bendigo****, Lieut. W. Jackson, R.A.N.V.R., *Woollongong****, Temp. Lt. J. Hare, R.A.N.R., *Cairns****, Temp. Lt. N.G. Webber, R.A.N.R, *Kalgoorlie*, Lt. E.J, Peel, *Ballarat****, Lt. L.G.C. Lever, R.A.N.R.

Victualling Stores Issuing Ships
Denbighshire, Fort Edmonton, Fort Alabama

Armament Stores Issuing Ships
Robert Maersk, Thyra S., Pacheco, Heron, Kheti, Prince de Leige

Combined Victualling Stores Issuing Ship
City of Dieppe

Naval Stores Carrier
Bosporus

Armament Stores Carrier
Gudrun Maersk

Destroyer Depot Ship
Tyne Capt. S. Boucher (flag of R.A.D., B.P.F.), Rear-Admiral J.E.H. Edelsten, C.B., C.B.E.

Heavy Repair Ships
Artifex, Capt. C.C. Flemming (act.), *Resource,* Capt. B.D. O'Connell (ret.)

Aircraft Repair Ship
Unicorn, Capt. G.M. Merewether (act.)

Aircraft Component Repair Ship
Deer Sound, Capt. R.H. Johnson, D.S.C., (act.) (ret.)

Fleet tug
Weasel, Temp. Act. Sub.-Lt. D. P. Budge.

Distilling ship and Naval Stores issuing ship*
Bacchus.

Air Stores issuing ship
Fort Colville.

Fleet Attendant Tankers
Brown Ranger, Cedardale, Arndale, Dingledale, Wave King, Wave Monarch, San Ambrosio, San Adolfo, San Amado, Aase Maersk.

* = Replenishment carrier
** = Ferry Escort carrier
*** = On loan to Royal Australian Navy

Appendix D

JOINT EXPEDITIONARY FORCE (TASK FORCE 51) (Vice-Admiral R. K. Turner – U.S.S. *Eldorado*, Flagship)

Note: (1) Lists of ships are as at the commencement of the operation.
(2) U.S. classification of types has been employed.

TASKS. (a) Capture, occupy, and defend the Kerama Retto, Keise Shima, Okinawa, IeShima, and other positions in the Nansei Shoto, if directed.

(b) Begin base development and establishment of military government at the objectives.

ORGANIZATION

Northern Attack Force (Task Force 53) (Rear-Admiral L. F. Reifsnider)
Landing Force (Major-General R. S. Geiger, U.S.M.C.) 111 Amphibious Corps.
1st Marine Division.
6th Marine Division.

TASK. Assault and support the landings on designated beaches on western Okinawa south of Hagushi

Expeditionary Troops (Task Force 56) (10th Army) (Lt.-Gen. S. B. Buckner, Jr.)
TASK. Seize and occupy objective islands and begin base development, Task Group 56.1.

Army Troops (Lt.-Gen. S. B. Buckner, Jr.).
H.Q., 10th Army and Headquarter Troops.
77th Army Division.
2nd Marine Division.
27th Army Division as Floating Reserve.

Area Reserve (under Cincpac until released).
81st Army Division.

Task Group 56.2. Northern Landing Force (Major-Gen. R. S. Geiger, U.S.M.C.).
III Amphibious Corps (reinforced).
Corps Troops.
1st Marine Division.
6th Marine Division.
Assigned Garrison Troops.

Task Group 56.3. Southern Landing Force. (Major-Gen. J. R. Hodge, U.S.A.)
XXIV Army Corps (reinforced).
Corps Troops.
7th Army Div.
96th Army Div.
Assigned Garrison Troops.

Gunfire and Covering Force (Task Force 54) (Rear-Admiral M. L. Deyo)
TASKS: (a) Assign ships to C.T.F. 52 for bombardment.
(b) Prevent enemy surface forces from interfering with landing operations.

10 old battleships, 23 destroyers, 9 heavy cruisers, 6 escort vessels, 4 light cruisers, 3 seaplane tenders (destroyers).

Amphibious Support Force (Task Force 52) (Rear-Admiral W. H. P. Blandy)
TASKS. Capture and defend Kerama Retto

Capture and defend Keise Shima.
Neutralize or destroy defence installations on Okinawa.
Fire support ships:

14 escort aircraft carriers. 10 destroyers. 17 escort vessels. 2 minelayers. 13 high speed minesweepers. 36 minesweepers. 13 light minelayers. 4 submarine chasers. 5 motor gunboats. 26 motor minesweepers. 20 Landing craft, personnel, ramped. 7 net-layers. 1 net ship. 14 high speed (destroyer) transports. 10 underwater demolition teams. 24 landing craft, infantry, gun. 3 landing craft (Senior Officers' ships). 11 landing craft, infantry, medium. 6 landing craft, infantry, rocket. 12 landing ships, medium, rocket.

Western Islands Attack Group (Task Group 51.1) (Rear-Admiral J. N. Kiland) (Under C.T.F. 52)

77th Infantry Division Landing Force (Major-General A. D. Bruce, U.S.A.)

TASK. Capture and defend Kerama Retto and begin the establishment there of an anchorage for the logistic support of fleet units and as a seaplane base.

Demonstration Group (Task Group 51.2) (Rear-Admiral J. Wright)

TASK. Diversionary feints of landings on S.E. Okinawa on L. and L+1 days.
Landing Force (Major-General T. E. Watson, U.S.M.C.).
2nd Marine Division, plus attached troops and one R.C.T. from Ill Amphibious Corps and XXIV Corps.

Expeditionary Force Floating Reserve (Task Group 51.3) (Cdre. J. B. McGovern)

27th Army Division (Major-Gen. G. W. Griner, U.S.A.) At Ulithi until called for by C.T.F. 51.
C.T.U. 51.3.1. (Transron 16) (Cdre. McGovern).

51.13.12 (Transdiv 46) (Cdre. McGovern)
Transports, attack: *Cecil, Devel, Darke, Hocking, Eldorado,*
Cargo ships attack: *Tolland, Whiteside.*

51.3.13 (Transdiv 47) (Capt. A. S. Wotherspoon)
Transports, attack: *Rutland, Highlands, Sandoral, Hansford.*
Cargo ship, attack: *New Hanover.*

51.3.14 (Transdiv 48) (Capt. C. L. Andrus, Jr.)
Transports, attack: *Talladega, Missoula, Lubbock, Dickens.*
Cargo ship, attack: *Yancey.*

51.3.6 (Landing Craft Unit) (Lt.-Cdr. Johnson)
L.S.M. Group 17 (10 Landing ships, medium).

51.3.7 (Expeditionary Force Floating Reserve) (Cdr. Rich).
Effective only until arrival at objective Cortdiv 61.
Escort vessels, destroyer: *Rall, Connolly, Finnegan, Grady, Halloran, McClelland.*

51.3.15 (Transdiv 27)
(Temp.) (Capt. A. J. Detzer)
Cargo ships, attack: *Lenawee, Carteret.*
Transport vessel, personnel: *Thurston.*
Cargo ships, attack: *Athens, Stokes*

Area Reserve (Task Group 51.4) (Commodore Loomis.)
(Not committed.)
81st Army Division

Transport Screen (Task Group 51.5) (Capt. F. Moosbrugger)

TASK. Protect vessels inside the screen against air, submarine and surface attack.

Ammen, Anthony, Bache, Bagley, Barton, Beale, Bennett, Bennion, Bradford, Boyd, Bryant, Bush, Capps, Callaghan, Cassin Young, C. J. Badger, Colhoun, Cowell, Daly, Gainard, Gregory, Evans, Hall, Halligan, H. L. Edwards, Hudson, Hutchins, Hyman, Ingraham, Irwin, Isherwood, Kimberley, J. D. Henley, Laffey, Laws, Leutze, Little, Longshaw, Lowry, Luce, M. L. Abele, Moale, Morrison, Mullany, Newcomb, O'Brien,Patterson, Paul Hamilton, Picking, Porterfield, Preston, Purdy, Prichett, Putnam, Ralph Talbot, Rooks, R. P. Leary, Sproston, Twiggs, Van Valkenburgh, Wadsworth, Wickes, W. D. Porter. (Destroyers, 63.)

Abercrombie, Chemson, Connolly, D. M. Cummings, Dennis, Eisde, Fleming, Finnegan, Foreman, Grady, G. E. Badger, Goldsborough, Goss, Halloran, K. C. Campbell, L.C. Taylor, Leray Wilson, Manlove, McClelland, Melvin R. Nawman, Oberrender, O'Neill, O'Flaherty, Oliver Mitchell, Hall, R. S. Bull, R. W. Powell, R. W. Suesens, Riddle,

R. F. Keller, S.S. Miles, Sands, Sederstrom, Seid, Stern, Swearer, Tabberer, Tisdale, U. M. Moore, Vammen, W.C. Wann, Wesson, Willmarth, Witter, W. Sieverling (45 escort vessels, destroyer.)

Chase, Crosby, Dickerson, Greene, Gosselin, Humphreys, Manley, Osmond Ingram, Overton, Ringness, Sims, Stringham, Tattnall (13 high speed (destroyer) transports).

Taney (Coastguard cutter), *Forrest* (Light minelayer), *PCE(R) 851, SC 636, SC 668.*

Service and Salvage Group (Task Group 51.6) (Capt. Curtis)

TASK. Provide salvage, fire-fighting and repair services.

Clamp, Gear, Shackle (3 salvage vessels), *Yuma, Tawakoni* (2 ocean tugs (fleet) *ATR 51, ATR 52* (2 rescue tugs), 4 ocean tugs (fleet) or ocean tugs (auxiliary), *Oceanus* (Repair ship battle damage), *Coronis, Egeria, Endymion* (3 Repair ship, landing craft, Landing ship, tank, assigned for fog oil storage, other vessels assigned.

1.

NORTHERN ATTACK FORCE (TASK FORCE 53) (Rear-Admiral L F. Reinfonider)

Force flagship *Panamint*. 1 Headquarters ship (Capt. E.E. Woods)

65.2 Northern Landing Force (Major-Gen. RS Geiger, U.S.M.C.)
III Amphibious Corps (Reinforced)

53.1 Transport Group Able (TransRon 12) (Cde. H.B. Knowles)
53.1.1 Trans. Div. 34: 6 Transports, attack, 2 cargo ships, attack.
53.1.2 Trans. Div. 35: 5 Transports, attack, 2 cargo ships, attack.
53.1.3 Trans. Div. 36: 5 Transports, attack, 2 cargo ships, attack, 1 landing ship, dock, 1 landing ship, vehicle.
56.2.1 Landing Group Able: 6th Marine Division, plus attached units, Corps, 10th Army and Garrison troops assigned

53.2 Transport Group Bake (TransRon 18) (Cdr. J.G. Moyer)
53.2.1 Trans. Div. 52: 5 Transports, attack, 2 cargo ships, attack, 1 landing ship, dock, 1 landing ship, vehicle.
53.2.2 Trans. Div. 53: 5 Transports, attack, 2 cargo ships, attack.

53.2.3 Trans. Div. 54: 5 Transports, attack, 2 cargo ships, attack, 1 landing ship, dock.
56.2.2 Landing Group Baker: 1st Division, plus attached units, Corps 10th Army and Garrison troops assigned.

53.3 Northern Tractor Flotilla (Capt. J. S. Laidlaw)
53.3.2 Tractor Group Baker: 1 landing craft (Senior Officer), 16 landing ships, tank.
53.3.1 Tractor Group Able: 1 landing craft (Senior Officer), 16 landing ships, tank, 16 landing ships, medium.
53.3.3 Tractor Group Charlie: 1 landing craft (Senior Officer), 14 landing ships, tank, 8 landing ships, medium, 1 landing ship, tank (medium).

53.4 Northern Control Group (Capt. Coleman)
53.4.1 Central Control Unit: 1patrol craft escort vessel, 180-ft., 1 submarine chaser, 136-ft., 2 submarine chasers, 136-ft.
53.4.2 Control Unit Able: 2 submarine chasers, 136-ft.

53.4.3 Control Green: 1 submarine chaser, 173-ft., 2 submarine chasers, 110-ft.
53.4.4 Control Red: 1 submarine chaser, 173-ft., 2 submarine chasers, 110-ft.
53.4.5 Control Unit Baker: 2 submarine chasers, 136-ft.
53.4.6 Control Blue: 2 submarine chasers, 136-ft.
53.4.7 Control Yellow:1 submarine chaser, 173-ft., 2 submarine chasers, 110-ft.

Northern Beach Party Group (Lt.-Cdr. Nelson)
2 Beach Party Units, Able and Baker.

Northern Defence Group (Capt. W. W. Weeden, Jr.)
1 Landing craft (Senior Officer), 21 landing ships, tank, 21 unclassified, 2 submarine chasers, 110-ft.
Northern Garrison Group (Capt. MacGowan)

Garrison Transport Group
1 transport vessel, personnel, 1 transport, attack, 2 ships converted to transports, attack, 5 civilian manned cargo ships, 1 landing ship, vehicle, 2 minelayers.

Screen Northern Garrison Group
4 escort vessels, destroyer.

Northern Support Craft
52.18.1 Gunboat Support Division: 6 Landing craft, infantry, gun.
52.19.3 LCS Division Three: 6 Landing craft, support, large.
52.19.4 LCS Division Four: 6 Landing craft, support large.
52.20.4 RCM and Rocket Division Four: 6 Landing craft, infantry, rocket (Radar counter measures).
52.20.5 RCM and Rocket Division Five: 6 Landing craft, infantry, rocket (Radar counter measures).
52.20.6 RCM and Rocket Division Six: 6 Landing craft, infantry, rocket (Radar counter measures).
52.21.2 LSM(R) Unit Two: 6 Landing ship, medium, rocket.
52.24. 2 Mortar Support Division Six: 6 Landing ship, infantry, mortar.
52.24.3 Mortar Support Division Seven: 6 Landing ship, infantry, mortar.
52.24.4 Mortar Support Division Eight: 4 Landing ship, infantry, mortar.

51.18.5 Northern Boat Patrol Unit (Lt.-Cdr. Nelson)
12 Landing craft, vehicle, personnel, 6 Armoured landing vehicles, tracked, 6 Landing vehicles, tracked, 2 submarine chasers, 110-ft, 2 Patrol craft escort vessels.

53.10 Northern Air Support Control Unit (Cdr. Perkins)

53.12 Northern Small Craft Group (Capt. C. H. Peterson, U.S.C.G.)

2.

SOUTHERN ATTACK FORCE (TASK FORCE 55) (Rear-Admiral J.L. Hall, Jr.)
Force Flagship *Teton* (communications HQ ship) (Capt. D.R. Tallman)

56.3 Southern Landing Force (Major-Gen. J.R. Hodge, USA)
XXIV Corps (reinforced).

55.1 Transport Group Dog (Trans. Ron 13) (Cdre. M.O. Carlson)
55.1.1 Trans. Div. 37: 4 Transports, attack, 2 cargo ships, attack.
55.1.2 Trans. Div. 38 4 Transports, attack, 1 landing ship, dock, 1 cargo ship, attack.
55.1.3 Trans. Div. 39: 4 Transports, attack, 2 cargo ships, attack.
55.1.4 Trans. Div. 13: 4 Transports, attack, 2 cargo ships, attack, 1 landing ship, vehicle.
56.3.1 Landing Group Dog: 7th U.S. Infantry Division plus attached units. Corps and Garrison Force Troops assigned for transportation.
55.2 Transport Group Easy (Trans Ron 14) (Cdre. C. G. Richardson)
55.2.1 Trans. Div. 40: 4 transports, attack, 2 cargo ships, attack, 1 landing ship, dock.
55.2.2 Trans. Div. 41: 4 Transports, attack, 2 cargo ships, attack.
55.2.3 Trans, Div. 43: 4 transports, attack, 2 cargo ships, attack, 1 landing ship, dock.
55.2.4 Trans Div. 14: 4 Transports, attack, 1 cargo ship, attack.
55.3.2 Landing Group Easy: 96th U.S. Infantry Division, plus attached unit. Tenth Army and Garrison Force Troops assigned for transportation.

55.3 Southern Tractor Flotilla (Capt. W. H, Brereton)
Flotilla and group flagship: 1 Landing craft infantry (Senior Officer).
55.3.1, 55.3.4, 55.5, 855.3.6 Tractor Group Dog: 14 Landing ships, tank, 2 landing ships, tank, hydrographic, 1 landing craft, infantry (Senior Officer), 13 landing ships medium.
55.3.2, 55.3.7, 55.3.8, 55.3.9 Tractor Group Easy: 14 Landing ships, tank, 2 landing ships, tank, hydrographic, 1 landing craft, infantry (Senior Officer), 5 landing ships medium.
55.3.3, 55.3.10, 55.3.11, 55.3.12, 55.3.13: Tractor Group Fox: 21 Landing ships, tank, 2 landing craft, infantry (Senior Officers), 10 landing ships medium.

55.4 Southern Control Group (Capt. Adeli)
55.4.1. Southern Flagship Unit: 1 Patrol craft escort vessel, 80-ft., 2 submarine chasers, 136-ft., 1 landing craft personnel (large).
55.4.2 Control Unit Dog: 2 submarine chasers, 136-ft., landing craft personnel (large) as assigned from 55.4.1.
55.4.3. Control Purple: 1 submarine chaser, 173-ft., 1 submarine chaser, 110-ft.
55.4.4 Control Orange: 1 submarine chaser, 173-ft., 2 submarine chasers, 110-ft.

55.4.5 Control Unit Easy: 2 submarine chasers, 136-ft., landing craft personnel, large, as assigned from 55.4.1.
55.4.6 Control White: 1 submarine chaser, 173-ft., 2 submarine chasers, 110-ft.
55.4.7 Control Brown: 1 submarine chaser, 173-ft., 3 submarine chasers, 110-ft.

55.5 Southern Beach Party Group (Cdr. Leever)
2 beach party units Dog and Easy.

Southern Attack Force Screen (Capt. E. W. Young)
Effective only until L-Day
Desron 24: 14 destroyers, 4 escort vessels, destroyer, 3 high speed (destroyer) transports, 1 patrol craft escort vessel (R).

Southern Defence Group (Cdr. Zelinka)
23 landing ships, tank, 14 landing ships, medium, 11 unclassified, 1 repair ship, battle damage, 1 oiler, 2 landing craft, infantry (large).

55.8 Southern Garrison Group (Capt. R. J. Townsend)
5 transports, attack, 1 Transport vessel, 1 ship converted tp transport, attack, 3 cargo ships, attack, 1 cargo vessel, 2 civilian manned cargo ships.
Screen: 5 high speed (destroyer) transports, 1 coastguard cutter.
Garrison troops assigned.

3.
GUNFIRE AND COVERING FORCE (TASK FORCE 54)
(Rear-Admiral M. L. Deyo)

Gunfire Support Group 54.1(Rear-Admiral B. J. Rodgers)

54.1.1 Fire Support Unit One (Rear-Admiral P. K. Fischler)
Old battleships *Texas* (Flagship), *Maryland*.
Heavy cruiser *Tuscaloosa*.
Destroyers *Laws, Longshaw, Morrison, Prichett*.

54.1.2 Fire Support Unit Two (Rear-Admiral O. T. Joy)
Old battleships *Arkansas, Colorado*.
Heavy cruisers *San Francisco, Minneapolis*.
Destroyers *Hall, Halligan, Paul Hamilton, Laffey, Twiggs*.

54.1.3 Fire Support Unit Three (Rear-Admiral B. J. Rodgers)
C.T.G. 54.1: Old battleships *Tennessee, Nevada.*
Heavy cruiser *Wichita.*
Light cruisers *Birmingham, St. Louis.*
Destroyers *M. L. Abele, Zellars, Bryant, Barton, O'Brien.*

54.1.4 Fire Support Unit Four (Rear-Admiral Le D. McCormick)
Old battleships *West Virginia, Idaho.*
Heavy cruisers *Portland, Pensacola.*
Light cruiser *Biloxi.*
Destroyers *Porterfield, Callaghan, Irwin, Cassin Young, Preston.*

54.1.5 Fire Support Unit Five (Rear-Admiral A. E. Smith)
Old battleships *New Mexico* (Flagship of Cdr. 5th Fleet), *New York.*
Heavy cruisers *Indianapolis, Salt Lake City.*
Destroyers *H.L. Edwards, Newcomb, Leutze, R.P. Leary, Bennion.*

54.1.6 Fire Support Unit Six (Cdr. Hinds)
Seaplane tenders (destroyer) *Williamson, Gillis.*
Escort vessels (destroyer) *S.S. Miles, Wesson, Witter, Willmarth.*

The following ships reported to T.F. 54 after L-Day:
Heavy cruiser *New Orleans*, Light cruiser, *Mobile*. Destroyers *C.J. Badger, W.D. Porter, Picking, Daly, Sproston, Beale, Rooks, Anthony, Wadsworth, Hutchins, Isherwood*. Light minelayer, *Forrest*.

4.
AMPHIBIOUS SUPPORT FORCE (TASK FORCE 52)

(Rear-Admiral W. H. P. Blandy)
Force flagship *Estes*, 1 Headquarters ship (Capt. B. O. Mathews).

52.10 Air Support Control Unit (Capt. Parker).
54.1 Fire support group (Rear-Admiral Rodgers).

52.1 Support Carrier Group (Rear-Admiral Durgin)

52.1.1 Support Carrier Unit One – Cardiv 36 and Screen (Rear-Admiral Sprague).
Escort carriers, *Makin Island*, Fanshaw Bay*, Lunga Point*, Sangamon**, Wake Island*.*
Destroyers, *Patterson, R. Talbot, Bagley, Moale.*

Escort vessels, destroyer, *R. M. Rowell, R. S. Bull, Dennis, O'Flaherty, Eiderstrom, Fleming*.

52.1.2 Support Carrier Unit Two – Cardiv 25 (Rear-Admiral G. R. Henderson).

Escort carriers, *Saginaw Bay*, Sargent Bay*, Rudyard Bay*, Petrof Bay*, Tulagi*, Natoma Bay**.

Des Div. 91 destroyers, *Capps, Lowry, Evans, J. D. Henley,* Ingraham.

Cort Div. 70, escort vessels, destroyer, *W. Seiverling, U. M. Moore, K. C. Campbell, Goss, Tisdale, Eisele*.

52.1.4 Support Carrier Unit Four – Cardiv 24 (Rear-Admiral F. B. Stump)

Escort carriers, *Marcus Island*, Savo Island*, Anzio**.

Des Div. 92 destroyers, *Boyd, Bradford*.

Cort Div. 72, escort vessels, destroyer, *L.C. Taylor, M.R. Nawman, O. Mitchell, R.F. Keller, Tabberer*.

* = Aircraft: 18 FM and 12 TBF or 42 FM or 30 F6F or F4U.
** = Aircraft: 24 F6F and 9 TBF or 42 FM or 36 F6F or F4U.

52.2 Mine Flotilla (Rear-Admiral A. Sharp)

52.3 D.M.S. Group (Capt. R. A. Larkin).

52.3.2 Sweep Unit Two – Min. Div. 58 (Cdr. Mitchell).

High Speed Minesweepers, *Forrest, Fitch, Hobson, Macomb, Hopkins*.

Light minelayer, *Groin*.

52.3.3 Sweep Unit Three – Mine Div. 59 (Capt. Larkin).

High Speed Minesweepers, *Ellyson, Hambleton, Rodman, Emmons*.

Light minelayer, *Lindsey*.

52.3.4 Sweep Unit Four – Min. Div. 60 (Cdr. Mathews).

High Speed Minesweepers, *Butler, Gherardi, Jeffers, Harding*.

Light minelayer, *Aaron Ward*.

52.4 A.M. Group One (Cdr. Donohue)

52.4.1 Sweep Unit Five – Min. Div. 10 (Cdr. Howard)

Minesweepers, *Champion, Defense, Ardent, Devastator*.

Light minelayer, *Adams*.

Submarine chaser, 173-ft., *P.C. 584*.

52.4.2 Sweep Unit Six – Min. Div. 13 (Lt.-Cdr. Pierce, Jr.)
Minesweepers, *Requisite, Revenge, Sage, Pursuit.*
Light minelayer, *Tolman.*
Submarine chaser, 173-ft., *P.C. 1128.*

52.4.3 Sweep Unit Seven (Lt.-Cdr. Estep)
Minesweepers, *Skylark, Shallow, Sterling, Heed.*
Light minelayer, *H. A. Wiley.*
Submarine chaser, 173-ft., *P.C. 1179.*

52.4.4 Sweep Unit Eight (Lt.-Cdr. Costello)
Minesweepers, *Gladiator, Impeccable, Vigilance, Spear, Triumph.*
Light minelayer, *Shea.*
Submarine chaser, 173-ft., *P.C. 1598.*

52.5 A.M. Group Two (Cdr. Freiburghouse)
52.5.1 Sweep Unit Nine – Min. Div. 35 (Lt.-Cdr. Kettering).
Minesweepers, *Skirmish, Signet, Scurry, Spectacle, Spector, Staunch.*
Light minelayer, *Tracy.*
Motor gunboat, *P.G.M. 9.*

52.5.2 Sweep Unit Ten – Min. Div. 36 (Lt. Hanson)
Minesweepers, *Serene, Shelter, Strategy, Strength, Success, Superior.*
Light minelayer, *J.W. Ditter.*
Motor gunboat, *P.G.M. 10.*

52.5. I Sweep Unit Eleven – Min. Div. 41 and 42 (Lt.-Cdr. McMillen).
Minesweepers, *Diploma, Density, Facility, Ransom, Rebel, Recruit.*
Motor gunboat, *P.G.M. 11.*

52.6 VMS Group (Lt.-Cdr. Bowes)
Sweep Units 12, 13, 14, 15: 26 motor minesweepers, 4 light minelayers, 2 motor gunboats. Mine Investigation and Disposal Unit: 1 light minelayer, 2 motor minesweepers, 4 landing craft, personnel (ramped), 1 motor gunboat.
Sweep Unit 20: landing craft personnel (ramped) embarked initially in high speed (destroyer) transports.

52.8 Net and Buoy Group (Cdr. King)
1 minelayer, 8 netlaying ships, 1 cargo ship, net.

52.11 Underwater Demolition Flotilla (Capt. Hanlon)

52.12 Underwater Demolition Group Able: 6 high speed (destroyer) transports, 4 underwater demolition teams.

52.13 Underwater Demolition Group Baker: 8 high speed (destroyer) transports, 6 underwater demolition teams.

52.25 Advance Support Craft (Capt. T.W. Rimer): 3 landing craft, infantry (Senior Officer), 24 landing craft, infantry, gun, 11 landing craft, infantry, medium, 6 landing craft, infantry, rocket (radar counter measures), 12 landing ship (medium), rocket.

5.

WESTERN ISLANDS ATTACK GROUP (TASK GROUP 51.1)

(Rear-Admiral I. N. Kiland)

Group flagship *Mt. McKinley* (Communications H.Q. ship) (Capt. W. N. Gamet).

51.1.10 Air Support Control Unit (Cdr. Buckley).

56.4 Western Islands Landing Force (Major-General A. D. Bruce, U.S.A.).

Army Troops: 77th Infantry Division, plus attached units.

Fleet Marine forces: 1 Amphibious R/C Battalion, less Coy. "B".

51.1.3 Trans. Div. 49 (Cdre. T. B. Brittain): Transports, attack, *Chilton, La Grange, Tasewell, St. Mary's,* cargo ships, attack, *Oberon, Torrance.*

51.1.4 Trans. Div. 50 (Capt. Kiehl): Transports, attack, *Henrico, Pitt, Drew, Natrona,* cargo ship, attack, *Tate,* evacuation transport (for wounded), *Rixey.*

51.1.5 Trans. Div. 51 (Capt. Willis): Transports, attack, *Goodhue, Eastland, Telfair, Mountrail, Montrose,* cargo ships, attack, *Wyandot, Suffolk*

51.1.7 Reconnaissance Section (Lt-Cdr. Street): High speed (destroyer) transports *Kinzer, Scribner* (Marine Amphibious R/C embarked).

51.1.6 Western Islands Tractor Flotilla (Capt. Webb): 1 landing craft, infantry (Senior Officer), 18 landing ships, tank.

51.1.9 Western Islands Reserve Tractor Group (Cdr. Anderson): 10 landing ships, tank.

51.1.14 Western Islands LSM Group (Cdr, Doe): 1 landing craft, infantry (Senior Officer), 11 landing ships (medium).

51.1.11 Western Islands Control Unit (Lt. Baker): 1 patrol craft escort vessel, 180-ft., 2 submarine chasers, 173-ft., 4 submarine chasers, 110-ft., 1 submarine chaser, 136-ft.

51.1.12 Western Islands Beach Party Unit (Lt.-Cdr. Lunt). 4 beach parties, I patrol craft escort vessel, 180-ft. (Rocket), 1 submarine chaser 110-ft., assigned.

52.12 Underwater Demolition Group Able.
Assigned from T.F. 52

51.1.15 Western Islands Fire Support Unit
Assigned from T.F. 52

51.1.15 Western Islands Support Craft Flotilla (Captain Rimmer)
Assigned from T.F. 52

51.5 Transport Screen (Capt. F. Moosbrugger) (effective 0600 L-Day). Screen flagship amphibious force, flagship *Biscayne.*

51.5.2 Kerama Retto Screen – vessels assigned by C.T.G. 51.5 after L-Day.

51.1.13 Western Islands Attack Group Screen (Capt. F. Moosbrugger). (Effective only until L-Day).
Des Ron. 49 (Capt. B. F. Brown): Destroyers, *Picking, Sproston, Wickes, W.D. Porter, Isherwood, Kimberly, Luce, C. J. Badger, Star.*
Cort. Div. 69 (Cdr. Phifer): Escort Vessels (Destroyer), *Abercrombie, Suesens, Oberrender.*
Cort Div. 44 (Lt.-Cdr. Hinds): Escort Vessels (Destroyer), *Riddle, Swear, Stern.* High speed destroyer escorts *Humphreys, Herbert, Dickerson.*

52.8 Net and Buoy Group (Lt.-Cdr. King) Assigned from T.F. 52.

51.20 Seaplane Base Group (Capt. G. A. McLean).
Seaplane tenders (large), *Hamlin, St. George, Chandeleur, Hamlin.*
Seaplane tenders (small), *Yakutat, Onslow, Shelikof, Bering Strait.*
Seaplane tenders (destroyers), *Gillis, Thornton, Williamson.*

51.17 Hydrographic Survey Unit (Lt. Woodke)
2 surveying vessels.

51.6 Service and Salvage Unit (Capt. Curtis).
Assigned from T.G. 51.6, 3 salvage vessels, 2 ocean tugs (fleet), 2 rescue tugs, 4 ocean tugs (fleet) or (auxiliary), 1 repair ship, battle damage, 3 repair ships, landing craft, 1 tank landing ship.

51.1.17 Western Islands Pontoon Barge and Causeway Unit (Lt. Zeigler).
7 causeways, 9 warping tugs, 4 barges.

51.1.18 LCT Group (Lt. Carncross).
18 landing craft, tank. 1

51.1.19 Kerama Retto Boat Pool (Lt.-Cdr. Pardee). (Included with Boat Pool Able.)
1 landing ship, tank (medium), *Egeria* repair ship, landing craft, *Gunston Hall* landing ship, dock.

56.2.5 Mine Investigation and Disposal Unit (Cdr. Clay).
Assigned from T.F. 52.

52.7.4 Sweep Unit Nineteen (Cdr. McEathron).
Minesweepers *Buoyant, Design, Device, Execute, Haggard.*

6.
DEMONSTRATION GROUP (TASK GROUP 51.2) (Rear-Admiral J. Wright)

Group flagship *Ancon,* 1st Headquarters ship (Capt. M. S. Pearson)

51.2.10 Air Support Control Unit (Cdr. Dickinson).

56.5 Demonstration Landing Group (Major-General T. E. Watson, U.S.M.C.).
From Army troops 2nd Marine Division, plus attached units.

51.2.1 Trans. Ron. 15 (Cdre. H. C. Flanagan).

51.2.11 Trans. Div. 43 (Cdre. H. C. Flanagan) – RCT No. 6 embarked.
Transports, attack *Bayfield, Mellette, Hendry, Sibley, Berrien.*
Cargo ships, attack Shoshore, *Theenim.*
Evacuation transport (for wounded) *Pinkney.*

51.2.12 Trans. Div, 44 (Capt. J.H. Seyfried) – RCT No. 2 embarked.
Cargo ships, attack *Hinsdale, Pickens, Sanborn, Kershaw, Bladen.*
Transports, attack *Logan, Newberry, Mifflin, Lowndes, Barrow.*
Cargo ships, attack *Lacerta, Muliphen*

51.2.6 Demonstration Group Tractor Flotilla (Cdr. Nickum).
2 landing craft, infantry (Senior Officer), 10 landing ships, tank, 1 landing ship tank (medium), 11 landing ships (medium).

51.2.7 Demonstration Group Control Unit (Cdr. Kuder).
1 submarine chaser 136-ft., 2 submarine chasers 173-ft., 4 submarine chasers 110-ft.

51.2.8 Demonstration Group Screen (Capt. A.D. Chandler).
(Effective only until L-Day.)
Destroyers *Van Valkenburg, Colhoun, Gregory, Little, Brown, Gainard, Cowell.*
Escort vessels (Destroyer) *Leroy Wilson, Seid.*
High speed (destroyer) transports *Chase, Ringness.*
Submarine chasers, 110-ft. *SC 636, 668.*

51.2.9 Demonstration Support Craft (Lt.-Cdr. McFadden).
2 Support Units – total 12 landing craft, infantry (medium), 6 landing craft, infantry, gun, 6 landing craft, infantry (large).

February 51. 2.19 Beach Party Group (Lt.-Cdr. Lippincott).
3 beach parties.

Appendix E

ORGANIZATION OF CARRIER FORCES, 1ST MAY

(1)

TASK FORCE 58

C.T.F. 58 Vice Admiral M. A. Mitscher (flagship *Bunker Hill*).

Task Group 58.1 (Rear-Admiral J.J. Clark)

Carriers: *Hornet, Bennington.*

Light carriers: *Belleau Wood, San Jacinto.*

Battleships: *Massachusetts, Indiana.*

Heavy cruisers: *Pittsburgh, Baltimore, Quiney.*

Light cruisers: *Vincennes, Miami, San Juan, Vicksburgh.*

Destroyers: *Haven, Mansfield, L.K. Swenson, Collett, Maddox, S.N. Moore, Blue, Brush, Taussig, John Rodgers, Harrison, McKee, Wedderburn, Twining, Stockham, Dashiell, Schroeder.*

Task Group 58.3 (Rear-Admiral F. C. Sherman)

Carriers: *Essex, Bunker Hill, Ranndolph.*

Light carrier: *Bataan.*

Battleships: *South Dakota, Washington.*

Light cruisers: *Pasadena, Astoria, Springfield, Oakland, Wilkes-Barre.*

Destroyers: *Owen, The Sullivans, Miller, Stephen Potter, Tingey, Ault, English, C.S. Sperry, Waldron, J.W. Weeks, W.L. Lind, Hank, Borie, Erben, Black, Bullard, Chauncey, Stembel.*

Task Group 58.4 (Rear-Admiral A.W. Radford)

Carriers: *Yorktown, Shangri-la.*

Light carriers: *Independence, Langley.*

Battleships *Iowa, Wisconsin.*
Large cruisers: *Guam, Alaska.*
Light cruisers: *San Diego, Flint.*
Destroyers: *McCord, Heermann, Hailey, Remey, Norman Scott, Mertz, Monssen, Melvin, McDermut, McGowan, Cushing, Colahan, Uhlmann, Benham.*

(2)

TASK FORCE 57
(Vice-Admiral Sir H. Bernard Rawlings, K.C.B., O.B.E.)

1st Battle Squadron
King George V (flag of C.T.F. 57-B.S.1).
Howe.
1st Carrier Squadron
Indomitable (flag of 2nd in command T.F. 57 and A.C.1 (38 Hellcats, 15 Avengers).
Victorious (37 Corsairs, 14 Avengers, 2 Walrus).
Formidable (Capt. P. Ruck-Keene, CBE) (36 Corsairs, 18 Avengers).
Indefatigable (40 Seafires, 12 Firefly, 21 Avengers).
4th Cruiser Squadron
Swiftsure (flag of C.S. 4) (9 x 6-in., 10 x 4-in.).
H.M.C.S. *Uganda* (Capt. E.R. Mainguy, OBE) (9 x 6-in., 8 x 4-in.).
H.M.N.Z.S. *Gambia* (12 x 6-in., 8 x 4-in.).
Euryalus (8 x 5.25-in.).
Black Prince (8 x 5.25-in.).

25th Destroyer Flotilla
Grenville (Capt. D. 25).
Ursa (Cdr. D.B. Wyburd, D.S.O., D, S.C).
Undine.
Urania.
Urchin (Lieut.-Cdr. A.F. Harkness, O.B.E., D.S.C.).
Undaunted.

4th Destroyer Flotilla
Quilliam (Capt. R.G. Onslow, D.S.O. (Capt. D. 4)).
Quiberon.

Queenborough.
Quickmatch.
Quality.

27th Destroyer Flotilla
Kempenfelt (Capt. D. 27).
Whirlwind.
Wessex.

Appendix F

TASK FORCE 54, ORGANIZATION FOR BATTLE, 7TH APRIL

Gunfire and Covering Force (Rear-Admiral M. L Deyo)

54.5 Battle Line (Rear-Admiral L. D. McCormick)

Battleship Division 3: *Idaho* (Flagship), *New Mexico* (Flagship of Com, Fifth Fleet), *Tennessee* (Flagship of C.T.F. 54).

Battleship Division 4: *West Virginia* (Flagship), *Colorado, Maryland.*

54.6 Right Flank Forces (Rear-Admiral Rodgers)

Cruiser Div. 13: *Birmingham* (Flagship), *Mobile, Biloxi.*

Destroyer Sqdn. 69: *Barton, Laffey.*

Destroyer Sqdn. 55: *Porterfield, Callaghan, Irwin, Preston, Longshaw.*

Destroyer Sqdn. 51: *Hall, Twiggs.*

Destroyer Div. 90: *Hutchins, Bennion.*

54.7 Left Flank Forces (Rear-Admiral Joy)

Cruiser Div. 6: *San Francisco* (flagship), *Minneapolis, Tuscaloosa, Portland.*

Destroyer Sqdn. 56: *R. P. Leary, H. L. Edwards.*

Destroyer Sqdn. 24: *Anthony, Beale, Wadsworth.*

Destroyer Sqdn. 59: *W.D. Porter, C.J. Badger, Rooks, Zellars.*

Appendix G

CHRONOLOGY OF THE OPERATION

9th October, 1944

Cdr. Fifth Fleet received Cincpoa preliminary warning order.

31st December, 1944

Cdr. Fifth Fleet received Cincpoa Operation Plan No. 14-44.

3rd January, 1945

Cdr. Fifth Fleet issued Operation Plan No. 1-45.

18th-19th March, 1945

Task Force 58 struck Kyushu, Kure and Inland Sea area.

23rd March, L-9 Day

Task Force 58 began strikes on Okinawa.

24th March, L-8 Day

Battleships of Task Force 58 bombarded Okinawa. Minesweeping operations at objective commenced.

25th March, L-7 Day

Amphibious Support Force (T.F. 52) and Gunfire and Covering Force (T.F. 54) arrived and commenced bombardment and covering operations. Underwater Demolition Group (T.G. 52.11) began operations at Kerama Retto. Com. Fifth Fleet in *Indianapolis* arrived at Kerama Retto. Fast Carrier Task Force Groups and Support Carrier Group (52.1) provided CAP and air support. T.F. 58 as yesterday.

26th March, L-6 Day

Western Islands Attack Group (51.1) arrived at Okinawa, and the 77th Division commenced occupation of the principal islands of Kerama Retto against light opposition. First air attack on shipping engaged in this operation damaged the light minelayer *Adams* and destroyer *Kimberly,* whilst other ships received minor damage. The destroyer *Halligan* was sunk by a mine in unswept waters 208° 14 miles from Sampa Misaki. British Carrier Force (T.F. 57) commenced strikes against Sakishima Gunto. T.F. 58 and T.G. 52.1 as yesterday.

27th March, L-5 Day

Landings on the islands of Kerama Retto continued. Many enemy suicide boats were captured in caves and destroyed. The battleship *Nevada,* light cruiser *Biloxi,* destroyer *O'Brien* were damaged by suicide air attacks. Minesweeping was slightly behind schedule, causing postponement of reconnaissance from L-4 to L-3 Day. Naval bombardment of Okinawa continued. Task Force 57 attacked Miyako and Ishigaki. T.F. 58 and T.G. 52.1 as yesterday.

28th March, L-4 Day

All organized opposition ceased on Kerama Retto. The minesweeper *Skylark* was sunk off Okinawa whilst sweeping. The Fast Carrier Force and Support Carrier Force continued to give air support, attacking ground targets. One group (58.1) of Fast Carrier Force despatched strike against Japanese Fleet, reported off Kyushu, but failed to find the enemy. T.F. 57 fuelling.

29th March, L-3 Day

Twenty-four enemy aircraft were destroyed in attacks on shipping off Okinawa to-day. The attack cargo ship *Wyandot* was damaged after dark by a suicide near miss. Air attacks on ships on patrol stations and in retirement areas during the night caused damage, but a number of enemy aircraft were destroyed. At least eight Japanese suicide boats were destroyed in attacks on shipping, slight damage being caused to one L.C.I. Fuelling and ammunitioning of ships commenced at Kerama Retto, and seaplanes began search and A/S operations from the Kerama Seaplane Base. U.D.T, reconnaissance of the Hagushi beaches and the demonstration beaches at Okinawa was completed. Fast U.S. carriers were absent from Okinawa, attacking shipping and targets on the Japanese mainland. Two battle cruisers with 4 A.A. cruisers and destroyers of T.F. 58 bombarded Minami

Oagari Shima last night. T.F. 57 fuelling. Part of Escort Carrier Group gave air support at Okinawa.

30th March, L-2 Day

All islands in Kerama Retto secured. Over 2,500 square miles around Okinawa had been swept for minutes to date. Enemy M.T.Bs. attacked ships on night patrol off Hagushi Beaches, without effect. T.F. 57 fuelling. Fast and support carriers gave air support at Okinawa.

31st March, L-1 Day

The Western Islands Attack Group occupied Keise Shima without opposition and landed field guns, which were in position and registered for the support of the main Okinawa landing at 1830. U.D.T. operations on the Hagushi beaches continued with the support of heavy bombing by aircraft of Task Force 58 and Task Group 52.1, who flew 1,176 sorties during yesterday and today. About 257 mines destroyed to date. A Japanese submarine (*I-8*) was sunk by U.S. destroyers *Stockton* and *Morrison* southeast of Okinawa, 25° 29′ N., 128° 35′ E. The heavy cruiser *Indianapolis*, flagship of Commander Fifth Fleet, was disabled by suicide air attack and proceeded to Kerama Retto for temporary voyage repairs. Task Force 57 attacked Ishigaki.

1st April, L-Day

Preceded by intense naval and air bombardment the Tenth Army landed over the Hagushi Beaches on Okinawa against light enemy resistance. The assault waves hit the beach at 0830, and by 1230 had captured both Yontan and Katena Airfields, suffering light losses. 50,000 troops were landed before night. The light minelayer *Adams* and assault transport *Alpine* were damaged by suicide air attacks, the battleship *West Virginia* was hit, but remained fully operational. The destroyer *Vammen* was damaged by a floating booby-trap. The Demonstration Group made a feint landing on the south-eastern beaches on Okinawa, in the course of which the assault transport *Hinsdale* and *L.S.T. 884* were damaged by suicide air attack. T.F. 57 attacked Sakishima Gunto. Destroyer *Ulster* damaged by air attack.

2nd April, L+1 Day

The advance of the troops on Okinawa severed the enemy's north and south line of communications. The Demonstration Group carried out a second feint off the south-eastern beaches. S.O.P.A. Kerama Retto was appointed, with designation C.T.G. 51.15. The cargo ships attack,

Achernar and *Tyrell*, on night retirement last night were damaged by suicide air attacks. This evening Transron 17 and screen on night retirement south of Kerama Retto sustained a heavy air attack; the assault transport *Henrico* and high speed destroyer transport *Dikerson* were seriously damaged. General cargo loading progressed rapidly under excellent beach conditions. T.F. 57 sent patrols over Ishigaki.

3rd April, L+2 Day

For the first time support of troops in the XXIV Corps zone was delivered by Fire Support ships from the eastern side of the island, which the Corps reached to-day: the Corps re-organized and re-grouped preparatory to attack to the south. The enemy continued his early morning air attacks on shipping; the destroyers *Prichett* and *Foreman*, and *L.S.T. 599* were damaged. Other ships were attacked during the day, though only the escort carrier *Wake Island*, operating to the east, sustained major damage *L.C.I. 82* was attacked by a suicide motor torpedo boat and sank next day. The enemy craft was sunk. Night retirement, except for hospital ships, was discontinued. Fast carriers of Task Group 58.1 covered Sakishima Gunto, whilst Task Force 57 (B.P.F.) fuelled.

4th April, L+3 Day

The XXIV Corps attacked to the south on Okinawa against light, but organized, resistance. Weather conditions began to deteriorate. Winds N. to N.N.E, increased to 20 knots in the evening. Surf increased to 4 to 6-feet by nightfall. Night unloading was discontinued on account of adverse sea conditions. A group from T.F. 58 covered Sakishima Gunto whilst T.F. 57 fuelled.

5th April, L+4 Day

The XXIV Corps assumed command ashore at 1000. In the north advance continued rapidly, but in the south increased resistance was met from more highly organized defences than had previously been encountered. Heavy weather and surf continued to hinder all naval operations throughout the day. Unloading on all beaches was stopped. During the night 15 L.S.Ts. and some landing craft were damaged in varying degrees at the beaches. At 1240 a submarine was sighted in the transport area, and two or more torpedoes were fired, but no ship was hit. Commander Fifth Fleet shifted flag to the *New Mexico*. T.F. 58 again covered Sakishima Gunto in the absence of T.F. 57. Japanese submarine *R.O.-41* was sunk near Kume Shima by U.S. destroyer *Hudson*.

6th April, L+5 Day

Strong resistance was encountered from prepared enemy defensive positions on the southern front on Okinawa. Weather clearing and there was an increase in all operations, partially unloading from ships into small craft. Unloading over the beaches was resumed. The Japanese made their first full-scale air attack. Coming about 1500 violent air attacks were made, an estimated total of at least 400 enemy aircraft being involved, of which at least 75 per cent were destroyed. The main targets were patrol and picket stations. The destroyers *Bush* and *Colhoun*, high speed minesweeper *Emmons*, and cargo ships *Hobbs Victory* and *Logan Victory*, and *L.S.T. 447* were sunk by suiciders, and the following ships received major damage: the destroyers *Howarth, Hyman, Leutze, Morris, Mullany* and *Newcomb*, battleship *Maryland* (from bomb), high speed minesweeper *Rodman* and destroyer escort *Witter*, whilst numerous other ships received lesser damage. Submarines reported two large ships and many escorts making a sortie from Bungo Suido, between Kyushu and Shikoku. Task Force 57 attacked airfields in Sakishima Gunto.

7th April, L+6 Day

In the south the XXIV Corps, confronted by exceedingly rough and cliff-like terrain, encountered the strongest resistance to date. The advance on the northern front continuous to be rapid and resistance light. The Tactical Air Force Tenth Army was established ashore at 1000. Satisfactory unloading over all beaches resulted from improved weather. In air attacks early this morning the destroyer *Bennett* and destroyer escort *Wesson* were damaged. The battleship *Maryland* was damaged by a suicider this evening.

Battle of East China Sea

Commander Task Force 58 was directed to permit the enemy force leaving Bungo Saido to proceed southward. When later information indicated that the force might not proceed towards Okinawa, C.T.F. 58 was directed to search for it and attack with aircraft. At 0815 an *Essex* reconnaissance aircraft reported one battleship, two light cruisers, and ten destroyers south-west of Kyushu, course 270°, At 1015 Task Force 58 launched attack by 38 aircraft against this force, which actually consisted of one battleship, one light cruiser and eight destroyers. At 1030 PBMs of Task Group 50.5 (Search and Reconnaissance Task Group) made contact with the enemy and held contact until 0430 on 8th. The strike by Task Force 58 reached the enemy at 1330, 50 miles south-west of Kyushu and in the ensuing attacks the battleship *Yamato*, the light cruiser *Yahagi* and four destroyers were sunk, and four destroyers escaped, some of them damaged. Task Force 57 attacked airfields in Sakishima Gunto.

8th April, L+7 Day

The attack on the southern front settled down to an assault against strong defensive positions, organized in depth. Major-General Mulcahy, U.S.M.C., Commanding General Tactical Air Force, assumed control of aircraft ashore on Okinawa. Yontan was all-weather and Katena dry-weather operational. The destroyer *Gregory* was damaged by air attack. Direct air support of troops was furnished by the fast carriers of T.G. 58.4, as well as escort carriers of T.G. 52.1. The latter also covered Sakishima Gunto in the absence T.F. 57. Control of direct air support of the XXIV Corps was passed from A.S.C.U. 55.10 in the *Teton* to Landing Force Air Support Control Unit 2 ashore.

9th April, L+8 Day

Enemy reaction to the occupation of Okinawa was evidenced by day and night air attacks, attempted attacks by 12 to 15 suicide boats and swimmers (15 of whom were killed), and increased gun, mortar and small arms fire along the southern front. The Tenth Army Military Government Section reported 73,000 Okinawan civilians interned. Owing to shortage of artillery ammunition ashore all units were limited to ⅓ unit of fire per day. 27th Infantry Division began landing over the Hagushi beaches and was assigned to XXIV Corps. The destroyer *C.J. Badger* received major damage from suicide boat attack and *Sterett* from suicide air attacks. The Expeditionary Force Floating Reserve arrived off the Western Beaches and commenced to unload. T.F. 57 fuelling. Japanese submarine *R.O.-46* was sunk S.E. of Okinawa by U.S. destroyers.

10th April, L + 9 Day

At 0840 a R.C.T. of the 27th Infantry Division preceded by naval gunfire and air bombardment, landed against light opposition on the southern beaches of Tsuken Shima (Eastern Islands) and by 1730 cleared the island of enemy troops who had guns mounted there, from which yesterday the high speed destroyer transport *Hopping* received six hits. The other Eastern Islands contained no garrisons. In the northwest part of Okinawa Unten Ko was captured, and with it, submarine pens (less boats) and a radar jammer. Heavy seas interfered with replenishment from assault shipping, and at 1233 all ships and craft were ordered to retract from the reef off the Hagushi beaches. Control of direct air support of III Corps was passed from A.S.C.U. 53.10 in *Panamint* to Landing Force Air Support Control Unit 1 ashore. T.F. 57 patrolling in southern area.

1st April, L-+10 Day

At 1200 the Island Commander of Okinawa assumed command of all troops in Kerama Retto. Unloading began over the Nago Wan beaches. High surf prevented unloading over the Hagushi beaches. Task Force 58 was subjected to enemy air attacks in force. The carrier *Enterprise* and one destroyer were seriously damaged, and the carrier *Essex*, battleship *Missouri*, and three destroyers received minor damage, all from suicide attacks. T.F. 57 strike of Formosa was weathered out.

April 12th, L+11 Day

Unloading was resumed, the highest priority of discharge being given to gun ammunition. Battleships rendered fire support for the first time to-day from inside Nakagusuku Wan, which had been swept for mines. Ships at Okinawa received heavy air attacks, commencing at 0000 and continuing, intermittently, until 2330. The destroyer *M.L. Abele* was sunk by suicide air attack and Baka bomb, and the battleships *Tennessee* and *Idaho* were seriously damaged by suicide attacks. Eleven escort types and several smaller craft were damaged in varying degrees. At least 208 enemy aircraft were destroyed. Three American light units were hit during the first employment by the enemy of jet-propelled Baka bombs. T.F. 57 struck Formosa (Shinchiku airfield and Kiirun harbour).

April 13th, L+12 Day

Ships assisted in repulsing a strong enemy counter-attack along the Kakazu ridge. Up to date, a total of 2,368 naval personnel casualties from 81 ships had occurred. Task Force 57 struck airfields in northern Formosa.

14th April, L+13 Day

Constant enemy artillery and mortar fire was reported to have lowered the morale of some units to a limited extent, though morale as a whole continued excellent. The battleship *New York* received minor damage from suicide air attack. Escort carrier aircraft of the Support Carrier Group attacked airfields on Ishigaki and Myako in Sakishima Gunto. T.F. 57 fuelling.

15th April, L+14 Day

Three battalions of the 77th Infantry Division Field Artillery were landed on Menna Shima for support of the landing on Ie Shima scheduled for tomorrow. No enemy resistance encountered. From to-day shore based aircraft of Task Group 99.2 assisted the escort carriers of Task Group 52.1 in direct air support of troops. The fast carrier force assisted and also attacked Kyushu. Support Carrier Group again attacked Ishigaki, whilst T.F. 57 fuelled.

16th April, L+15 Day

At 0830 the 77th Infantry Division, supported by naval gunfire, air bombardment and guns previously emplaced on Menna Shima, landed on the southern beaches of Ie Shima on a two R.C.T front. Opposition was light, though bitter resistance to mopping up was subsequently encountered. Suicide aircraft and bombers made a heavy attack on the transport area this morning. The destroyer *Laffey* received four suicide hits and two direct bomb hits: she had 94 casualties, but shot down six enemy aircraft, and did not sink. The destroyer *Pringle* was sunk in the north, and *Hobson* and *Harding* (high speed minesweepers), *Bryant* (destroyer), *Bowers* (destroyer escort), the oiler *Taluga* and some landing craft received severe damage. 270 enemy aircraft were destroyed. Direct air support of the troops was given by the same forces as yesterday until cancelled in favour of defence of ships. Task Force 57 attacked Sakishima Gunto. Fighter sweeps were launched against Kyushu by Task Force 58 to break up a major enemy air attack. The fast carrier *Intrepid* was heavily damaged in an air attack on Task Force 58.

17th April, L+16 Day

Fire support ships remained all night in Nakagusuku Wan for the first time, rendering support to the troops ashore. Landing ships and craft were anchored last night in Chim Wan. Task Forces 57, 58 engaged in same areas as yesterday. Task group 58.2 was dissolved.

18th April, L+17 Day

Lieut.-General Buckner, U.S.A., Commanding General Tenth Army, established headquarters on shore at Okinawa. Cincpoa released the 81st Infantry Division from the area reserve for the Okinawa operation. Patrols up the coasts of the northern part of the island under no resistance. As Forces 53 and 55 were dissolved, Rear-Admiral Reifsnider (C.T.F. 53) became C.T.G. 51.22 and S.O.P.A., Ie Shima, with authority north of Zampa Misaki; Rear-Admiral Hall became (C.T.F. 55), and S.O.P.A. Hagushi, with authority north of Zampa Misaki. All assault shipping was reported unloaded, except for some Tenth Army troop supplies loaded in one transport. Fast carriers of T.F. 58 co-operated with the escort carriers of T.G. 52.1 in furnishing direct air support of troops. The latter group also made an attack on Sakishima Gunto. T.F. 57 fuelled. Japanese submarine *I-56* was sunk East of Okinawa by U.S. destroyers.

19th April, L+18 Day

XXIV Corps began a major assault on the enemy defence line in southern Okinawa; an advance of 800 to 1,000 yards was made along the entire front. Before the attack the entire southern section of Okinawa was plastered by the fire support ships, who were reinforced by the battleships *Washington, North Carolina,* and *South Dakota* from Task Force 58. A feint landing was made on this coast. The fast carriers assisted in furnishing direct air support of the troops until this was cancelled at 1500 through bad weather. An especially heavy series of strikes was made on south Okinawa. The first aircraft operated from Ie Shima. T.F. 57 remained in the replenishing area.

20th April, L+19 Day

XXIV Corps renewed the attack and made further gains to-day. All assault shipping was completely discharged. Direct air support of troops was furnished by the same forces as yesterday. Task Force 57 attacked Sakishima Gunto, and at 1910 set course for Leyte, for replenishment. The Escort Carrier Force took over the duty of neutralizing the airfields of the Sakishima Gunto,

April 21st, L+20 Day

Ie Shima was secured at 1059, after bitter resistance. Thus, Phase II of the operation was completed, although Phase I continued.

April 22nd, L+21 Day

Organized resistance at an end in northern Okinawa. Sesoko Shima (north of Nago Wan) was occupied without opposition. An attack was made by some 80 enemy aircraft this evening. 54 were destroyed, and none penetrated to the transport area. But the minesweeper *Swallow* was sunk, and the destroyer *Isherwood* was heavily damaged, and six other destroyer types received lesser damage on picket station.

23rd April, L+22 Day

Tankers connected with off-shore pipe lines began pumping oil into storage tanks on Okinawa. Direct air support of troops was assisted by fast carriers of T.F. 58.

24th April, L+23 Day

Unloading continued at a satisfactory rate over all beaches. Bad weather caused the cessation of direct air support of the troops.

April 25th, L+24 Day

Direct air support of the troops was held to a minimum through bad weather. T.U. 52.1.3 attacked Sakishima Gunto, Ishigaki, Miyako and Nobara runways. The first shore-based air search was made from Okinawa. Katena field was put out of action at 2032 through rain. New carrier *Shangri-la,* which joined T.G. 58.4 yesterday, launched strike against Okino Oagari Shima.

April 26th, L+25 Day

T.G. 52.1, fast carriers of T.F. 58 assisted with direct air support of troops.

April 27th, L+26 Day

Katena airfield became operational again during daylight. During the last night the destroyer *Hutchins* was badly damaged by a suicide boat whilst giving fire support to the 7th Division. Rear Adm. Fischler relieved Rear Adm. Smith as C.T.G. 51.19. The heavy cruiser *Wichita* was damaged by shell-fire at 2350 whilst engaged in a support mission in Nakagusuku Wan. Evening suicide attacks by 25 enemy aircraft sank the cargo ship *Canada Victory,* which was in a rift in the smoke cover, and damaged the destroyer escort *Ralph Talbot* and high speed destroyer transport *Rathburne.* These were the first large scale night suicide attacks. Direct air support of troops was furnished by the same forces as yesterday. Task Group 58.1 proceeded to Ulithi for replenishment and overhaul, a regular schedule having been instituted.

28th April, L+27 Day

An emergency landing strip became available on Ie Shima. Enemy small boat activity increased during last night and 19 were reported destroyed off the southwest coast, nine of them by the cruiser *St. Louis.* Several of them penetrated the screen and three of them were destroyed, one of which damaged a cargo ship. The suicide air attacks of yesterday evening continued from midnight to 0400 to-day on radar pickets and forces ashore by about 50 aircraft, but no ships received serious damage. Raids recommenced about 1400 and continued until 0200 on 29th, about 200 enemy aircraft being concerned. None of them reached the transport area before dark. 98 were destroyed in the objective area, in addition to 20 shot down near Task Force 58, where two destroyers were damaged. The destroyers *Daly* and *Twiggs*, a transport and a cargo ship were damaged in the objective area, in addition to minor damage to other ships. The hospital ship *Comfort*, observing full hospital ship procedure, was hit by a suicide aircraft 50 miles southeast of Okinawa at 2000. Direct air support of troops as yesterday. T.U. 52.1.1 attacked Sakishima Gunto.

29th April, L+28 Day

Machinato airfield was captured. Direct air support of troops as yesterday (T.F. 58, T.G. 99.2, T.G. 52.1). T.U. 52.1.3 attacked Sakishima Gunto. Air attack on T.F. 58 badly damaged two destroyers; 25 of the enemy were destroyed. Japanese submarine *R.109* was sunk S.E. of Okinawa by aircraft from *Tulagi*.

30th April, L+29 Day

The 1st Marine Division began relieving the 27th Infantry Division on the western sector of the southern front. The minelayer *Terror* at Kerama Retto was heavily damaged by suicide air attack at 0400, with 173 casualties. T.F. 58, T.G. 99.2, T.G. 52.1 operated similarly to yesterday.

1st May, L+30 Day

T.F. 58, T.G. 99.2, T.G. 52.1 were engaged on similar duties to yesterday.

2nd May, L+31 Day

Unloading over beaches at Nakagusuku Wan was begun. Bad weather reduced direct air support of troops to a minimum.

3rd May, L+32 Day

20-25 enemy aircraft attacked at sunset; the light minelayer *Aaron Ward* and high speed minesweeper *Macomb* were damaged and the destroyer *Little* and *L.S.M. 195* were sunk.

4th May, L+33 Day

Last night and this morning were marked by closely co-ordinated enemy air, sea and land attacks in an attempt to effect counter-landings behind the American lines on both sides of Okinawa. At 0200 some 500 to 600 enemy troops landed from barges west of Machinato Airfield, and 300 attempted to land on the east coast. 15 suicide boats were destroyed near the transport area last night; the only damage was to the cargo vessel *Carina*. The first air attacks began at 0130 and lasted until 0445 but caused no damage to ships. In a second series of

14 raids, from 0745 to 0915, by about 70 aircraft, the destroyers *Luce* and *Morrison*, and two L.S.Ms., were sunk by suiciders, and the light cruiser *Birmingham*, destroyer *Ingraham*, and light minelayer *Shea* were seriously damaged, the last named by Baka bomb, and many other light craft were slightly damaged. In the evening a third air attack damaged the escort carrier *Sangamon* and light minelayer *Gwin*. 137 enemy aircraft were destroyed during the day, including 12 suicide hits. Task Force 58 fighters assisted in defence of Okinawa area against enemy air attacks and shot down 98 out of the 137 enemy destroyed, losing only five aircraft. Task Force 57 resumed strikes on Sakishima Gunto, which was still being attacked by TU. 52.1.3, and the battleships with cruisers and screen bombarded Miyako. Naval patrol bombers operating from Yontan and Kerama Retto began today attacks on Japanese shipping in Tsushima Straits and round the southern coast of Korea.

5th May, L+34 Day

The ground situation, which showed little change, began to improve and small advances were made as the result of aggressive attacks and some lightening of the enemy resistance. Rear Adm. A.E. Smith (ComCruDiv 5) in *Salt Lake City* relieved Rear Adm. Deyo as Commander, Task Force 54. Task Force 57 struck Sakishima Gunto.

6th May, L+35 Day

Steps were taken to increase the volume of supplies and equipment which was considered to be somewhat less than was required to support the number of troops ashore and provide for the base development programme. Enemy air attacks this morning inflicted only minor damage on shipping. An evening attack caused no damage. Naval patrol bombers from Kerama and Yontan operated again off the coast of China, Korea and Kyushu.

7th May, L+36 Day

In the south, a two-corps front was established. A revised plan for naval gunfire went into effect. Service Squadron 10 (T.G. 50.9) began the movement of its principal base of operations from Ulithi to Leyte. T.F. 58, T.G. 99.2, T.G. 52.1, T.U. 52.1.3 and naval patrol bombers from Yontan and Kerama operated as yesterday.

8th May, L+37 Day

Activity limited by bad weather. At 1200 V.E. Day was celebrated by the firing at the enemy of one round from every gun ashore, accompanied by a full gun salvo from every possible fire support ship.

9th May, L+38 Day

The destroyer *England* and destroyer escort *Oberrender* were badly damaged by suicide air attacks at dusk whilst on radar picket stations. The aircraft carriers *Victorious* and *Formidable* were damaged by suiciders, but remained operational. After this attack, the striking position of T.F. 57 was moved further to the eastward.

10th May, L+39 Day

"A high snooper who flew over Okinawa at 0900 was brought down by an F4U of TG 99.2, who climbed to 38,000 feet and, after a chase of 165 miles, chewed the tail off the enemy plane with his propeller when his guns froze." In an air raid this evening the destroyer *H.W. Hadley* was hit by a torpedo which did not explode: the *H.W. Hadley* was undamaged. The destroyer *Kimberly* was missed by a torpedo.

11th May, L+40 Day

The Tenth Army launched a co-ordinated attack on the entire front, heavily supported by T.F. 58, T.G. 52.1 and T.G. 99.2, and made substantial gains on both flanks. In heavy air attacks this morning the destroyers *H.W. Hadley* and *Evans* received major damage. 3 of the enemy were shot down. Task Force 58, operating 80 miles east of Okinawa shot down 35 aircraft during a heavy attack in which the carrier *Bunker Hill,* flagship of Commander Task Force 58, was seriously damaged by a suicide hit. C.T.F. 58 shifted flag to *Enterprise,* Task Group 58.4 left for replenishment at Ulithi.

12th May, L+41 Day

Tori Shima was occupied without opposition and secured for the purpose of establishing an air raid warning station. Enemy small boat activity increased, and at least seven were destroyed in the early hours of to-day in the Naha area. Two enemy aircraft penetrated to the transport area this evening and crash-dived the battleship *New Mexico,* causing considerable structural damage. Thereafter, until his departure from the combat area on 28th May, Commander Fifth Fleet remained at anchor in the Hagushi anchorage, where repairs to *New Mexico* were effected. Task Force 57 and T.U. 52.1.3 continued strikes on Sakishima Gunto.

13th May, L+42 Day

An attempted enemy counter landing from six boats in the Machinato Airfield area was defeated, all six boats being destroyed. Airfield on Ie

Shima in full operation. 25 out of 35 enemy aircraft which approached the transport area this evening were shot down. The destroyers *Bache* and *Bright* were hit and damaged. The fast carriers of T.F. 58 destroyed between 92 and 154 enemy aircraft in operations against Kyushu airfields to-day. T.G. 52.1 and T.G. 99.2 gave direct air support of troops. Task Force 57 bombed the Sakishima Gunto airfields.

14th May, L+43 Day

Task Force 58 continued its strikes on Kyushu, destroying 73 aircraft, including over the Task Force, and probably destroying 46. During enemy attacks on the task force the carrier *Enterprise* was seriously damaged by a suicide crash, and C.T.F. 58 shifted his flag to the *Randolph*.

15th May, L+44 Day

Naval craft operating off the west coast of Okinawa were instrumental in breaking up another attempted enemy counter-landing near Machinato Airfield. Simultaneously, the enemy counter-attacked the left of the 22nd Marines. A second counter-attack at 0730 was stopped by artillery and ships' gunfire, but continued throughout the morning.

16th May, L+45 Day

Yontan and Katena Airfielda were bombed before dawn, bat little damage resulted. Task Unit 52.1.3 and Task Force 57 attacked Sakishima Gunto.

17th May, L+65 Day

At 0900 Vice-Admiral Hill (Com. Fifth PhibFor) relieved Vice-Admiral Turner as Commander Task Force 51. Coincident with this change, the command of all forces on shore in the Okinawa area passed to the Commanding General Tenth Army, who assumed responsibility to Commander Fifth Fleet for the defence and development of captured positions. C.T.F. 51 was responsible to Commanding General Tenth Army for control of the Air Defence of Okinawa and of naval forces present. The destroyer *D.H. Fox* was seriously damaged by suicide ait attack, but shot down four of the enemy. Task Force 57 attacked Sakishima Gunto. Task Force 58 assisted with air support of troops.

18th May, L+47 Day

Enemy air was active in the early hours and one raid did considerable damage to aircraft and runways at Yontan. The destroyer *Longshaw*, whilst aground southwest of Naha air strip, was destroyed by an enemy shore battery. *L.S.T. 808* was damaged by aerial torpedo this evening, and was beached, air support of troops as yesterday.

19th May, L+48 Day

Machinato Beach operational (designated Brown 5).

20th May, L+49 Day

Unloading crisis aggravated by bad weather. In dusk air attacks, 26 out of 35 attacking enemy aircraft were destroyed. Suicide hits causing major damage, were made on the destroyer escort *J.C. Buller*, destroyer *Thatcher*, and high speed destroyer transport *Chase*, all in the transport screen, and *LC.T. 808* whilst beached as the result of damage from air attack on 18th. Several sound contacts west of the transport area were attacked, with possible destruction of two or three midget submarines. T.F. 58 assisted in air support of troops.

21st May, L+50 Day

Bad weather limited air support of troops by T.G. 52.1 and 99.2.

22nd May, L + 51 Day

Bad weather prevented any air support missions.

24th May, L+53 Day

The objective area – the Shuri line – was under heavy enemy air attack, coming at dusk, 24th May, and continuing intermittently until 1200, 25th, most attacks being concentrated on the airfields. About 300 aircraft were involved, of which at least 181 were destroyed. One enemy aircraft landed about ten enemy troops on Yontan field at 2225 to-day, who did considerable damage to parked aircraft and installations before being killed. Improved visibility enabled artillery and fire support ships to operate with greater destructive effect against enemy positions and material. Task Force 57 covered Sakishima Gunto, Task Force 58 launched a clean up sweep against airfields in Southern Kyushu and covered Amami Gunto; and 28 TA.F. P. 47s struck Kyushu.

25th May, L+54 Day

Enemy artillery fire during the night was exceptionally heavy, and during the early morning and forenoon under cover of air attacks Japanese troops attempted counter-attacks and infiltrations, which were repulsed. On account of the weather, only a single air support mission could be carried out. From soon after midnight 24th/25th American ships began to suffer heavily from suicide air attacks. The high speed destroyer transport *Bates* and *LS.M. 135* were sunk, and the following received major damage: destroyer escort *O'Neill*, high speed destroyer transports *Barry* and *Roper*, destroyer *Stormes*, high speed minesweeper *Buller*, minesweeper *Spectacle*, cargo ship *W. Allinson*, whilst several other ships received minor damage. Task Force 58 was weathered out on the Amami Gunto strike. Task Force 57 struck Sakishima Gunto for the last time and retired to Manus via the refuelling area.

26th May, L+55 Day

The American lines had advanced only about four miles since April 4th, but to-day the enemy began withdrawing troops from the Shuri line along most of its length. Bad weather restricted air operations and all aircraft were grounded until 1315. Heavy rain severely curtailed unloading and supply. Critical shortage of artillery ammunition caused reduction of maximum daily expenditure allowance to 0.3 U/F for 155 mm. guns and 0.2 U/F for howitzers.

27th May, L+56 Day

Rain and mud, with consequent supply difficulties, prevented any large scale offensive operations. Ground conditions grew steadily worse during the day, and many emergency measures were taken to get supplies through the mud to the troops. Enemy suicide air attacks during the forenoon caused major damage to the destroyer *Braine* and high speed minesweeper *Forrest*. Recommencing in the evening, raids continuous all night. By midnight two high speed destroyer transports, *Loy* and *Rathburne*, and two L.C.S. had been heavily damaged, and other ships had minor damage. Task Group 58.4 re-joined T.F. 58 from Ulithi.

28th May, L+57 Day

At 0000 operational control of all naval forces then attached to the Fifth Fleet passed to Commander Third Fleet. Task Force 54 became Task Force 34 (Gunfire and Covering Force). At the same time Commanding General Tenth Army became directly responsible to the C-in-C. Pacific Ocean Areas for the defence and development of captured positions in the Ryukus. Enemy air raids continued from yesterday. The destroyer *Drexler* was sunk, but only one ship received severe damage, the cargo ship *T. Snelling*, though a number of others were slightly damaged. 76 enemy aircraft were destroyed. From to-day the enemy air raids began to decline in weight. T.A.F. sent a fighter sweep to Kyushu. Vice-Admiral J.S. McCain relieved Vice-Admiral Mitscher as C.T.F. 38. Task Group 38.3 left for Ulithi for rotation replenishment.

29th May, L+58 Day

Marines occupied all of Naha north of the harbor and captured Shuri Castle. The destroyer *Shubrick* was severely damaged by suicide air attack. Task Force 38 assisted in close support of troops.

30th May, L+59 Day

The 27th Division in northern Okinawa was meeting considerable enemy resistance at Onnataki. Torrential rains, accompanied by electrical storm, slowed all naval operations during the day. For the first time, no enemy aircraft were detected in the area for the 24-hour period. T.A.F. Kyushu sweep was stopped by weather and hit Amami instead.

31st May, L+60 Day

The 1st Marines and 77th Infantry Division units completed the reduction of the Wana Ridge position which had delayed the American advance for many days. The entire Shuri stronghold was occupied by the end of the day.

1st June, L+61 Day

Task Force 38 assisted T.G. 99.2 and T.U. 32.1.1 in giving close support of troops.

2nd June, L+62 Day

The 27th Division seized Onnataki. There were no air alerts during the period. Task Force 38 long-range fighter sweeps against Kyushu were impaired by bad weather.

3rd June, L+63 Day

The Chinen Peninsula was cut off. A special landing force (R.C.T. of 2nd Marine Division) landed unopposed at Iheya Shima. Vice-Admiral Hill, C.T.F. 31, shifted flag to the H.Q. ship *Auburn*. 48 enemy aircraft were destroyed, but the only damage caused to ships was minor to one cargo vessel and one landing craft.

4th June, L+64 Day

Elements of the 7th Division swept the entire Chinen Peninsula, encountering no enemy resistance. Preparations were made to meet a typhoon, which weather reports indicated as approaching from the south. There were no enemy air alerts during the period. T.F. 38 manoeuvring to avoid typhoon.

5th June, L+65 Day

The expected storm passed 300 miles south-east. At 0456 storm danger was considered and over and all units were directed to revert to normal. Suicide air attacks this evening caused only minor damage to the battleship *Mississippi* and heavy cruiser *Louisville*. Three cruisers, two carriers and one destroyer of Task Force 38 were seriously damaged by the typhoon.

6th June, L+66 Day

Naha airfield was secured. The light minelayer *J.W. Ditter* was damaged by suicide air attack. 40 enemy aircraft were shot down on evening raids.

7th June, L+67 Day

20 enemy aircraft were destroyed. Only minor damage to two ships was caused. T.U. 32.1.1 made 306 sorties against Sakishima Gunto. T.A.F. and Task Force 38 gave close support to troops.

8th June, L+68 Day

15 enemy aircraft were destroyed. No ships were damaged. T.U. 32.1.1 and T.A.F. in close support. T.F. 38 aircraft made a final attack on southern Kyushu and struck Okino Oagari Shima, whilst cruisers of the force bombarded the island.

9th June, L+69 Day

A special landing force landed on Aguni Shima and secured the island by noon. T.A.F. supported the landing on Aguni Shima, attacked Koniya Seaplane Base on Amami, and T.A.F. and T.U. 32.1.1 provided close support to front lines on Okinawa. Battleships and cruisers of T.F. 38 bombed Minami Oagari Shima.

10th June, L+70 Day

The destroyer escort *Gendreau* received major damage from a shore battery. The destroyer *W.D. Porter* was sunk by suicide air attack this forenoon; 21 of the enemy attackers were destroyed. At 1600 Vice-Admiral Oldendorf relieved Rear-Admiral McCormick as C.T.F. 32. Task Force 30.2 bombed Minami Oagari Shima. Fast carrier force left for Leyte Gulf for replenishment and repair.

11th June, L+71 Day

C.T.F. 32 assumed control of all naval gunfire support, exercising direct control for both sides of the island. Typhoon Plan "W" was put into force at 1400. 13 enemy aircraft were destroyed, but no ship received serious damage.

12th June, L+72 Day

Typhoon Plan "W" was cancelled at 0640. High seas and swell caused cessation of unloading at 1800 after a day of difficulty.

13th June, L+73 Day

Radar and F.D. stations on Tori Shima began operating.

15th June, L+75 Day

T.A.F. attacked Amami Gunto, Kyushu being weathered out.

16th June, L+76 Day

The destroyer *Twiggs* was sunk by aerial torpedo and possibly suicider this evening.

17th June, L+77 Day

The T.A.F. strike to Kyushu was forced by bad weather to attack Amami Gunto instead.

18th June, L+78 Day

Lieut.-General S.B. Buckner was killed by enemy shellfire.

19th June, L+79 Day

Major-General R.S. Geiger, U.S.M.C., assumed command of the Ryuku Forces and Expeditionary Troops, vice the late Lieut.-General Buckner. Elements of the 1st Marine Division in an advance of 2,600 yards reached the south coast of Okinawa and split the remainder of the enemy held territory into two regiments.

20th June, L+80 Day

Preparations were made to meet possible approach of typhoon.

21st June, L+81 Day

The island of Okinawa was secured at 1305 to-day. Com. Fifth Phib Force continued in command of T.F. 31 until 0900, 1st July. Typhoon danger was past by 1845.

INDEX OF VESSELS

ALLIED VESSELS

JAPANESE VESSELS